Sixty Years of Hollywood

Sixty Years of Hollywood

John Baxter

SOUTH BRUNSWICK AND NEW YORK: A. S. BARNES AND COMPANY
LONDON: THE TANTIVY PRESS

© 1973 by A. S. Barnes and Co., Inc.

A. S. Barnes and Co., Inc.
Cranbury, New Jersey 08512

The Tantivy Press
108 New Bond Street
London W1Y OQX, England

Library of Congress Cataloging in Publication Data

Baxter, John, 1939–
  Sixty Years of Hollywood.

  1. Moving-picture industry—Hollywood, Calif.
I. Title.
PN1933.5.U65B355   791.43   70-37804
ISBN 0-498-01046-5

SBN 90073 062 5 (U.K.)

Printed in the United States of America

This book is for Douglas White.

Contents

Author's Note

By tradition, literature on the American film industry falls into precise categories, ranging from the reverent accolades of the fan magazines through works of aesthetic or industrial analysis to the meticulous reportage of the trade press. This polarisation hinders an appreciation of the whole Hollywood, not merely an art centre, industrial complex or social symbol, but an organic artistic and commercial community. With Hollywood now in a state of flux from which it will certainly emerge in a different form, it is more appropriate than ever to look back on its history and analyse its birth, growth and senescence.

This book is neither a detailed history of the American film industry nor a scrapbook of its best films and greatest stars, but rather a survey of how films and stars were created. Many existing books list the most successful Hollywood films of each year, either by the criterion of profit, as in the "Film Daily Yearbook," or on aesthetic, nostalgic or other grounds. That the lists differ one from another suggests the problems of any such approach to film evaluation. Rather than become involved in minute measurements of artistic or commercial merit, I have analysed Hollywood's output in the context of the times, choosing films for their importance to the industry and its image rather than because of outstanding merit in modern critical terms. Emphasis has been laid on aspects of Hollywood history often glossed over—the evolution of a performer's cinema after the director-oriented early Twenties, Hollywood's disastrous involvement with the American financial establishment, the growth of a political conscience—and it is to these themes that specific films are often related. In this way, I hope to show Hollywood as an organism; one which, like any living thing, was born, flourished and, when its time came, died. In Hollywood's case, it was a bad death, in anger and despair.

Many people assisted me in researching *Sixty Years of Hollywood,* and I am particularly grateful to the following: René Clair, John Cromwell, Miss Bette Davis, Edward Dmytryk, Douglas Fairbanks Jnr., Dustin Hoffman, Dennis Hopper, Charles Katz, Rex Lipton, Ben Lyon, David Niven, Miss Marion Nixon and Donald Ogden Stewart for their reminiscences of film-making in Hollywood; to Colin Ford and Jeremy Boulton of the National Film Archive, London, the staff of the Information and Stills Departments of the British Film Institute, Bob Baker and Terry Billings of the American Embassy, London, Jacques Ledoux of the Cinémathèque Royale de Belgique, and the Cinémathèque Française; and Eric Rhode, Colin Shindler, John Kobal, Barrie Pattison, Ian Klava, Joel Finler, Scott McQueen, and William K. Everson. Certain sections of this book, in a different form, were originally prepared for or published by *Film Digest,* the *Sunday Telegraph, The Silent Picture* and the National Film Theatre, London. Portions of the material on Sixties films are taken from *Hollywood in the Sixties* (Tantivy/Barnes, 1972).

Sixty Years of Hollywood

1894

Horace Henderson Wilcox moved from Kansas and bought 120 acres in the flat, waterless country beyond Los Angeles to establish a country residence. His wife named their ranch "Hollywood."

1908

Though Hollywood was to become synonymous with the American motion picture industry, its early days as a centre of movie manufacturing were modest. Following Thomas Edison's patenting of his Kinetoscope and the flurry of patents on similar machines by independent inventors, cinema changed from penny-arcade trick to national institution, with storefront "Nickleodeons" luring sharp speculators into this new and lucrative field. By 1907, the men who were to shape Hollywood had seen the potential profit of film exhibition. In that year, William Fox abandoned cloth sponging to start a Nickleodeon chain, Adolph Zukor left furs for a similar enterprise, while Carl Laemmle and Robert Cochran formed Independent Motion Pictures Inc.—IMP. IMP and others later merged, creating Laemmle's famous Universal.

Henry Aitken, film salesman, John R. Freuler, real estate dealer, and Samuel Hutchinson, druggist, formed Mutual which, after absorbing companies like Thanouser, all but broke up in the formation of the revolutionary but short-lived Triangle (see 1915). Adam Kessel and Charles Bauman, bookmakers hampered by new laws against betting, founded the New York Motion Picture Co., later Keystone, and another arm of Triangle. Some companies produced their own films, others relied on independent producers. Edison continued to make films, and licensed a number of companies to use his equipment. Biograph in New York, which itself owned some important patents and had, in D. W. Griffith, a major innovator, Selig in Chicago, Vitagraph at Flatbush and other licensees paid a percentage of their profits monthly to the Wizard of Menlo Park. Less legally, other companies operated with cameras from England, where Edison omitted to patent his designs, or France, where the Lumière brothers had beaten him to it with their combined camera/printer/projector,

the Cinématographe, while the bulk of producers worked outside the law, using copied or stolen equipment. Patents taken out on individual mechanisms and improvements to cameras or projectors further confused the position. Woodville Latham's patent on the incorporation of a loop of loose film into the camera to prevent breakage by sharp movement caused endless litigation. Cameraman Charles Rosher recalls taking his camera indoors to open it so as to prevent Edison spies from glimpsing its "Latham Loop." Legality often resided in a producer acquiring, through purchase or agreement, enough individual patents to make his cameras at least partly legal, but Edison's agents were indefatigable in seeking out those who failed to do so. The search for a conveniently remote location to make films—Florida and Cuba were both tried—led some producers to think of California.

The first was "Colonel" William Selig. Having made the interiors for a version of Dumas's *The Count of Monte Cristo* in 1908, Selig director Francis Boggs and his cameraman/editor/unit manager/assistant director Thomas Persons travelled to California for the climax, where the count, escaping from prison, triumphantly bobs up out of the waves. Boggs and Persons went by train, stopping off at appropriate locations to shoot exterior footage that might be useful later. Arriving in Los Angeles, they persuaded an out-of-work hypnotist to don a wig and stand in for the escapee, a performance that nearly cost the actor his life and Boggs the hired wig. Impressed with the sunshine, freedom from Chicago fogs and unlimited room for expansion, Boggs, with Selig's approval, stayed on to make more films.*

---

* Boggs died dramatically a few years later when a Japanese gardener, irritated by the noise of film production, ran amok with a pistol, killing Boggs and also wounding Selig in the first of Hollywood's many shooting dramas.

The Selig Company at work in California, 1908.

Recruiting Hobart Bosworth, an actor who had lost his voice as a result of tuberculosis and was recuperating in California, Boggs hired a vacant lot next to a Chinese laundry on Olive and Seventh Streets and shot *The Power of the Sultan* (1908), probably the first dramatic film made entirely in California. It starred Stella Adams, Tom Santschi, Frank Montgomery, and Robert Leonard (later to become, as Robert Z. Leonard, a major director). A few weeks later, Boggs leased the roof of an office building in downtown Los Angeles and set up the state's first studio.

1909

More producers discovered California's possibilities. Some, like "Broncho Billy Anderson" (actually Max Aronson), Western star and founder with George K. Spoor of the Essanay company (from the principals' initials), an Edison-licensee, were driven, as Boggs had been, by the desire for realism and California's promised 350 sunny days per year. In a train fitted with a laboratory to ensure quick processing of film, Anderson chugged through the West, shooting a one-reel Western each week, using himself as star, locals as supporting cast and one of seven proven plots. In this way he produced 376 films in Montana, Colorado and California before settling down at Niles, California, where Essanay, later the studio of Chaplin, made its permanent home.

Fred Balshofer opened West Coast operations for Kessel and Bauman's New York Motion Picture Co., then releasing its films with the trade mark "101 Bison," an emblem adapted from the famous "101 Ranch" Rodeo, whose services it had hired for a series of Westerns, and the design of the $10 note. When Laemmle took over their "101" contract, they adapted the symbol of the Pennsylvania Railroad and named their company "Keystone" (such plagiarism was privileged by custom, Lubin having taken the Liberty Bell as a trademark and Essanay the Indian head of the US penny). Keystone studios at Edendale, a Los Angeles suburb, became the centre of the comedy world.

But 1909's most important event for America's film industry was the formation of the Motion Picture

"Broncho Billy" Anderson in *Broncho Billy and the Redskin*, 1914.

Patents Co. in January. Pressed by George Kleine, the "K" of Kalem, firms that held Edison licences or controlled key patents banded together to freeze out illegal producers: Edison, Vitagraph, Biograph, Kalem, Lubin, Selig, Essanay, the French Pathé Frères and Méliès were the initial signatories. Action against the fugitives was stepped up, and successful prosecutions dramatised the fact that unless some refuge could be found not only from the Patents Co. agents but also from the risk of arrest and imprisonment, many film-makers were doomed to extinction.

1910

The Patents Co. consolidated its power by founding a distribution arm, General Film, which monopolised film supply to exhibitors, and levied $2 per projector weekly, plus a fee for prints ranging from 10¢ a foot to $1 for better films. An indignant Carl Laemmle was moved to address his colleagues in a trade advertisement; "Good Morrow! Have you just paid $2 for sitting on your hands?" Meanwhile the exodus to California quickened, even MPPC members like Biograph seeing the value of a sunny winter location. In January, D. W. Griffith and company arrived in Los Angeles, having hired a vacant lot at Grand Ave. and Washington St. (hence the word "lot" to describe any film studio), floored fifty square feet for a stage and erected huts for changing. Twenty-one films were made in their first three month stay, beginning with exteriors for *The Newly-Weds,* a knockabout comedy of surprising violence in which Jack Pickford elopes with fiancée Mary Pickford in a flight that, after the explosion of their car, a canoe accident in which she is dumped into the river, and other painful experiences, ends in their marriage. Later films used Verdugo, Brentwood and Edendale backgrounds, and although, as Griffith actor Mack Sennett remarked, Hollywood in those days was "just a crossroads out in the country," Griffith's second Californian film,

In Old California, with Marion Leonard and Frank Grandin, used locations in what was later the Hollywood area.

1910 saw the "star system" begin. Though actors were seldom identified by name (most stage players felt ashamed at appearing in "galloping tintypes"), Biograph's Florence Lawrence was nationally known, but only as "The Biograph Girl." When she broke with Biograph over their refusal to employ her husband, director Harry Salter, IMP's Carl Laemmle hired both, and leaked the story that Miss Lawrence had died in a street accident. When interest was at its peak, he denounced this "vicious lie," implying a Biograph trick, and made public for the first time that Miss Lawrence had become "The IMP Girl." (She was replaced as "The Biograph Girl" by Mary Pickford.) Film players seldom received such respect. $5 a day was the usual fee, or $3 for extra parts, and actors were expected to pitch in with the chores. Florence Turner, "The Vitagraph Girl," helped paint scenery and keep the company's petty-cash. At Biograph, Wallace Reid, who could play the violin, was pressed into providing "mood music," and both Mary Pickford and Mack Sennett developed their film sense by writing scenarios at Biograph under Griffith.

1911

October 1911: Hollywood's first studio was opened by the Centaur Company, owned by two Englishmen, William and David Horsley, leaders in the fight against the Patents Co. Already shooting in Bayonne, N.J., their chief director, Al Christie, was tired of false backgrounds for their Westerns and suggested moving to California. David Horsley nominated the more accessible Florida, but Christie won on the toss of a coin. On the way out, David Horsley and Christie met a theatrical producer who advised them to see Frank Hoover, owner of a Los Angeles photographic business. After showing them properties in Edendale and Santa Monica, Hoover drove them to Hollywood, then eight miles from town. On the corner of Sunset Boulevard and Gower Street, they found a hall that had previously been a Salvation Army meeting place, and originally a tavern. It then belonged to Frank Blondeau, the town's only barber and later a rich man from property speculation. Centaur bought the building, and a barn behind it where film could be processed. The first film shot there, and therefore Hollywood's first, was *The Best Man Wins*, a drama starring Victoria Forde (later Mrs. Tom Mix) and Harold Lockwood, completed on October 27, 1911. The company's cameraman was Charles Rosher, later Mary Pickford's lighting man. Centaur's West Coast branch, renamed Nestor Films, became one of California's most prolific production companies until the following year, when it was taken over by Universal. Christie later left to establish himself as a successful manufacturer of broad comedies: the Columbia Broadcasting System offices now stand on the site where Nestor created its historic first.

While Horsley and Christie had only debated whether to try Florida, Carl Laemmle of IMP had loaded a film crew and cast on a boat and sailed for Cuba in the hope of escaping the MPPC spies, but returned when conditions proved too primitive. Among those he took was Thomas Harper Ince, an actor who made his *début* as an IMP director in 1910. Leaving IMP, he joined Kessel and Bauman and directed *The New Cook* at their Edendale studio, starring Ethel Grandin whom he had stolen from his old company. Ince immediately distinguished himself as an imaginative but prodigal technician. "My first picture had fifty-three scenes and it was freely predicted I would be fired for wasting so much time and film . . . It took three days to make." Vitagraph also opened a California studio, though production was mainly centered at their Flatbush lot. Later, Vitagraph's principals, James Stuart Blackton and Albert Smith, were to become Hollywood luminaries before their company was absorbed by Warner Brothers in 1920.

1912

The motion picture boom was bringing a fortune to its instigators—Vitagraph grossed between $5-$6 million in 1912—and they expanded accordingly. Most companies opened studios in Los Angeles less to avoid the MPPC police than to guarantee continuity of production during the winter. Some of the new lots were ramshackle affairs. The irreducible minimum, like that of Kalem, was a platform two feet high with canvas diffusers above to control the light and movable flats to act as sets, but the ambitious Kessel and Bauman, pressed by Ince, bought twenty thousand acres of land in Santa Ynez Canyon, between the mountains and the sea, and, handing Edendale over to Mack Sennett for his comedies, moved to what would become famous as "Inceville." Visitors faced "a road leading from Santa Monica, choked with dust in summer, and impassable with mud in winter. On rainy days everybody used to ride horseback from the Japanese fishing village where the car line ended." ("Photoplay," Nov., 1929) By 1913, Ince employed seven hundred people and had $35,000 worth of buildings: with director Francis Ford (brother of John) who also acted, Ince began the series of remarkable films that were to make him a major figure of the early cinema.

Few directors shared Ince's independence from studio control. At Biograph, Griffith was meeting opposition to his ambitious four-reel *The Battle of Elderberry Gulch* and *Judith of Bethulia,* although producers, while restricting artistic experiment, were adventurous in exploring the by-ways of film manufacture. Kalem, which specialised in location shooting, made part of *From the Manger to the Cross* (Sidney Olcott, 1911) in Palestine, and, at the other extreme, Adolph Zukor in 1912 founded his Famous Players Company to produce film versions of successful Broadway plays starring the actors who had appeared in them. On September 23, Mack Sennett released his first two Keystone productions, *Cohen Collects a Debt* and *The Water Nymph,* but neither had immediate public success. The golden age of screen comedy, like that of Griffith's genius, had yet to arrive.

1913

William Fox. Because of poor medical work on a broken left elbow, his left arm was permanently stiffened.

Cecil B. DeMille (on running board) and cast of *The Squaw Man.*

Incensed by Biograph's refusal to release *Judith of Bethulia* and *The Battle of Elderberry Gulch* (neither emerged until 1914) and by the company's decision to film a series of stage successes in collaboration with Klaw and Erlanger, Broadway entrepreneurs (a response to Zukor's pioneering Famous Players concept), Griffith left to join Mutual on October 1, taking with him all his major players, including the Gish sisters, Mae Marsh and Bobby Harron. A first shot in the independents' war against the MPPC was fired when exhibitor William Fox, backed by wealthy politician Tim Sullivan and lawyer Gustavus A. Rogers, sued the company and persuaded the Federal government that it was "an unlawful conspiracy in restraint of trade." Initially an irritation to the Edison interests, Fox's suit and the chink it revealed in MPPC's armour led to an erosion of its standing and eventual demise in 1917, by which time its power had been destroyed. Meanwhile an exodus towards California by MPPC members and independents continued, including one man later to create many of Hollywood's traditions and much of its characteristic style—Cecil Blount DeMille.

THE SQUAW MAN. Jesse L. Lasky Feature Play Co. Directed by Cecil B. DeMille and Oscar Apfel. Script by Apfel and DeMille from play by Edwin Milton Royle. Photographed by Alfred Gandolfi. Edited by Mamie Wagner. Assistant Director: Alvin Wyckoff. Players: Dustin Farnum, Winifred Kingston, Redwing, Dick La Strange, Foster Knox, Monroe Salisbury, Joe E. Singleton. Billy Elmer, Fred Montague, Babe de Rue, Dick La Reno, Hal Roach.

Legends about DeMille's first production of *The Squaw Man* (he remade it in 1918 and 1930) have proliferated, fanned by the director, who never hesitated to inflate his own reputation and historical importance to the film industry. It was the first venture of a company formed by Jesse L. Lasky and his brother in-law, glove salesman Samuel Goldfish, who later, as Sam Goldwyn, became a major Hollywood figure. Hoping to exploit Zukor's Famous Players concept, Lasky succeeded so well that the former took over control of the new company. *The Squaw Man* has often been claimed as the first film made in Hollywood, which is clearly not so. One is equally doubtful whether DeMille, as he claims, chose Hollywood purely by chance after having intended to shoot the film in Denver; news of the Californian studios was by then common knowledge. Certainly he did rent a barn on the corner of Vine Street and Hollywood Boulevard, turn most of it into a studio—actors changed in the horse stalls—and shoot his adaptation of the stagey Broadway success in which he had persuaded Dustin Farnum (not, as DeMille claimed, the play's star but a supporting actor in it) to appear.

No print of this original version exists, but one assumes it followed closely the approach of later productions, Farnum playing an aristocrat who abandons high life after his girl has left him and goes out West, where he marries an Indian girl with whom he makes a new life. Shooting began on December 29, and immediately ran into trouble, instigated, DeMille implies, by MPPC agents. The film's negative was tampered with, and portions ruined; happily, DeMille had shot a second for safety. Attempts were twice made to kill him as he rode to the studio from his home on Cahuenga Boulevard, then well out in the country, though the greatest problem came when he found that the film, when projected, yielded only a blur. Two theories as to why this was so suggest the technical confusion under which pioneer producers operated: using unsprocketted film stock, as did all film-makers at the time, DeMille had unwittingly bought a punching machine that operated to the European standard of sixty-five holes per foot rather than the usual sixty-four; the cameraman had not correctly regulated his cranking speed nor taken into account the problems of working with two cameras. DeMille's difficulties were solved by Selig in Chicago, who showed him how the film could be rescued, and shortly afterwards Bell and Howell introduced a perforator that stan-

Cecil B. DeMille displays the camera used to shoot *The Squaw Man.*

dardised sprocket holes. Meanwhile, *The Squaw Man* was successfully released, setting the scene for the establishment of the giant Paramount company.

1914

Charlie Chaplin made his film *début* in Keystone's *Making a Living* and in New York another film legend was created when William Fox, still deep in litigation against the MPPC, began film production with *Life's Shop Window*. Later, he made *A Fool There Was* (Frank Powell, 1914), an adaptation of Porter Emerson Browne's melodrama starring a young actress named Theodosia Goodman, who, under her new name of Theda Bara and with the famous line "Kiss me, my fool" created The Vamp. In the midwest, a theatre owner named William Wadsworth Hodkinson was, like Fox, taking steps to destroy the tyranny of the MPPC. Tired of the variable material forced on him by General Film and of "block booking," in which good films were offered only in blocks with bad, Hodkinson joined other exhibitors to form Paramount, a distribution company determined to acquire the best films, whether from Edison licensees or independents. (Soon after, Vitagraph, Selig, Lubin and Essanay broke from MPPC to form VLSE, betraying growing disquiet within the Edison ranks.) Paramount's name came from that of an apartment block Hodkinson passed on his way to California on a film buying trip, and the emblem of a snow-covered peak from the Wasatch Range near his Utah home. In Hollywood, Hodkinson found that Broadway producer David Belasco had recently sold film rights to ten of his most successful plays to Lasky, and that DeMille had imported Wilfred Buckland, Hollywood's first art director, to improve the appearance of Lasky product. Hodkinson promptly contracted for thirty films a year from Lasky, fifty-two from Zukor's Famous Players, and twenty-two from the best remaining independents like Morosco and Bosworth. While America paused cautiously on the brink of war, the European cinema petered out, and France, England and the Commonwealth turned to Hollywood for films. The great days had begun.

TILLIE'S PUNCTURED ROMANCE. Keystone. Directed by Mack Sennett. Script by Hampton Del Ruth from *Tillie's Nightmare*, a musical comedy with book and lyrics by Edgar Smith. Players: Charles Chaplin (The City Slicker), Marie Dressler (Tillie), Mabel Normand (Charlie's Girlfriend), Charles Bennett (Rich Uncle, two minor characters), Charlie Chase (Detective), Chester Conklin (Society Guest), Charles Murray (Detective), Mack Swain (Tillie's Father), Edgar Kennedy (Café Owner), Al St. John, Slim Summerville, Eddie Sutherland, Hank Mann (Keystone Cops), Phyllis Allen, Billie Bennett, Joe Bordereaux, Alice Howell, Gordon Griffith, G. G. Ligon, Harry McCoy, Wallace MacDonald.

An ex-vaudeville comic and boilermaker, Mack Sennett (real name Michael Sinnott) began directing at Biograph in 1911 after two years of experience as a Mary Pickford foil in one-reel comedies. On location in California for *One Round O'Brien*, assistant director Frank Powell became ill and Sennett deputised. Joining Kessel and Bauman in 1912, Sennett proved himself capable of sustaining an output on cheap one-reel comedies relying on the simple, even brutal comedy of violence, and over the following two years he gathered a notable team of ex-circus and vaudeville comics at Keystone's Edendale studios, including Roscoe "Fatty" Arbuckle, Mabel Normand, Chester Conklin, Mary Miles Minter and his star, Ford Sterling. Sterling soon announced his intention to enter independent production with Universal (his film failed) and in December 1913 Sennett hired English comedian Charlie Chaplin when his tour with the Fred Karno troupe ended. Sterling had received $200 a week; Chaplin got $150 a week for three months and $175 for the rest of his one-year contract. During his year with Keystone, Chaplin made thirty-five short comedies, beginning with a secondary role in *Making a Living* (Henry "Pathé" Lehrman, 1914).

Charlie Chaplin in *The Face on the Barroom Floor*.

takes a job as maid. On the level of invention at which Chaplin was then working, Sennett's simple knockabout comedy offered little stimulus, and he rightly considers the film to be without much merit. Most of the comedy relies on straight pratfalls, beginning with a playful duel between Charlie and Tillie with bricks, and continuing through a messy restaurant sequence where Tillie, as a waitress, inundates everybody with soup, to the climax in which the Keystone Cops' car bumps her into the sea, leading to a lively speedboat chase.

Tillie's importance lies in its status as Hollywood's first comedy feature. After fourteen weeks in production, the film was delayed until November 1914 because of doubts about its acceptance, but proved an immediate hit. Soon afterwards, Miss Dressler was hired by exploitation producer Sig Lubin in Phila-

His second, *Kid Auto Races at Venice,* introduced the famous tramp, with Fatty Arbuckle's hat and trousers, Ford Sterling's boots (on wrong feet because of their size), painted moustache, and walk copied from a London cabbie with bad feet. Initially doubtful about Chaplin's ability and finding him egotistical and difficult (for some time he was known derisively at Keystone as "Edgar English"), Sennett's low opinion was revised when, at a time when other Keystone films merited only twenty or thirty prints each, Chaplin's sold twice that. Chaplin quickly graduated to writer/director/star on Sennett productions like *The Face on the Bar-room Floor, Dough and Dynamite* and *The Property Man;* he also starred in the first feature comedy ever made and one of Hollywood's first important productions, *Tillie's Punctured Romance.*

Sennett conceived *Tillie* to exploit the popularity of Marie Dressler, who starred in the stage version and made famous the song "Heaven Protect the Working Girl." $2,500 persuaded her to make the film. Chaplin showed a special aptitude for even the most robust comedy stunts, and Mabel Normand, who plays his girl and accomplice, made a charming foil. Sennett also added his team of comic policemen, shortly to be world-famous as the Keystone Cops. *Tillie* imitated the original's stage style, including "asides," with Dressler as a farmer's ugly daughter wooed by Chaplin, and lured into eloping with her father's bankroll which he promptly steals. When his discarded victim becomes an heiress, Charlie reappears, marries her and moves into a huge mansion, only to have his paradise destroyed when a jealous Mabel

Tillie's Punctured Romance. **Mabel Normand, Charlie Chaplin and a cheap advertisement for Keystone.**

delphia to make *Tillie's Tomato Surprise* but her career declined until revived in the early Thirties with character roles in *Dinner at Eight* (George Cukor, 1933) and Clarence Brown's *Anna Christie* (1930). The reckless Sennett prospered during the early Twenties, but his refusal to acknowledge the star system's power—few of his discoveries were placed under long-term contract since he argued he could manufacture a new star whenever he needed one—as well as reckless spending on gold mines, mansions and a large studio, led to his downfall.

24

1915

A group of distributors unhappy with available films formed the Metro Production Company from the ruins of Al Lichtman's Alco organisation, with Richard Rowland as president and Louis B. Mayer, a minor Boston exhibitor only recently out of the fur business, as secretary. Chaplin, after unsuccessfully demanding $750 a week from Keystone, joined Essanay at $1,250 a week plus $10,000 bonus. His first film at Essanay's Chicago studios—disliking the cold, he quickly insisted all future productions be done at the Niles, California, location—was *His First Job*. Making their cinema *débuts* in it were Ben Turpin and Gloria Swanson. Mary Pickford signed with Famous Players at $2,000 a week, plus half the profits of her films. But as two stars rose, another fell. Florence Lawrence, whom Miss Pickford replaced as "The Biograph Girl," was injured in an accident, and never regained her former eminence. After minor acting roles in the Twenties and jobs as a cosmetician, she committed suicide in 1939.

Technical developments multiplied. Carl Laemmle opened Universal Studios on March 15, two-hundred-and-thirty acres on the Taylor Ranch by the Los Angeles River, five miles from Hollywood. Thomas Edison and Henry Ford christened the first film stage to be electrically lit (though arcs had been used on location for prize-fight films as early as 1899, and Vitagraph had experimented with Mercury-vapour tubes, whose violet light was ill-suited to photography). The lights, unmasked carbon-arc Klieg lamps, had their problems. They threw off carbon dust that caused painful "Klieg eyes," and since film stocks were still insensitive (see 1924) and the electrical current was likely to waver, sunlight remained the best and most reliable illumination; consequently, few studios immediately followed Laemmle's lead. The cunning DeMille exploited his camera problems by inventing the phrase "Rembrandt Lighting" to justify some in-

differently exposed shots in *The Warrens of Virginia* the same year.

Nineteen-fifteen was the year of *The Birth of a Nation* which, apart from setting the seal on D. W. Griffith's reputation, had important industrial repercussions. After leaving Biograph in 1913, Griffith had joined Mutual at the invitation of one of its principals, Henry E. Aitken, and it was to Mutual he suggested a long film of Thomas Dixon's "The Clansman." Only Aitken saw its potential, and when Mutual refused the project, he withdrew from the company and financed it privately with Griffith and Dixon. Aitken then secretly approached Thomas Ince, allied to Mutual through his company Reliance, and Sennett, Kessel and Bauman of Keystone, to form a separate company producing the ambitious features pioneered by directors like Griffith and Ince. The company, called Triangle, gave, as the name suggested, equality to its three principals, Griffith, Ince and Sennett, allowing them to retain their own staff, stars and studios. William S. Hart, Ince's strongest star, worked at "Inceville" in Santa Ynez Canyon while Ince moved into larger Hollywood studios. Griffith continued to occupy the Fine Arts Studios at 4500 Sunset Boulevard, and Sennett the enlarged Edendale lot, while Kessel and Bauman (KayBee) joined Hart at "Inceville" and, via their New York Motion Picture Company, handled the release of some Triangle productions.

Aitken made immediate raids on Broadway to recruit for Triangle, and massive investment was made in talent, often for failing stars or those unsuited for films. Sir Herbert Beerbohm Tree joined the company for $110,000 for six months work, and the declining comedy team of Weber and Fields for $2,500 each per week. DeWolf Hopper, Billie Burke and many other Broadway stars were hired, as well as a promising juvenile, Douglas Fairbanks. Triangle's directors included many who were to become famous: Christy Cabanne, Allan Dwan, John Emerson and scenarist wife Anita Loos. Joseph August was a cameraman, William Daniels an assistant, Lee Garmes a painter's helper. W. S. Van Dyke, Jack Conway, Raoul Walsh and Sidney Franklin, all later major figures, were assistant directors. More than just one new company among many, Triangle used unique production methods based on its stage and director orientation, planning to release a complete three-film programme each week, one from each arm of the company. To sustain such an output, its artistic principals would not direct but "supervise" their films—an approximation of the stage policy of the time in which a producer/writer like David Belasco would exert total control over his plays from conception to presentation by establishing a strong personal style and training assistants to follow it. High rentals restricted Triangle films to the best cinemas, and exhibitors were encouraged to improve amenities as a means of extracting from customers an unheard-of $2 a seat. Films ran a week rather than the customary two days, and an adequate musical backing was facilitated by the composition of sophisticated scores by Triangle staff musicians like Victor Schertzinger, later a talented director himself. The seeds of Sixties "hard ticket" and "road show" techniques were in Triangle's methods.

On September 23, Triangle offered its first programme: *My Valet,* with Raymond Hitchcock, directed by Sennett; *The Lamb,* Douglas Fairbanks's film *début,* supervised (with distaste) by Griffith; and Dustin Farnum and Louise Glaum in *The Iron Strain* (Reginald Barker, under Ince supervision). Though doomed to collapse in a few years through internal dissension, Aitken's overexpenditure on stage "names" and the desire of Griffith and Ince for independence, Triangle

Birth of a Nation. D. W. Griffith's vision of the Civil War.

marked the end of the MPPC trust concept and the beginning of competitive studio production which Zukor of Paramount, Laemmle of Universal and Mayer of Metro-Goldwyn-Mayer were to perfect.

THE BIRTH OF A NATION. Epoch Film Corporation. Directed by D. W. Griffith. Script by D. W. Griffith, Frank Woods from the novels "The Clansman" and "The Leopard's Spots" by Rev. Thomas Dixon Jnr. Photographed by G. W. Bitzer. Players: Lillian Gish (Elsie Stoneman), Mae Marsh (Flora Cameron), Henry B. Walthall (Col. Ben Cameron), Miriam Cooper (Margaret Cameron), Mary Alden (Lydia, Stoneman's Housekeeper), Ralph Lewis (Hon. Austin Stoneman), George Seigmann (Silas Lynch), Walter Long (Gus), Robert Harron (Rod Stoneman), Wallace Reid (Jeff, the Black-Smith), Joseph Henaberry (Abraham Lincoln), Elmer Clifton (Phil Stoneman), Josephine Crowell (Mrs. Cameron), Spottiswoode Aitken (Dr. Cameron), J. A. Beringer (Wade Cameron), Maxfield Stanley (Duke Cameron), Jennie Lee (Mammy), Donald Crisp (General U. S. Grant), Howard Gaye (General Robert E. Lee).

Griffith saw his film of "The Clansman" as a statement more ambitious and overwhelming than anything the cinema had achieved until then, the crystallisation of history and his own Southern heritage into one perfect visual saga. At forty, with a background as actor, playwright and film director none of his contemporaries could remotely equal, Griffith was uniquely qualified to create the first truly modern film, in which all the technical and stylistic advances of the cinema's first decade were to be combined, an initial statement in what was to become the basic film language. Griffith's "invention" of the close-up, the techniques of editing for impact, the tracking shot and other technical devices (claims open to question), has less importance than his integration of all these elements into a coherent whole, and his presentation of them, almost as a primer of film grammar, in this remarkable work.

The Birth of a Nation's philosophical standing is less sure. Griffith sees the decline of Southern power, the Confederate defeat and the agonies of Reconstruction with a Tennessee romantic's sense of injustice, sincerely believing in the rightful rule of the landed aristocracy, the solid (though, to him, lesser) worth of the black minority and the viciousness of integration and miscegenation, the latter representing to Griffith, as it does to John Ford (who was an extra in the Klan charge), an assault on the almost divine value of white social institutions. His saga of the Camerons explores these ideas through the character of Henry B. Walthall's "Little Colonel," gracious Southern host to his rival Northern counterparts, the Stonemans, before the war, courageous adversary during the superbly directed battles,* bereaved casualty in the aftermath and then prime mover in the Ku Klux Klan movement that sweeps in with Biblical righteousness to expunge the carpetbaggers and their Negro helpers, establishing "Liberty and Union, One and Inseparable, Now and Forever." All Griffith's chauvinism is on display in the plot, and even allowing for the conviction with which he expresses himself it is the technique of *The Birth of a Nation* that guarantees its immortality.

---

* All the more remarkable for the primitiveness of the equipment with which they were shot: Bitzer's camera had a mere two lenses, changeable only by removing one and screwing in the other. The necessity for working close-in meant he was in frequent danger from the prop bombs used to duplicate shell bursts.

1916

Searching for a drawcard to replace the lost Ince and Griffith, Mutual hired twenty-six year old Chaplin for $10,000 a week plus $150,000 bonus. Jesse Lasky, anxious to facilitate the merger with Hodkinson's Paramount, bought out his partner Samuel Goldfish for $900,000: Goldfish promptly joined Arthur Hopkins, playwright Margaret Mayo and Broadway producers Edgar and Arch Selwyn to form Goldwyn, a name he later adopted for himself. As part of a general rationalisation as MPPC crumbled, Vitagraph bought out its VLSE partners Selig, Lubin and Essanay, the last ruined by Chaplin's defection to Mutual, and acquired ailing Kalem. Recognising the danger of giving too much power to a star, Adolph Zukor of Famous Players met Mary Pickford's request for $1 million guaranteed profit each year by suggesting that she form her own company, Artcraft, which would then distribute its films through Zukor; Mary could charge Zukor what she liked for the films (and keep all the profit) while Famous Players passed the cost on to exhibitors in the form of high rentals. Lewis J. Selznick, who had already used a similar system in handling the films of Clara Kimball Young, rightly saw Zukor behind it and led the attack of exhibitors alarmed at the triple rentals Artcraft imposed. Nevertheless Artcraft (and thus Famous Players) prospered, and the Zukor empire grew. Meanwhile, at Triangle, Ince and Griffith, with their epics *Intolerance* and *Civilization*, were leading the company towards artistic immortality and financial ruin.

CIVILIZATION. Triangle. Supervised by Thomas H. Ince. Directed by Raymond B. West (additional material by Irvin Willatt, Scott Sidney, Reginald Barker and J. Parker Read Jnr.) . Script by Thomas H. Ince. Photographed by Robert Newhard and Irvin Willatt. Music score by Victor Schertzinger. Players: Howard Hickman (Count Ferdinand), Katherine (Enid Markey), J. Frank Burke (Luther Rolfe), George Fisher (Christ), J. Barney Sherry, Lola May.

One of the most extraordinary of early American films, Thomas Ince's *Civilization* shows how long-standing and complex a form the epic is, and the degree to which its success depends on management, engineering and timing rather than creative control. Made by Ince shortly after his departure from Reliance, it was, in his words, "an allegorical story about war (dealing) with those ranks that are already paying the grim penalty—the ranks of humanity," and intended to cash in on the prevailing pacifist sentiment of a United States as yet unwilling to enter the First World War. Ince's shrewdness eventually backfired when the US declared war just as the film went on release, but he still made $700,000 on his $100,000 investment, and did much to guarantee Wilson's re-election for a second term on an anti-war platform.

Civilization shows Ince as a skilful showman sharing much of Griffith's technical genius and judgement of popular taste without his visual flair. After a reverent introduction—"Civilisation has been misnamed in our modern times. Not until hatred, greed, envy is plucked from the heart of man can we hope for universal peace, for Civilization"—it shows the peaceful city of Nurma with its inhabitants—a happy blacksmith, farmers in their fields—unaware that in "the Seat of Pomp and Power" the government is preparing to go to war. Luther Rolf, described in various copies of the film as a socialist, a pacifist and a christian, argues with the king and council for peace, but his pleas are rejected since, as the king puts it, "war is necessary to any nation that wishes to survive." Meanwhile, Count Ferdinand, an inventor, demonstrates his submarine to the council, and is encouraged to perfect it as a weapon of war, something his fiancée Katherine re-

Charlie Chaplin: *The Cure.*

sists, preparing us for her later recruitment into a group of underground pacifists identified by hidden crosses stitched to their clothing. As the war begins, invaders destroy the tranquil life of Nurma. Ferdinand's submarine is ordered to sink a liner, the *Propatria*, but, remembering Katherine's protests, he holds the crew at gunpoint and sinks his own craft, killing himself in the process. A fantasy sequence follows in which he descends into Hell, sees a vision of Christ and is absorbed, Ince using an intricate series of dissolves to suggest that Christ has become Ferdinand. Reappearing in Nurma, Ferdinand speaks against the war, is jailed and sentenced to death but, after the pacifists have held mass prayer meetings before the palace, the king visits Ferdinand in his cell, and Christ appears and shows him the horrors of war for which he is responsible. Repenting, the king sues for peace, the shepherd returns to his sheep, and a dove settles on the barrel of an overturned cannon.

Stories vary about the production of this remarkable film. Ince wrote the script, and supervised the production in line with Triangle practice. During shooting, the master print was destroyed in a fire, and although the negative survived, Ince was dissatisfied

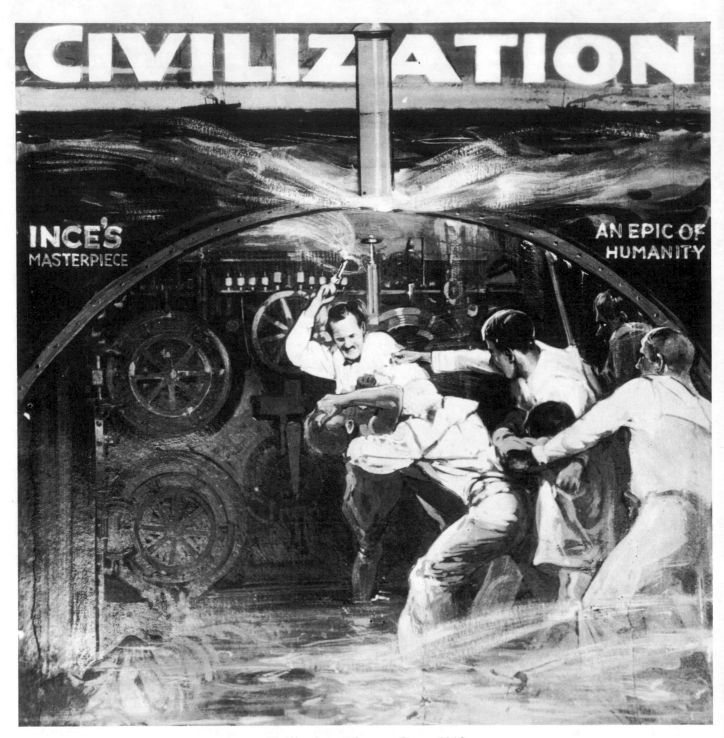

Civilization. Thomas Ince, 1916.

with the completed film, and asked Irvin Willatt, a talented cameraman and assistant director, to revise it. Willatt added the prologue and epilogue, and stiffened the central story by inserting portions of another Triangle film, *The Ice Bullet*, which used the same stars and costumes. (Most of Count Ferdinand's story is presumably from this source.) It is a tribute to Ince's management that despite an often lumbering pacifist allegory, the result seldom flags. Battle scenes with buildings shattering under gunfire (Willatt claimed he also improved these by enlargement with an optical printer he built himself) contrast with insets of war's horror: a horse pawing the dead body of its rider, women begging for bread, a tiny girl toddling out to welcome the returning army. Throughout, the photography shows a surprising virtuosity, with memorable images like the ranks of female pacifists marching silhouetted against the evening sky, and light flooding through a church window to glow on a nun's white coif. Both the sequence in Hell, with writhing souls in torment, and the *Propatria*'s destruction (visualised by Ferdinand as he prepares to torpedo it) have a technical skill that, whoever may be responsible, shows the true beginnings of Hollywood big-budget film-making.

HELL'S HINGES. Triangle/New York Motion Picture Co. Supervised by Thomas H. Ince. Directed by Charles Swickard. Script and titles by C. Gardner Sullivan. Photographed by Joseph August. Players: William S. Hart ("Blaze" Tracy), Clara Williams (Faith Henley), Jack Standing (Rev. Robert Henley), Alfred Hollingsworth ("Silk" Miller), Robert McKim (Clergyman), J. Frank Burke (Zeb Taylor), Louise Glaum (Dolly).

Although the Western had been a cinema staple since Edwin S. Porter's *The Great Train Robbery* (1903), its value as a vehicle for philosophy and morality began only with William Shakespeare Hart. Already a Western hero through his stage role as "The Virginian" (he also played on Broadway in "Camille," and was Messala in a lavish 1899 stage version of "Ben-Hur"), his hiring by Ince in 1914 began the screen's exploration of American mythology. His first Ince film, *The Bargain* (1914) was the first Western ever written specifically for the screen (by Ince and William H. Clifford) and Hart's subsequent two-reelers showed unusual realism. He insisted on accuracy in settings and costume, emphasising that his own clothing on screen minutely copied that of the working cowboy. Though Ince and Hart were barely on speaking terms for most of their association, the partnership produced films of great and lasting worth.

Supplanted in the Twenties by the more flamboyant Tom Mix and Buck Jones, Hart's studied style, reflecting a stage background, earned his undeserved demotion to a primitive if interesting pioneer. Yet his most ambitious Triangle production, *Hell's Hinges*, the most moving of all early Westerns whose violence

and realism are sustained by a poetic imagination and restraint in acting, is a uniquely modern work. It is not only Hart's resemblance to Randolph Scott that brings to mind the Boetticher/Scott/Harry Joe Brown "Ranown" Westerns of the Fifties; Boetticher's choice of the sparse desert setting also recalls the moral rigour of Hart and Ince.

William S. Hart (as *Wild Bill Hickok*, Clifford F. Smith, 1923).

Placer Center, nicknamed "Hell's Hinges," is a miserable collection of desert shacks to which the bishop sends Henley, a self-indulgent young minister, hoping to correct his tendency to become a "society priest" with, as a caption says, "an actor's delight in swaying his audience." After Henley has been initially beguiled—a clever dream sequence shows his vision of Western life, a group of admiring señoritas—the reality of Placer, traded upon by dance-hall owner "Silk" Miller and his girl Dolly, makes him turn to drink. Meanwhile, the town bad man, "Blaze" Tracy—"an embodiment of the best and worst of the early West" —has fallen in love with Henley's sister and joined the congregation, but despite his efforts Miller's customers burn the drunken Henley's church and, in a running gunfight through the streets, kill him and many of his followers. A furious Tracy burns "Hell's Hinges" to the ground, buries the young minister and sets off into the desert sunrise with the girl.

At a time when most Westerns were excuses for lively gunplay, fights and chases, Hart and Ince respected the form as a vehicle for ideas. A few wide streets clinging to a dusty hillside above the desert, Placer Center has a drab frontier featurelessness, and the gunfights in its streets, including an initial duel whose newsreel immediacy carries a legitimate chill, are, like the rowdiness of Miller's clients, natural results of a boring, meaningless existence. Hart, laconic, tough, handles both extremes of the story, from the amusement with which he leans down out of his saddle to grab a riddled tin can on which town sports have pasted a caricature of Henley, to his conversion, where he looks up from his Bible to the new church standing four-square against the desert: the director cuts to the shot of a rabbit quivering with fear, a remarkable image of a man facing unsuspected reality. One sees Ince's theatrical imagination in another of the symbolic representations of religious experience: hearing Faith Henley sing a hymn, Tracy visualises an ocean pounding on rocks, and a woman in white clasping a cross and looking out to sea, a symbol of "the white flame that shone over the blood-drenched arena and the racks of the Inquisition." The climax of revenge on the doomed town, and the image of two figures walking away from the smouldering ruins with a corpse slung over Tracy's horse, emphasised by high shots of the confusion, and sunbeams cutting through the smoke (a grotesque mixture of beauty and ruin a caption calls "Hell's Crown"), sustain this almost Wagnerian fantasy. Hart's film career was relatively brief. Quarrelling with Ince, he made fewer and fewer films, then, pleading he had made too much money, retired in the early Twenties to concentrate on ranching and writing inspirational books for boys. *Tumble-*

Intolerance. The Babylonian Episode.

weeds (King Baggott, 1925) with its exciting land-rush climax, is the fitting end to a notable and successful career.

INTOLERANCE. Director: D. W. Griffith. This epic dominated American film-making of the year as the enormous sets for the Babylonian episode monopolised the Hollywood skyline. All the town's extras, most of its technicians, including the entire staff of Triangle, and dozens of stars, current or future, took their place in Griffith's vast parable of human cruelty and its eventual destruction by love, a film that, despite violent opposition from the entrenched reactionaries, mutilation in which sections were lopped off to be released as individual features, and harsher criticism from intellectuals that Griffith's vision was simplistic and excessively literary in its basis, has triumphantly survived its time.

1917

The Patents Company was finally declared illegal, but Hollywood had long since ceased to respect it or its rules. After the Pickford/Artcraft *coup,* Zukor acquired Hodkinson's equity in the Paramount theatre chain and also bought up the Jesse Lasky studios, merging them in December 1918 with his own Famous Players to create the empire of modern Paramount. Beginning another empire, Louis B. Mayer left Metro to form Mayer Productions, stealing Vitagraph's Anita Stewart as his first star. Mayer's raid had an important side-effect. Ordered by Vitagraph to work the remaining months of her contract, Miss Stewart pleaded illness, but the court ruled that any days on which she was unavailable for work could be added to the period of the contract. Mayer was forced to buy up the balance for $70,000. This decision, giving studios the right to keep stars under contract almost indefinitely, suspending them if they proved intractable and adding the period of suspension to the end of the contract, was not over-ruled for twenty-seven years (see 1944).

To escape the dictatorship of Zukor and others, and the practice of block-booking, twenty-five owners of one hundred theatres formed First National Exhibitors' Circuit, shortly to become the largest US theatre chain and an ambitious production company. First National raided other studios for stars, acquiring Chaplin from Mutual by offering him relative autonomy and an effective release. The company provided $125,000 for each film, with an additional $15,000 a reel for productions longer than the customary two or three-reelers; profits were divided equally between the two sides after distribution costs were deducted. The deal offered Chaplin more than $1 million a year, making him the first super-star, reasonable recognition for an artist then at his peak; during 1917 he released four classics—*Easy Street, The Adventurer, The Cure* and *The Immigrant.*

Triangle, ruined by excessive investment in stage stars and the resignation of Ince who, quarrelling with Aitken, left to found his own studio, collapsed. Sennett, whose films had become the only continuously profitable part of Triangle's operations, returned to slapstick production, while Griffith, Fairbanks, Hart, Arbuckle, Emerson/Loos and also Ince, despite varying responses to the failure, all allied themselves with the ambitious Zukor, now Hollywood's most important figure.

WILD AND WOOLLY. Fairbanks/Artcraft-Paramount. Directed by John Emerson. Script by Anita Loos from story by Horace B. Carpenter. Photographed by Victor Fleming. Players: Douglas Fairbanks (Jeff Hillington), Eileen Percy (Nell), Sam de Grasse (Steve).

Few of Triangle's stars adjusted as well to the collapse as Douglas Fairbanks, whose aptitude in business matters did not always match his physical deftness. Seeing the company in difficulties, he negotiated a release from his contract and formed the Douglas Fairbanks Film Corporation with his brother Robert as Production Manager and half-brother John as business head. The Corporation then signed with the Zukor/Pickford Artcraft for a series of five-reel comedy-adventures exploring the light-hearted character he had created under Griffith's dour supervision. Three more Triangle graduates, director John Emerson, his wife, writer Anita Loos, and cameraman Victor Fleming became his regular team. In his first film after the break, *In Again, Out Again,* (John Emerson, 1917) he played the embodiment of Teddy Roosevelt's "preparedness" (his character was even named "Teddy Rutherford"), foiling burglars and other menaces through agility and alertness. *Wild and Woolly* continued this theme, with Fairbanks the son of a railroad magnate who, even in his father's city mansion, sustains the spirit of the old West, recreating it in his

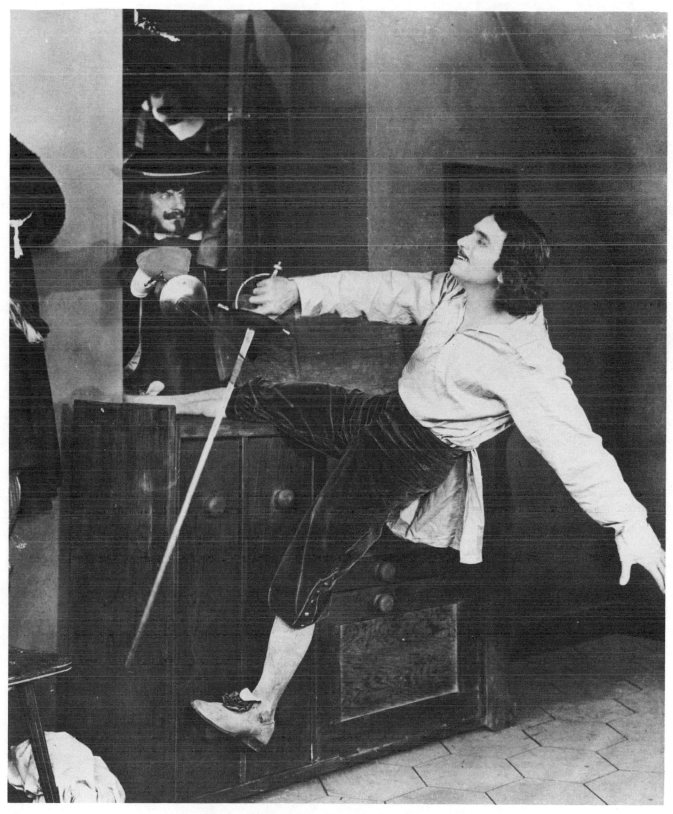

Douglas Fairbanks's energetic persona developed fully only in his self-produced historical romances; *The Three Musketeers* (Fred Niblo, 1921).

bedroom: he sleeps in a tent by a campfire, "rides" a saddle hung over a hurdle, and ropes the butler who calls him for meals. When his father, desperate for peace, sends him out West to decide whether a district should have a new line, obliging locals remake their town in the image of forty years earlier, judiciously loading all guns with blanks to avoid accidents, a move they regret when angry Indians from the local reservation attack the town; Fairbanks, however, with his enthusiasm and energy, vanquishes them and wins the girl.

"The main problem with writing for Douglas Fairbanks," Anita Loos has said, "was in finding new places for him to jump from." *Wild and Woolly* has him leaping on a horse's back, spinning a lariat with Will Rogers-like skill, escaping from a locked room by kicking holes in the ceiling and swinging up through the gap, and engaging in spirited fights with crowds of renegade Indians, a prescription that was to sustain him until ambition and the changing cin-ema, as well as his association with United Artists, led to major productions like *Robin Hood* and *The Thief of Bagdad* (see 1924).

THE BUTCHER BOY. Director: Roscoe "Fatty" Arbuckle. Buster Keaton's first film came in a year when Chaplin had reached his peak. Actually starring Arbuckle, with Keaton in a supporting role to Josephine Stevens and Luke the Dog, the film's best scene has Buster, the butcher boy, go to Fatty's grocer shop for a pail of treacle, omitting to tell him that the coin to pay for it is at the bottom of the pail. Arbuckle, having filled it, gropes for the coin, empties the treacle into Keaton's hat, then back into the pail, licking up the remains. Keaton's blank consideration of these actions, and the falls and flour fight that follow, show the timing and physical skill that was later to put him in a class above all other screen comedians.

1918

Ince was too adept to be caught in the Triangle collapse he had helped to bring about. Throughout his association with the company, he retained ownership of the studio in which his films were made, and of W. S. Hart's personal contract. When he withdrew, both went with him, and Aitken only persuaded him to relinquish the studio after paying $250,000. Signing a profitable deal with Zukor for the release of Hart's future films, Ince began building a new studio down the road from the Triangle lot, on sixteen acres of ground he had obtained free from property developer Harry Culver in 1915 on the promise to build a film studio there (an offer Culver made to all film producers, with meagre results). It is a measure of Ince's grandiose vision that the main office imitated George Washington's Mount Vernon home, and that its facilities were among Hollywood's best. But the investment overstretched Ince, and he was forced to sell the studio almost immediately to Goldwyn, who moved in in 1918. It was absorbed in the Metro-Goldwyn-Mayer merger (see 1924) and became the nucleus of M-G-M's Culver City lot. Ince's original building became David O. Selznick's office, and its facade, with the slogan "In a Tradition of Quality" superimposed, the Selznick company emblem.

The myth of Zukor's uncanny business sense was shaken when Mary Pickford showed signs of accepting an offer from the growing First National company to join its list of stars, and Zukor, on the advice of Cecil B. DeMille and other associates, declined to meet her new price, $250,000 each for three films. He did offer her $250,000 merely for an undertaking that she would appear in no films for five years but, recognising that her immense popularity would almost certainly evaporate if she delayed her career even for one year, Miss Pickford left to join the company that was to stop Zukor in his progress towards complete Hollywood domination.

STELLA MARIS. Artcraft/Paramount. Directed by Marshall Neilan. Script by Frances Marion from the novel by William J. Locke. Photographed by Walter Stradling. Art direction by Wilfred Buckland. Players: Mary Pickford (Stella Maris/Unity Blake), Conway Tearle (John Risca), "Marcia Manon"—Camille Ankewich—(Louise Risca), Ida Waterman (Lady Blount), Herbert Standing (Lord Blount), Josephine Crowell (Gladys Linder), "Himself" (The Dog).

Mary Pickford's sunny one-reelers for Biograph in 1909 and 1910 show little of the intensity of her first Hollywood films, and while *Rebecca of Sunnybrook Farm* (Marshall Neilan, 1917), despite its light exterior style, presages the drama of *Stella Maris* in its storm scenes, the impact of this production on audiences accustomed to "Little Mary, America's Sweetheart" was profound. Even today, its realism and lack of sentiment are impressive. Pickford plays a double role: in one persona she is Stella Maris, a young cripple whose guardians protect her childish view of the world, in which she is the Princess of Happiness and those who visit her, even unhappily married journalist John Risca, are her adoring servants; in the other, she is Unity Blake, a poor-house orphan. Unknown to her husband, Risca's feckless wife Louise, already an alcoholic and shortly to be a heroin addict, takes Unity from the orphanage to be her servant, and when her purchases are stolen on a shopping trip, beats the girl with a red-hot poker. The wife is jailed, and Risca adopts Unity. Meanwhile, Stella Maris, cured of her paralysis, has learned to walk; she and Risca fall in love, but when, hoping to surprise him, Stella visits his house—which, child-like, she still thinks of as a knight's castle—her illusions are shattered by a meeting with the drunken Louise. Appalled by her new discovery of the world's misery, she berates her guardians for failing to expose her to it earlier and Risca, despairing, decides to kill himself. It is only the hardened Unity, long since stripped of illusions by her ugliness and hopeless life, who sees the logical solution by which she can help the people she loves: she murders Louise and then kills herself.

Zukor, who left Pickford's films largely in her hands under the Artcraft deal, was horrified when, returning from a business trip, he arrived on the *Stella Maris* set to find it a realistic recreation of a poorhouse dormitory and his star's hair plastered flat with vaseline, one hip lower than the other (Pickford having reasoned that a slum girl from a large family would slouch from carrying younger brothers on her hip), dressed in calico and swathed in bandages. "It's OK," she is said to have told Zukor consolingly, "I die before the picture's over." She had encouraged actor Marshall Neilan, her co-star in *Madame Butterfly* (1915), to try directing, and found him a sensitive stylist with an instinctive understanding of her sentimental manner. Like most of their collaborations, *Stella Maris* shines in its Pickford set-pieces: the moment when Unity peers at the framed portrait of Stella, then looks at her reflection in a mirror, fails to relate it to Stella's misty beauty, and collapses weeping, is a scene of which no dramatic actress need be ashamed, just as the murder of Louise, with Unity moving through the darkened house and into close-up so that only her eyes are lit, conveys haunting despair and malevolence. Stella's scenes, less intense, show Neilan's taste for formal arrangements of rural beauty: a moonlight interlude between John and Stella with halating light in the lens; a love scene framed with an arch of flowers, a decorative effect borrowed from *Rebecca*. The beauty of *Stella Maris*, its double-exposures, masks and wipes show Neilan, who later deteriorated into a bland stylishness, as the most interesting and unassertive of early Hollywood artists in the smooth studio style.

THE HIRED MAN. Ince. Directed by Victor Schertzinger. Script by Julien Josephson. Players: Charles Ray (Ezry Hollins), Doris Lee (Ruth Endicott), Karl Ullman (Stuart Morley), Lydia Knott (Ma Endicott), Charles French (Pa Endicott), Robert Gordon (Walter Endicott).

A failure to understand their limitations has ruined many Hollywood actors, but none so tragically as Charles Ray. Discovered by Ince and cast as shy country boy in a series of films between 1912 and 1920, Ray remained out of sympathy with such roles even when his popularity was at its height. Later he said

his goal had always been "artistic, uplifting psychological drama," and though Ince often hardened Ray's characters, making him a Confederate deserter in *The Coward* (1915) and a dishonest employee in *The Family Skeleton* (1918), the last reel always saw his redemption. An attempt to succeed in his chosen field after leaving Ince led to an independent production of *The Courtship of Miles Standish* (Frederick Sullivan, 1923) which failed disastrously, and Ray, after the typically flamboyant gesture of throwing a huge party on the eve of his bankruptcy, declined to playing extra roles and died penniless in 1943.

The Hired Man. Charles Ray.

Ray's expressed contempt for his performances as an amiable rustic hardly squares with the skill and conviction he brought to them. In *The Hired Hand*, countless opportunities to let action carry the film are rejected, Ray investing his scenes with unforced sentiment and humanity to which one instinctively responds. Into the story of a shy farmhand who earns community respect and the girl he loves despite misunderstandings and his own reticence, Ray instills an Ince-like streak of rural dignity, echoed in the director's accurate depiction of the flat Mid-Western farm country and of events like a district agricultural fair, recorded with a documentary sharpness that contrasts with the pastoral delicacy of *The Old Swimmin' Hole* (Joseph de Grasse, 1921), Ray's best known film, shot for First National after his break with Ince, but inferior in most respects to the harsher *The Hired Man.*

1919

Even without Pickford, Zukor held the balance of Hollywood power, and might have established a monopoly had not his own general manager, Benjamin P. Schulberg, teamed up with Hiram Abrams, Paramount president until a dispute with Zukor, and approached Hollywood's biggest names, Griffith, Chaplin, Pickford and Fairbanks, to form a company to distribute their own films and those of major independent producers. The four agreed, and William Gibbs McAdoo, President Wilson's son-in-law and Secretary of the Treasury, became financial head of United Artists, which put film-making resources and profits into the artists' hands. The preponderance of actors in its make-up, and in that of companies formed in its wake, points to a major shift in emphasis from the director's cinema, which Triangle, essentially a directors' consortium, represented, to the performer's cinema which dominated Hollywood for thirty years. Griffith, significantly, was the first to feel ill at ease in the UA hierarchy (prior commitments also complicated his full participation) and he preferred to work alone, while Chaplin, whose ambition lured him to feature direction, did not fully exploit the UA machine. It was Mary Pickford and Douglas Fairbanks who made most use of their freedom, setting up a studio, hiring the best cameramen and designers—Charles Rosher, Miss Pickford's personal photographer, did much to perfect Hollywood visual style, and William Cameron Menzies its design techniques on the Fairbanks costume romances—and acquiring the best new stars. Buster Keaton, Rudolph Valentino (who had his first featured role in *The Married Virgin*—Joseph Maxwell, 1918—after graduating, like Clifton Webb and Mae Murray, from New York exhibition dancing) and countless other creative performers were to find United Artists a congenial and stimulating studio.

Frustrated in his attempt to dominate film production, Zukor turned to exhibition where, he reasoned, the industry's real power lay. Helped by cultivated Broadway patron and financier Otto Kahn, he issued $10 million in Famous Players-Lasky stock to finance the construction of major cinemas in locations where First National had hitherto held total control. As well as beginning the rush to buy and build cinemas that dominated the next five years, this issue had long-term effects. Hollywood had never before offered shares in itself nor become deeply involved in the commercial world, except for unpromising flotations of Triangle and World Film stock, both of which had failed. Zukor stock was, however, gilt-edged, and its quotation on the stock exchange opened the way for other producers to seek outside finance. Hollywood soon shared all American industry's reliance on New York banking houses, whose conservatism was to have a direct effect on film content and policy in future years.

MALE AND FEMALE. Famous Players/Lasky. Produced and directed by Cecil B. DeMille. Script by Jeanie Macpherson based on "The Admirable Crichton" by J. M. Barrie. Photographed by Alvin Wyckoff. Edited by Anne Bauchens. Players: Gloria Swanson (Lady Mary Lasenby), Thomas Meighan (Crichton), Lila Lee (Tweeny), Theodore Roberts (Lord Loam), Raymond Hatton (Hon. Ernest Wolley), Mildred Reardon (Agatha Lasenby), Bebe Daniels (The King's Favourite), Robert Cain (Lord Brocklehurst), Julia Faye (Susan), Rhy Darby (Lady Eileen Dun Craigie), Maym Kelso (Lady Brocklehurst), Edward (Edmund) Burns (Treherne), Henry Woodward (McGuire), Sydney Deane (Thomas), Wesley Barry ("Buttons").

DeMille's version of Barrie's gentle social satire in which, among the members of an aristocratic yachting party shipwrecked on a Pacific island, only Crichton, the butler, proves a natural nobleman and leader, was predictably boosted with stars and production values into a garish distortion of the original. With it, De-Mille popularised the bath scene, exploiting Gloria Swanson's Latin beauty in a sunken-bath interlude whose luxury and veiled eroticism established a tradition, culminating in Claudette Colbert's bath, with real milk, in *The Sign of the Cross* (1932). He also exercised his *penchant* for historical spectacle by inserting a lavish flashback, feebly excused by Lady Mary speculating that she and Crichton may have been antagonists/lovers in some previous existence. The verse "When you were a king in Babylon/And I was a Christian slave" justifies the sequence in which Miss Swanson rejects the overtures of Meighan's emperor and goes to a glamorous death in a lion pit, the animals pawing nervously at elaborate costumes of *lamé*, sequins and pearls created by Mitchell Leisen. Never a good comedy director, DeMille is heavy-handed in the island scenes, interesting mainly for the Robinson Crusoe methods used by the castaways to restore the necessities of life; but in sex and spectacle he had few competitors.

BROKEN BLOSSOMS. United Artists. Directed by D. W. Griffith. Script by Griffith based on "The Chink and the Child" by Thomas Burke. Photographed by G. W. Bitzer. Players: Lillian Gish (Lucy Burrows), Richard Barthelmess (The Yellow Man), Donald Crisp (Battling Burrows).

Absent from Hollywood for two years, during which time he had produced his flawed anti-war melodrama *Hearts of the World* in Britain and France, Griffith returned to make a film which was unconventionally European in sensibility and style. Taken from a story in Thomas Burke's "Limehouse Nights," sketches of life in what had been London's Asian quarter in the 1890s, it cast Richard Barthelmess as a Chinese shop-keeper and Lillian Gish as the brutalised daughter of broken-down prizefighter Battling Burrows. Shot in only eighteen days, after long rehearsal, and on simple

Broken Blossoms. Lillian Gish (centre).

sets duplicating London slums of a generation before, *Broken Blossoms* has the dream-like elegance of a Wiene or Murnau work: Lillian Gish's waif shuffling through the fog, crushed by the misery of her existence, while Barthelmess's black-clothed Yellow Man, movements as fluid and alien as those of Conrad Veidt's somnambulist in *The Cabinet of Dr. Caligari (Das Kabinett des Dr. Caligari,* made the same year), watches silently as she moves by, unaware of his existence and love. The film's set-pieces are made for Miss Gish—her desperate forgery of a smile, pushing up the corners of her mouth with two fingers, and her terror as, locked in a closet with Burrows pounding at the door, she whirls in hysteria within the constricting space—but Barthelmess, in a role demanding the most rigid restriction of mannerism and movement, is its true star.

1920

After having dissolved their respective marriages—Fairbanks was divorced by Anna Beth Sully in 1918; Pickford divorced director Owen Moore in 1920—Douglas Fairbanks and Mary Pickford married on March 28. Their house, "Pickfair," became the movie colony's social heart, where they entertained visiting aristocracy and the *élite* of both coasts. The image of a "golden couple" persisted even away from home, where Doug and Mary requested they should always be seated together at dinner parties. Hollywood finally left such mythological relationships behind; the two stars, both rich but forgotten by their world, were divorced in 1936.

As if in contrast with the "Pickfair" circle and announcing the more business-like Hollywood to come, four brothers named Warner moved into films from their Chicago scrap-metal and wholesale butchery business. Initially interested only in exhibition, they were encouraged to enter production by the youngest, Jack L. Warner, who had tried his hand at producing and acting with *Open Your Eyes* (Gilbert P. Hamilton, 1919), an anti-venereal disease film in which Ben Lyon, previously an extra, played his first featured role as a boy led astray by bad companions, one played by Warner himself. Lyon recalls the film was made on New York streets only one step ahead of the police, and that Warner, although showing production flair, was a poor actor (see 1925).

The unstable Metro company, after rashly spending large amounts on a "Screen Classics" series of prestige pictures that failed to return their cost—with between six and eight hundred features a year from Hollywood, the market was oversupplied, especially since the European cinema was now back to full production—offered its assets to Zukor and, when he turned it down, sold out to New York theatre chain owner Marcus Loew, who wanted a production end to his operation. Among the properties owned by Metro at the time were the film rights to what seemed, in the post-war decline of interest in war pictures, an unfilmable story—Ibanez's "The Four Horsemen of the Apocalypse." The mammoth success of this film (see 1921) was later to repay almost all of Loew's investment in the company. Meanwhile, First National had effectively outlawed the "block booking" system previously forced on exhibitors by the studios, and was succeeding with its policy of booking the best available films for its 3,000 cinemas. This success angered Zukor, who set out to stop the spread of this disconcerting independent chain.

THE PENALTY. Goldwyn. Directed by Wallace Worsley. Script by Charles Kenyon from the novel by Gouverneur Morris. Players: Lon Chaney (Blizzard), Claire Adams (Barbara), Kenneth Harlan (Dr. Wilmot), Charles Clary (Doctor), Ethel Grey Terry (Rose), Edouard Trebaol (Bubble), Milton Rose (Lichtenstein), James Mason (Pete), Wilson Hummell (Crook).

Lon Chaney died in 1930 with his perplexing and private personality unpenetrated, a mass of vague studio propaganda obscuring a man whose motives were plainly unique. Forbidding any publicity except in connection with his current film and retiring after each production to fish and meditate, he seemed less one man than a shifting set of *personae* in which his own was intentionally lost. His favourite film was *Tell It to the Marines* (George Hill, 1927), almost his only starring role without make-up, in which he played a Marine sergeant (at the hour of his funeral the M-G-M flag was lowered by a Marine, while another blew "Taps.") Sound films were to him a threat. "When you hear a person talk," he said, "you begin to know him better. . . . It has taken me years to build up a sort of mystery surrounding myself . . . and I wouldn't sacrifice it by talking." ("New York Times," July 6,

The Growth of a Studio: a) Warner Brothers first
studio, 1920; b) First National Studios at Burbank,
with whom Warners merged in 1929; c) Warner
Brothers in the 1940s.

a

b

c

1930) When he finally made his only sound film, a re-make of *The Unholy Three* in 1930, he used five voices, none of them his own. Shortly afterwards, on August 26, he died, paradoxically of bronchial cancer.

The Penalty shows clearly the twin aspects of Chaney's career and character. His almost masochistic ingenuity in finding ways to twist his body into grotesque shapes, and the bitter emphasis on sexual frustration, loneliness and despair all his films reflect. (Chaney was brought up with parents who were deaf-mutes.) In the film, Blizzard has had both legs amputated after a childhood accident in which a fractured skull also affected his sanity. Years later, the rich and feared boss of the Barbary Coast brothels, he sets out to ruin the career of the doctor responsible for his mutilation, a task from which he is diverted when the doctor removes a blood clot from his brain, restoring his sanity. Both legs strapped up behind him (with an agonising effect on his circulation) and moving on crutches with a dexterity bespeaking a lifetime's practice, Chaney makes Blizzard almost too believable, notably in a key scene where he visits his mistress, playfully takes her on his knees in a gesture that has elements of the girl's intentional humiliation, then plays the piano with her below him on the floor working the pedals, telling her of his plans to control San Francisco, and to exact from it "the pleasures of a Nero, the powers of a Caesar." Both his earlier grotesque triumph in *The Miracle Man* (George Loane Tucker, 1919) where he metamorphoses from twisted cripple to whole man before an astonished crowd, and the more extravagant romances (*The Phantom of the Opera*, Rupert Julian/Edward Sedgwick, 1925) and *The Hunchback of Notre Dame* (Wallace Worsley, 1923) had greater publicity, but *The Penalty* reveals Chaney at his most adept and disturbing.

Lon Chaney as "Blizzard" in *The Penalty*.

1921

Zukor's empire-building activities in acquiring new cinemas for the Paramount chain and his continuing battle with First National brought him into conflict with the Motion Picture Theatre Owners, an organisation of independent theatre owners and small chains formed to protect its members against Paramount's increasingly ruthless practices. Cinemas that refused to sign with Zukor were bankrupted by the construction of a large Paramount theatre nearby, and Zukor's "dynamiters" frequently moved in on new additions to the chain, fired the employees and replaced them with company men. At the MPTO convention in Minneapolis, Zukor finally agreed to curtail his activities. The high-water mark of Paramount expansion had been reached, and the Federal Trade Commission's 1922 suit against him for monopolistic practices, taken with the growth of M-G-M and Fox, doomed Zukor's plans for wholesale domination of Hollywood, though until the early Thirties "Paramount" justified its name.

On September 5, at a party in San Francisco's St. Francis Hotel, young actress Virginia Rappe, girl friend of Henry "Pathé" Lehrman, was taken ill, allegedly as a result of having had sexual intercourse with comedian Roscoe Arbuckle. She died shortly afterwards of peritonitis, and on September 14 Arbuckle was charged with manslaughter. The juries in two subsequent trials were unable to agree, largely because of a violent public outcry fed by fanciful rumours as to the circumstances of the girl's injury, but a third jury acquitted him eight months later. Although he made a few films as director (under the rueful alias "Will B. Good"), went into the restaurant business (his Hollywood club "The Plantation Room" closed after the 1929 Crash), and even appeared on Broadway in a play, "Baby Mine" (some provincial tours had to be cancelled because of public resistance), he never regained his former standing.

By 1932, Warners were sufficiently certain of his rehabilitation to offer a contract to appear in short comedies, but he had made only one when he died on April 24, 1933.

TOL'ABLE DAVID. Inspiration Pictures/First National. Produced by Charles H. Duell. Directed by Henry King. Script by Edmund Goulding and King from the novel by Joseph Hergesheimer. Photographed by Henry Cronjager. Edited by Duncan Mansfield. Players: Richard Barthelmess (David Kinemon), Gladys Hulette (Esther Hatburn), Edmund Gurney (Hunter Kinemon), Marion Abbott (Mrs. Kinemon), Lawrence Eddinger (John Galt), Walter Lewis (Iska Hatburn), Ernest Torrence (Luke Hatburn), Ralph Yearsley (Buzzard Hatburn), Forrest Robinson (Neighbour Hatburn).

One of the most famous and enduring examples of Hollywood Americana, Henry King's classic used authentic Virginia locations to echo the story's rural charm. Originally to have been made by D. W. Griffith, Hergesheimer's story was bought from him by King who, with financier Averell Harriman, Richard Barthelmess and producer Charles Duell formed Inspiration Pictures to make it for a low $86,000. Barthelmess, then twenty-six, played teenager David Kinemon, a farm boy whose ambition is to drive the mail coach from the nearest town to his village of Greenstream. When his dream finally comes true, he accidentally drops the mail bag, which is stolen by the brutish Hatburn brothers, led by towering Luke, played by English character actor Ernest Torrence in his first Hollywood role. The fugitive Hatburns have imposed themselves on their relative and his daughter Esther, with whom David is in love, and, returning to the Hatburn house, David fights the brothers, defeats or kills them all and, despite injuries, carries the mail to Greenstream. Melodrama is neutralised by un-

Ernest Torrence. (M-G-M photo by Ruth Harriet Louise)

spoiled locations (King was brought up in the same area) and by Barthelmess's restrained playing as the cheerful, simple David. Whether losing his pants to a playful dog in the opening scene and then encountering the curious Esther with horrified embarrassment, dreaming of being the mail driver, only to have his dream shattered when the fence on which he is leaning collapses, or being driven by a steely spirit to recapture the mail bag from the sadistic Hatburns in a bloodily violent sequence, he conveys accurately the innocence and strength of rural life.

THE FOUR HORSEMEN OF THE APOCALYPSE. Metro Pictures. Directed by Rex Ingram. Script by June Mathis from the novel by Vincente Blasco-Ibanez. Photographed by John F. Seitz. Art direction by Joseph Calder. Edited by Grant Whytock. Special effects by Amos Myers. Art titles by John W. Robinson. Players: Rudolph Valentino (Julio Desnoyers), Alice Terry (Marguerite Laurier), Pomeroy Cannon (Madriaga, the Centaur), Joseph Swickard (Marcelo Desnoyers), Brinsley Shaw (Celendonio), Alan Hale (Karl von Hartrott), Bridgetta Clark (Dona Luisa), Mabel Van Buren (Elena), Brodwitch "Smoke" Turner (Argensola), Nigel de Brulier (Tchernoff), John Sainpolis (Laurier), Mark Fenton (Senator Lacour), Virginia Warwick (Chichi), Derek Ghent (René Lacour), Stuart Holmes (Capt. von Hartrott), Jean Hersholt (Prof. von Hartrott), Henry Klaus (Heinrick von Hartrott), Edward Connelly (Lodgekeeper), Georgia Woodthorpe (Lodgekeeper's Wife), Kathleen Key (Georgette), Wallace Beery (Lt. Col. von Richthoffen), Jacques D'Auray (Capt. D'Aubrey), Curt Rehfeld (Major Blumhardt), Mlle. Dolorez (Lucette, the Model), Bull Montana (Barber), Noble Johnson (Conquest), Beatrice Dominguez (Dancer).

When Blasco-Ibanez's fevered novel of the European war and Spanish nobility appeared in America in 1918, its popularity was immense, but peace, which had caught studios producing war films for which the public had little interest, made its filming difficult. When Metro's Richard Rowland, impressed by the novel's sales if not its story, bought it for $20,000 plus 10% of the gross, his own executives and especially theatre tycoon Marcus Loew, Metro's major shareholder, were hostile. But June Mathis, top scenarist to whom the project was entrusted, saw its potential, and also that of young actor Rudolph Valentino, whom she suggested to star as Julio Desnoyers instead of the nondescript Carlyle Blackwell. Her faith in both was fulfilled: *The Four Horsemen* became one of Hollywood's all-time financial successes and Valentino a great star.

Slow and mannered by modern standards, Rex Ingram's film echoes the sweep of its subject in the classic style of development, following the decline of a noble Argentinian family, the sisters of which marry a German and Frenchman respectively. The German, regimented and unfeeling, produces three sons, hardened Junkers reflecting their father's militaristic principles, while the Frenchman, a visionary forced to flee Europe because of his socialist ideas, produces Julio, sensitive, cultivated and weak. Moving to Paris, Julio plays at being an artist, entertaining models and finally the bored Madam Laurier in his studio until her husband finds them. Meanwhile, war is declared and Laurier becomes a blinded cripple. Julio, realising his worthlessness, joins the French army, fighting the invading German army in which his three cousins are officers. In the battle around his father's *château*, the castle and its art treasures are destroyed, and Julio killed. Reeling from the smoke of battle, his spirit sees the four horsemen of the Apocalypse—Famine, Pestilence, War and Death—riding across the sky, and the ghost, clothing scorched and smoking, appears to Marguerie Laurier as she tends her husband, a dramatic symbol of war's destruction of youth and love.

Ingram's virtuosity balances the plot's *longueurs*, and he gives the film all the visual beauty of which he and Seitz were masters. The use of arches to frame compositions and of gauze to soften close-ups of Alice Terry, his leading lady and later wife, show the influence of European film-making, and of stylists like

The famous tango from *The Four Horsemen of the Apocalypse.*

Neilan who pioneered such techniques with Pickford. Few sequences lack some bizarre detail from Ingram's vivid imagination: a casual street scene becomes a symbol of the risk the lovers run when a wagon's wheels pass on either side of an oblivious baby, leaving it unharmed; Valentino's famous tango in an Argentinian bar is handled with great *panache,* with the bar a high-ceilinged cellar and the feet of passing pedestrians glimpsed in narrow. windows high above the dancers' heads. Julio, visited by his father at a soldiers' roadside rest station, carries a monkey that mischievously inspects the heads of his comrades for lice, while a Red Cross nurse emerges with a long stick looped with doughnuts which she distributes among the men. Draped nudes in Julio's Paris studio suggest his dissipation, and a surprising scene in which the Junker cousin is seen luxuriating in a bubble bath with a patent band to protect his waxed moustache (a

detail reminiscent of the mature work of von Stroheim, as is a later scene of Germans drinking champagne from jackboots and parading in women's under-clothes) show Ingram's ability to convey personality through gesture and background, a skill that places him in the forefront of Hollywood creators.

When Rowland and Loew sensed in the rushes the potential of Valentino, additional material was shot to expand his part, but by this time Metro was over-committed and Loew stepped in to buy total control (see 1924). After being cast in some routine melodramas by Rowland, Valentino asked for $100 increase to his $350 salary and when Metro countered with a $50 offer left, with June Mathis, to join Jesse Lasky at Paramount, where he was promptly cast in *The Sheik,* which established his career. *The Four Horsemen of the Apocalypse* remains, however, his finest film.

1922

"I was the spark that lit up flaming youth," F. Scott Fitzgerald wrote. "Colleen Moore was the torch." When the Western Associated Motion Picture Advertisers (WAMPAS) held their first annual elections for the "baby stars" of Hollywood in 1922, it was Miss Moore who topped their list, above Mary Philbin, Patsy Ruth Miller, Jacqueline Logan, Lila Lee and Bessie Love. Hollywood took the jazz age to its heart. Clara Bow began her career in *Beyond the Rainbow,* her prize for winning a beauty contest. Films were advertised with a breathless style redolent of the age: "Brilliant men, beautiful jazz babies, champagne baths, midnight revels, petting parties in the purple dawn . . ." and "Neckers, petters, white kisses, red kisses, pleasure-mad daughters, sensation-craving mothers . . ." "Jazz tinting," in which alternate feet of film were tinted or toned different shades (see 1935), gave sequences of such films an eye-straining psychedelic quality not seen again until the Sixties. Despite Prohibition, bootleggers thrived in Hollywood, often using studio prop departments to give bathtub brandy spurious authenticity with sprayed-on cobwebs and dust. Hard drugs, still not illegal, were widely available, and many films featured their use. But the Arbuckle scandal, combined with the murder of Famous Players-Lasky director William Desmond Taylor on February 2 and the implication in his death of stars Mabel Normand and Mary Miles Minter, the revelation of Wallace Reid's drug addiction (he died in 1923) and other disasters forced Hollywood to accept self-censorship as an alternative to federal control. Will H. Hays, Postmaster-General under Harding, a traditional reward for political services rendered, was offered $100,000 annually— Harding paid only $12,000—to head the Motion Picture Producers and Distributors of America (MPPDA) which formally began operations in March. A seasoned politician despite his hayseed appearance, deeply in-

Wallace Reid (left) in one of his most popular appearances as a resourceful young man. *The Dancing Fool* (1920).

volved in Harding's landslide victory and highly praised for modernising the outdated postal system, Hays, who had proved his usefulness to Hollywood with some string-pulling on behalf of Zukor and the Schencks, was an ideal choice. Among his first moves was the establishment of an index of prohibited books and plays; by 1929, it contained 125 titles, including at least fifteen Broadway hits.

Hays also set up an official actor employment agency, Central Casting. Officially opened in 1925 as a company wholly owned by the MPPDA, Central Casting removed such practices as the "casting couch" system of seduction and that of prostitutes avoiding vagrancy charges by claiming to be film extras. All extras were required to register with Central Casting, and studios

The breadline of Hollywood. Extras check out of the Goldwyn studio.

agreed to employ only its members. An elaborate coding system made obsolete the old "bull pen" method in which extras gathered in a studio compound each day in the hope of work, often wearing their own evening dress ("dress extras" were paid a higher rate than the usual $3.50–$5.00 a day) or sporting bizarre make-up to catch an action director's eye (Lon Chaney began his career in this way). In *The Last Command* (1928) Josef von Sternberg, an ex-assistant director, showed the iniquities of this system, describing the mob of eager and humiliated extras as "the bread-line of Hollywood."

FOOLISH WIVES. Universal. Presented by Carl Laemmle. Direction, story and script by Erich von Stroheim. Titles by Marian Ainslee and von Stroheim. Photographed by Ben Reynolds and William Daniels. Are direction by E. E. Sheeley and Richard Day. Musical score by Sigmund Romberg. Players: Erich von Stroheim (Count Sergius Karamzin), Rudolph Christians (Andrew J. Hughes), Miss DuPont (Helen, his wife), Maude George (Princess Olga Petschnikoff), Mae Busch (Princess Vera Petschnikoff), Dale Fuller (Maruschka, a Maid), Al Edmundsen (Pavel Pavlich, a Butler), Cesare Gravina (Ventucci), Malvine Polo (Marietta), Louis K. Webb (Dr. Judd), Mrs. Kent (His Wife), C. J. Allen (Prince of Monaco), Edward Reinach (Secretary of State).

Carl Laemmle's flirtation with the declining "Famous Players" concept pioneered by Zukor and Lasky led him to support Erich von Stroheim in the production of his ambitious masterpieces. Trips to Europe kept him aloof from Stroheim's bizarre working methods and lavish expenditure, and it was to young studio manager Irving Thalberg that the responsibility fell of regulating a director to whom the commercial realities of Hollywood mattered not at all. On *Foolish Wives,* Stroheim shot most scenes at night when the studio was quiet and he could achieve more effectively his subtle lighting effects; the electricity and overtime bills were enormous. The villa had an electric bell system, never seen or heard but justified by Stroheim as a means of guaranteeing that Dale Fuller's performance as the maid had the necessary verisimilitude. The caviare he piles on his boiled eggs in a breakfast scene is also real, presumably for the same reason.

The completed film ran to twenty-one reels and was designed to be shown in two parts. In it, Stroheim cut to the core of corruption in social and marital relations, showing, as Von Sternberg was later to do in his best films, that personality is merely a set of deceptions and love the expression of one person's desire to be absorbed and destroyed by the other. His own Count Karamzin, installed in a Monaco villa with two shadowy "cousins" who seem variously to be mistresses, confederates and employees, exploits women ruthlessly—even his maid, whose savings he steals, and the idiot daughter of a counterfeiter from whom he obtains fake money to sustain his excesses. Intriguing the wife of the American ambassador to Monaco, he seduces her, makes her pregnant, then abandons her. He is at last stopped by the counterfeiter, who kills him in revenge for attempting to rape his daughter and stuffs the corpse into a sewer where it is carried out to sea with other *débris.*

Recognising that *Foolish Wives* had negligible commercial value, Thalberg cut it from twenty-one reels to fourteen, compromising it as a work of art and making the message broader and more harsh. What remains is nevertheless impressive, notably Von Stroheim's vicious, self-indulgent but oddly amiable Count, wolfing ox blood and caviare for breakfast, scenting eyebrows and buffing nails with the care of a *débutant,* then potting pigeons from his balcony like a born sportsman. After seducing the Ambassador's wife, he lures her to a hovel during a rainstorm, where, after courteously turning his back as she undresses, he appraises her charms in a hand-mirror—a goat tethered in the hut suggests Karamzin's ruttish instincts, while the mysterious monk, commenting on the gullibility of women who can be peeled as easily as a fruit, predicts his downfall. When his safety is at stake, Karamzin discards her, leaping from his burning villa, ignited by the jealous maid, and leaving her inside. (Later he claims to have jumped first "to give her courage.") Whether callously dripping water on the hands of the soft-hearted maid to suggest tears and thus extort her savings, creeping through a window to contemplate with relish the sleeping idiot whom he proposes to rape, or manipulating the romantic wife who sees his attentions as part of the romance of European sophistication, Stroheim's Karamzin is a monument to self-interest, at his most charming when he cares least for those he preys upon.

Universal's exhibitors greeted the film with reactions ranging from enthusiasm to shocked horror. In March

Foolish Wives. Erich von Stroheim.

1922, "Photoplay" called it "an insult to every American," mainly because an American diplomat was chosen as the cuckolded husband. One distributor even rewrote the titles to call Hughes a travelling salesman, making unaccountable the Naval honours on his arrival in Monte Carlo and audience at the Court of Monaco. The premature birth of Mrs. Hughes's child by Karamzin, his murder and the girl's attempted rape were also deleted in most release prints. Von Stroheim went on to make *Greed* at M-G-M, his greatest work but one as hopelessly compromised by its studio as *Foolish Wives* was by a producer later to make M-G-M industrially supreme in Hollywood.

SALOME. Director: Charles Bryant.
THE YOUNG RAJAH. Director: Philip Rosen.

One of Hollywood's most unconventional and short-lived talents, designer Natasha Rambova was the *protégée* of Alla Nazimova, the Russian Art Theatre actress and classic interpreter of Ibsen who established a reputation during the early Twenties for the intense, restrained acting-style developed by Stanislavski and Reinhardt's "Kammerspiel" as an alternative to the stylised extravagance of Expressionist dramaturgy.

After designing a lush version of *Camille* (Ray C. Smallwood, 1920) for Nazimova and Rudolph Valentino, Miss Rambova and the young Valentino struck up a passionate relationship and later married; her remarkable graphic style, more reminiscent of Vienna's Secessionist artists like Klimt or the Russian Tairov Theatre than of Hollywood, influenced his choice of film subjects until his death.

The forty-minute *Salome* was made independently by Nazimova as a showcase for Miss Rambova, who exploited the opportunity by designing sets that followed Aubrey Beardsley's erotic *art nouveau* illustrations for Oscar Wilde's play. Nazimova's tense style was subordinated to design, both in the pearl-studded costumes she wore and in the complex screens and props with which she was surrounded. The actress, seeing the film as "a kind of dream or phantasmagoria," wrote the script herself under the name "Peter M. Winters," basing it on a new translation of the play by Wilde's son Vyvyan Holland, from which the titles are drawn. The music was taken from Richard Strauss's opera "Salome," and issued in a form suitable for playing on a typical cinema organ.

Though a commercial failure, *Salome* sufficiently impressed Paramount to agree, at Valentino's insistence, to let Miss Rambova conceive his next film. *The Young Rajah* was a film of extraordinary eccentricity, casting Valentino as the son of an Indian prince who is brought to the United States and raised as a farmer's son in order to protect him from his father's enemies. Despite his love for an American girl, he is drawn back to India by his ability to foretell events, and sacrifices happiness to govern his people. Using pearls and elaborate *art nouveau* arabesques similar to those in *Salome,* Miss Rambova capitalised on Valentino's physical beauty, and despite the nonsensical plot it achieved a minor success; but the popularity of *The Sheik* persuaded Paramount that it was in his Arabic *persona* that Valentino's primary appeal lay.

1923

Thirty minute "prologues" had became an accepted part of first-run cinema programmes in the big cities. Often crude *mélanges* of vaudeville acts, they occasionally, for a film of greater quality, employed elaborate effects. For the American release of *The Cabinet of Doctor Caligari* in 1923 (after a brief 1921 showing in some cities), they aided acceptance of Wiene's film by providing dramatic justification for its illogical story (at least, to American eyes). For *A Woman of Paris* (1923), Chaplin, tired of trite prologues, designed and produced his own, based on a sentimental print called "Beethoven's Sonata," depicting bohemians, oblivious of the audience, sitting in a half-lit studio listening to a violinist who, after *apache* dancers had performed and a *chanteuse* sung, played "Après de ma Blonde" while the guests wandered off into the night, leaving the room in moonlight. (The production of prologues was used as the basis for Lloyd Bacon's *Footlight Parade* in 1933.)

1923 marked the beginning of Hollywood's major importation of European artists. The German economy had crumbled, and though stability returned shortly afterwards, the Jewish/socialist artistic *élite* that had flourished in the great days of the Weimar Republic felt itself threatened. Max Reinhardt and Erwin Piscator had developed their radical theories of stage production, and under Erich Pommer Ufa had become one of the world's major production studios. For these men, only America offered any real hope of advancement, and after Mary Pickford imported Viennese Ernst Lubitsch in 1922 to direct *Rosita*, a test case to prove American patriotism had declined sufficiently to allow German artists to work in Hollywood once again, studio chiefs made regular head-hunting visits to Europe. In 1925, Jack L. Warner signed Mihály Kertész (Michael Curtiz) and Wilhelm Dieterle, and Louis B. Mayer, who preferred Scandinavian artists and had previously hired Swedish director Victor Sjöström (Seastrom), acquired Mauritz Stiller, agreeing without enthusiasm also to sign up his *protégée*, a dumpy actress he had re-named Greta Garbo: "Tell her in America men don't like their women fat" he is said to have warned Stiller. Fox imported F. W. Murnau, M-G-M the Dane Benjamin Christensen, Universal Paul Leni. Most brought a few colleagues, but Lubitsch's arrival seemed part of a Viennese invasion, with cameraman Theodore Sparkuhl, writers Edward Knoblauch (Knoblock), Heinrich (Henry) Blanke and regular collaborator Hanns Krähly (Hans Kraly) all arriving in his wake. When Lubitsch moved to Paramount, this team was to contribute much to that studio's opulent Thirties style, aided by the brilliant Hans Dreier who had been hired as head of studio design. (Anton Grot and Carl-Jules Weyl at Warner Brothers had a similar influence.)

There were initial teething problems. Heavy accents such as those possessed by Lubitsch and Curtiz often confused stars, and autocratic European methods offended actresses used to more deference. The differences in technique could be grotesque: Marion Nixon recalls that, on *The Chinese Parrot* (1928) Paul Leni introduced the unannounced striking of a gong at a moment of tension to achieve a realistic start from actors. Aided by other Viennese *émigrés* like Josef von Sternberg and Erich von Stroheim who had been in Hollywood for years, European subtlety, sexual sophistication and visual style became established as part of the Hollywood product.

In February, Irving Thalberg left Universal to join Louis B. Mayer at Metro when Carl Laemmle refused his appeal for a rise to $600 a week. His replacement, Laemmle's nephew Julius Stern, alienated stars like Eddie Polo and greatly impaired the profitable machinery Thalberg had built up. Cecil B. DeMille also left Paramount after criticism of his expenditure of

¶ Curtains part to disclose a spacious room with the glow from a lighted fireplace at left, while through a large library window at the rear streams soft moonlight. At a table between the window and fireplace the figures of two men are outlined but not fully disclosed. The dialogue begins as soon as the curtain has risen.

CRANFORD.

"I believe you know that I am not given to imagining things—I deal in facts and ignore fancies—and yet I cannot express to you in words the intense distaste that grew on me the nearer I drew to my goal. There was something positively malignant and unnatural in the density of the twisted creepers and shrubbery. That I continued to force my way through the dank, green foliage was due entirely to my pride and not to any liking for my adventure. As I struggled on in the tangled thicket suddenly the green wall in front of me parted easily to my touch and I plunged breathless, confused and shivering with a nameless dread, out of that unhealthy green welter on to a gravelled path which wound away toward the house. Facing me on a marble seat green with mould sat a young man who appeared in no wise surprised at my advent, but more as if he had been expecting me. He was tall and slender, with haunted eyes set in a sad and sensitive face. As I went toward him, he arose and greeted me simply. Being somewhat of a recluse, he said, it was rarely visitors came his way; but they were none the less welcome. He seemed

Written by
KATHERINE
HILLIKER

PRESENTED BY
S. L. ROTHAFEL
AT THE

CAPITOL
THEATRE
NEW YORK

AND AT

THE ALHAMBRA
LEICESTER SQ, LONDON
On FRIDAY
Nov. 2nd, 1923

like a man sleep-walking in a horrid nightmare, and his need to talk was so apparent that despite the warning of danger that prickled my skin I sat down beside him on the ancient seat. 'Did you ever hear of 'The Cabinet of Dr. Caligari?'' he asked me abruptly. As I shook my head and started to reply he laid an admonitory hand on my arm and looked toward the house. Along the pathway came a maiden moving as if in a dream—''

¶ Curtains close, lights out, fade into first scene of picture, showing two characters in garden, with girl in white coming slowly down path.

EPILOGUE.

Same scene as in Prologue. Fire has banked down to glowing embers. On the table the great candles are low

in their sockets. A blue haze of cigar smoke rests lightly on the atmosphere. As the scene is disclosed Cranford rises to his feet, stretches his arms high above his head, then turns quickly to Janes as the latter, who has been comfortably sprawled out in his chair presumably throughout the narrative, struggles up alertly into a sitting posture. Janes' whole attitude expresses intense questioning, but before he can speak Cranford raises an emphatic finger.

CRANFORD.

"And he did! Francis Purnay is to-day a prosperous jeweller in Holstenwall, happily married, with a couple of healthy, normal children. And the strangest thing about his recovery is the lapse of memory that accompanies it. He is like a man suddenly awakened from a bad dream and unable to remember any detail of its horror. The name 'Dr. Caligari,' to-day means no more to him than Smith or Jones. He has completely forgotten his hallucination!''

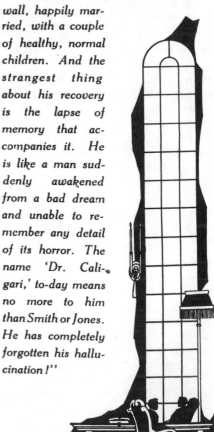

Prologue for *The Cabinet of Dr. Caligari.*

$1 million on *The Ten Commandments*. A $11½ million profit on the film encouraged Zukor to lure him back with powers for independent production that made him a major figure. Unknown to most, the Federal Trade Commission opened investigations into theatre/producer monopolies in the cinema—the first shot in a struggle that was not to end until 1948, when the great combines were finally destroyed. And on April 15, the Rivoli Theatre in New York presented a programme of short films with synchronised sound provided by the Case-Sponable method. There was little interest, and the experiment was not repeated.

ROSITA. Mary Pickford Co./United Artists. Directed by Ernst Lubitsch. Script by Edward Knoblock and Hans Kraly from Knoblock's adaptation of the play "Don Caesar de Bazan" by Adolphe D'Ennery and P. S. P. Dumanoir. Photographed by Charles Rosher. Set direction by Svend Gade. Players: Mary Pickford (Rosita), Holbrook Blinn (The King), Irene Rich (The Queen), George Walsh (Don Diego), Charles Belcher (Prime Minister), Frank Leigh (Prison Commandant), Mathilde Comont (Rosita's Mother), George Periolat (Rosita's Father), Bert Sprotte (Jailer), Snitz Edwards (Little Jailer), Mme. de Bodamere (Servant), Phillipe de Lacey, Donald McAlpin (Rosita's Brothers), Mario Carrillo (Major-domo), Doreen Turner (Rosita's Sister).

Mary Pickford's career shows a curious vacillation between the familiar image of "America's Sweetheart," created with Biograph and Artcraft, and her ambitions as a serious actress, which she exercised in her independent productions without quite losing touch with her "Little Mary" persona. Throughout her career, she hired dramatic directors—on one occasion in 1924, she even commissioned a film from Josef von Sternberg, but was horrified at the grim tragedy in which he proposed to star her—only to reject them if their ideas or style ran counter to hers. One of the first to suffer

Rosita. Mary Pickford. Design by Svend Gade.

this was Lubitsch who, after the success of *Madame Dubarry* (1919) (released as *Passion* in the US, where it made First National $1 million for a $30,000 investment) and *Anne Boleyn* (1920) (*Deception* in US) was hired by Miss Pickford to create a mature new costume film. He wished to shoot a script by himself and Edward Knoblock based on "Faust," while Miss Pickford suggested the sentimental "Dorothy Vernon of Haddon Hall," the rights to which she owned. They compromised on *Rosita*, a Spanish melodrama with many resemblances to the plot of "Tosca." Although, because of her disagreements with Lubitsch, Miss Pickford considers *Rosita* "the worst film I ever made" and has prevented its circulation since the early Thirties, it compares favourably with both her best work and that of Lubitsch. Moreover, in the script, design and Rosher's glowing, razor-sharp photography, it is a technical achievement of immense skill.

Set in Nineteenth century Toledo, *Rosita* is a comedy-romance about urchin street-singer Rosita who, falling in love with Don Diego, a young officer who kills another in a fight over her, attracts the attention of the king through her singing of a ballad attacking him and his profligate court. As in *Madame Dubarry*, the king "acquires" the girl by marrying her to an anonymous nobleman—unwittingly, it is Don Diego he chooses to marry Rosita at a blindfold ceremony in Toledo's lavish cathedral. Despite subsequent efforts by the king to have Diego removed, including a dramatic false execution, he is outmanoeuvred by the queen, and Rosita and her lover are reunited.

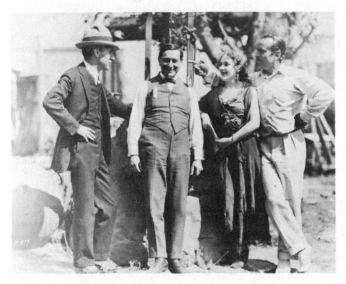

Chaplin, Lubitsch, Pickford and Fairbanks on *Rosita* set.

Gade recreates Toledo with theatrical flair, gloomy gothic alleys leading to wide plazas with elaborate cascades of steps and cornices around which Rosita skips, singing. The palace, with its lofty rooms, shining expanses of floor and elegantly veiled *boudoir* is sunny and light, ideal as a background to the king's earnest attempts at seduction and the calm machinations of the queen (played with regal detachment by Irene Rich) to foil him, though it is contrasted with the medieval jail, high walls slit by towering off-centre arches, and dank cells whose jailers are straight out of some German fantasy. Gade, who designed Asta Nielsen's *Hamlet* in 1920 and was also an imaginative minor director, did not work again on a project of this size, but his designs show a great decorative talent. An impeccable cast supports Miss Pickford. The king, played in imitation of Emil Janning's Louis XV in *Madame Dubarry* by Holbrook Blinn, is suave and corpulent, cruising greedily from one group of girls to another. George Walsh overplays the sturdy Diego, but there is a marvellous group performance from Rosita's family, at its best when she returns home in expensive clothes and passes around a scented handkerchief sniffed reverently by everybody but the last little boy, who uses it to blow his nose. Only in Pickford's performance is there a sense of strain, and a failure to realise the mocking satirist in Rosita that balances the charming waif. More scenes like the one in which, during the carnival, a man stabs another in the back and grabs the girl he had been passionately kissing, she submitting as readily to him as she did to her recently murdered lover, would have made *Rosita* a film of greater merit.

SAFETY LAST. Pathé. Directors: Fred Newmayer, Sam Taylor. Among Hollywood's many comedians of the early Twenties, Harold Lloyd did not stand out, and in retrospect his one-reelers for Hal Roach and other producers show no particular flair. His career took off only when he added two unique features to his *persona;* the bespectacled "college boy" image that replaced his "Lonesome Luke" character, a variation on the Chaplin tramp, and the concept of the "thrill picture," again an adaptation of existing models, notably Henry Lehrman's "Sunshine Comedies" in which humour depended mainly on lions chasing Negroes. In *Look Out Below, High and Dizzy* and *Never Weaken*, mild-mannered Harold clambered over skyscrapers, completed and half-built, hung from flagpoles or teetered above every kind of abyss; *Safety Last*, his first "thrill feature," established him as the master of this dangerous form.

Safety Last. Harold Lloyd.

1924

One of the early cinema's greatest artists, Thomas Harper Ince, died at forty-three after dining with newspaper magnate William Randolph Hearst on his yacht. Rumours surrounded his death, variously described as murder and manslaughter, but it seems certain that Ince, who had visited Hearst to discuss acquiring film rights to certain stories in "Cosmopolitan" magazine and the prospect of directing films starring Hearst's mistress Marion Davies, foolishly drank champagne that aggravated the stomach ulcers and heart condition from which he suffered. He died shortly after of a thrombosis.

Alarmed by Zukor's growing monopoly, theatre owner Marcus Loew, who had acquired the Metro company in 1920, as well as Louis B. Mayer and his partners, financial genius J. Robert Rubin and production manager Irving Thalberg, merged it with the Goldwyn company to create Metro-Goldwyn-Mayer (Sam Goldwyn declined to participate and left to form his own studio with the proviso that his name remain permanently in that of the new firm). Its first film was *He Who Gets Slapped* (Victor Sjöström) with Lon Chaney.

Panchromatic film came into general use, beginning the era of a personal style in cinematography. The crude film stocks of the early days had lacked sensitivity, responding only to harsh blue-white light, which resulted in exterior shooting, a shallow depth of focus (caused by wide-open apertures) and heavy make-up to define features as black on a white ground. Orthochromatic film, common after the First World War, had recorded blue and green, but red registered as black, and pink, light blue and yellow as white. Such deficiencies had caused countless problems, not least of which had been the tendency for very light blue eyes to photograph as colourless. Since most babies' eyes are blue, Biograph had regularly hired a light-skinned Negro baby with black eyes to appear in films like *The Battle of Elderberry Gulch* (1913). Stan Laurel had been hired by Hal Roach as a comic, but because of his blue eyes was employed as a writer until panchromatic film came into use.

THE THIEF OF BAGDAD. United Artists. Directed by Raoul Walsh. Script by Elton Thomas (Douglas Fairbanks). Photographed by Arthur Edeson. Set direction by William Cameron Menzies. Scenario editor: Lotta Woods. Research direction by Dr. Arthur Woods. Technical director: Robert Fairbanks. Special effects by Ned Mann. Players: Douglas Fairbanks (The Thief), Snitz Edwards (His Evil Associate), Charles Belcher (Holy Man), Julanne Johnston (Princess), Anna May Wong (Mongol Slave), Winter-Blossom (Slave of the Lute), Etta Lee (Slave of the Sand Tray), Brandon Hurst (Caliph), Tate du Crow (Soothsayer), So-Jin (Mongol Prince), K. Nambu (His Counsellor), Sakakichi Hartmann (Court Magician), Noble Johnson (Indian Prince), C. Comont (Persian Prince), Charles Stevens (His Awaker), Sam Baker (The Sworder), Jess Weldon, Scott Mattraw, Charles Sylvester (Eunuchs).

After his success with *Robin Hood* (Allan Dwan, 1922), the massive sets, light-hearted fantasy and agile central performance of which delighted America, Douglas Fairbanks looked for a subject allowing similar scope. Months were spent researching a pirate story (which surfaced in 1926 as *The Black Pirate*—Al Parker—his first colour film), but after reading Burton's translation of "The Arabian Nights" Fairbanks abruptly decided on an Oriental fantasy exploring Burton's aphorism "Happiness Must Be Earned." Always a man of the theatre, Fairbanks signed Broadway producer Morris Gest to stage the film, but when Gest withdrew to concentrate on presenting Reinhardt's lavish production of Vollmoeller's "The Miracle," Raoul Walsh took over. *The Thief of Bagdad*

Advertisement for Universal's directors, 1924.

Stan Laurel.

took seven months to shoot and fourteen to complete, using four thousand extras and six-and-a-half acres of sets, built by William Cameron Menzies, most versatile and imaginative of Hollywood production designers. Agreeing that they should appear fantastic and beautiful rather than real, Menzies adopted the illustrator's style, adapting decorative ideas from Aubrey Beardsley, Gustav Klimt and *art nouveau.* When the massive city buildings looked too solid on film, Menzies had the four-acre Bagdad plaza covered in four inches of cement which was then heavily painted with black enamel to reflect the walls and make them appear to float. The surface was repainted weekly throughout the production, and a sign reminded visitors "Are Your Feet Clean?".

Thief of Bagdad. **Douglas Fairbanks Sr.**

No hint of this contrivance is evident in the film, which captures one instantly with its beauty and excitement. Fairbanks plays an expert thief, light-heartedly lifting the purses of Bagdad's honest citizens and, after entering a mosque to escape an irate victim, mocking the moralisers: "What I want, I take. My paradise is here. Heaven is a fool's dream and Allah a myth." His opinions change when he falls in love with the Princess on a midnight robbery attempt in the palace. Impersonating a prince, he wins her love, only to be betrayed by her Mongol servant, beaten and ejected. Disconsolate, he accepts the teacher's advice to compete with her other three suitors in finding the rarest gift in the world. After fights with a dragon and the perils of a burning cave, he gains the magic box containing a powder that grants any wish, and returns to win the princess and defeat a Mongol army threatening to capture Bagdad.

Fairbanks's reputation as a daredevil stunt-man is largely based on supposition and carefully-chosen excerpts from his films. In fact he was more acrobat than stunter, giving relatively simple tricks the air of the miraculous by clever stage management. In *Robin Hood* a concealed slide allowed him to slip nonchalantly down an enormous drape, while in *The Thief of Bagdad* he bounces in and out of three huge jars with the help of trampolines concealed inside. Careful engineering of window fittings (like all Fairbanks sets, they are precisely adjusted to his height, reach and strength) allows him to grasp almost invisible rods and slide into a room, or run elegantly about the palace as if he knows every stair and alcove. Little photographic process work is used, but midgets and miniatures make a chimpanzee appear enormous, and clever substitutions allow the thief's companion to become light enough to be lifted on his head, or turn him via a collapsible screen into a convincing decorative jar. The style fits Fairbanks's exaggerated acting style, with its balletic movements, often in profile to achieve a two-dimensional effect, and extravagant mime. The result is an Arabian Nights comic strip, visually beautiful, exciting and, most important, totally involving. It is Fairbanks at his peak, the last good-natured innocent in Hollywood cinema, but since *Thief* cost three times the budget of *Robin Hood* yet earned less, he never again attempted such extravagance.

SHERLOCK JR. Buster Keaton Productions/Metro. Produced by Joseph M. Schenck. Directed by Buster Keaton. Script by Clyde Bruckman, Jean Havez and Joseph Mitchell. Photographed by Byron Houck and Elgin Lessley. Art direction by Fred Gabourie. Costumes by Clare West. Players: Buster Keaton (Sherlock Jr.), Kathryn McGuire (The Girl), Ward Cane (The Rival), Joseph Keaton (Father), Horace Morgan, Jane Connelly, Erwin Connelly, Ford West, George Davis, John Patrick, Ruth Holly.

Sherlock Jr., Keaton's *tour de force* and perhaps his

The "star row" of bungalows at United Artists in the late 1920s: from left to right, those of John Barrymore, Corinne Griffith, Mary Pickford and Douglas Fairbanks, and Norma and Constance Talmadge.

background (his vaudevillian father has a role in the film): before entering the thieves' lair, he directs Reginald to hold a flat suitcase full of women's clothing against the open window. Diving out, he somersaults and comes up fully dressed as an old lady. Another old lady appears with a tray of knick-knacks and, standing against the fence, urges Buster to leap through the tray. He does so, and disappears. Both are popular illusionist's tricks; the paper suitcase holds a loose-fitting smock which covers Keaton sufficiently to make the illusion convincing, and the man playing the old lady is actually supported above ground with only his head showing through the fence. Below him is a trapdoor hidden by the dress. Less trickery is employed in the dangerous chase which has Buster, balanced on the handlebars of a motor cycle whose rider, unknown to him, has fallen off (Keaton doubled both rider and passenger), race across railroad crossings feet ahead of a moving train and flip off the bike through an open window, stunts achieved only through Keaton's remarkable athletic ability.

most perfect exercise in the "comedy of objects" of which he was a master, gives Buster as a daydreaming movie projectionist opportunities to joke both with the idea of a dreamer turned daredevil and with the conventions of cinema. Dozing in his projection box, he imagines himself within the film he is showing: wandering into a seaside scene, he perches on a rock and dives off, only to end buried in a snowdrift when the scene changes. As if the dream has entered his own life, he responds to the faked theft of his prospective father-in-law's watch and his girl's kidnapping by turning into the perfect detective, accompanied everywhere by the faithful, indispensable Reginald, a sequence in which Keaton parodied John Barrymore's appearance in *Sherlock Holmes* in 1922.

For these scenes, Keaton falls back on his vaudeville

Sherlock Jr. Buster Keaton.

61

1925

The Warner Brothers bought Vitagraph, last surviving Patents Company studio, to form, with their theatre chain, the nucleus of Warner Brothers, which immediately followed the popular trend and went public. One of the oldest Hollywood companies, Vitagraph, founded by J. Stuart Blackton, Albert E. Smith and Joe "Pop" Rock before the turn of the century, was responsible for the early careers of John Bunny, Florence Turner, Norma and Natalie Talmadge and Rudolph Valentino. Its new owners acquired, as well as the studio and film library, the inventive spirit it had long represented in Hollywood. The Warners lacked polish, but not business acumen. Financial head Harry Warner controlled the business from New York, aided by Albert, head of sales. Sam Warner, the champion of sound film, died in October 1927, the day after *The Jazz Singer* was first shown. Jack L. Warner remained in Hollywood as production manager, one of the industry's smartest and, superficially, most light-hearted personalities.

Having been hired by Mayer in order to acquire Stiller—he arrived in July—Greta Garbo used her success in *The Torrent* (Stiller, 1925) to demand an increase in salary from $500 a week to $5,000. Examining her contract, M-G-M found she had been under age when it was signed and were forced to renegotiate, to her advantage. As Garbo's popularity increased, that of Stiller, emotionally unable to adjust to Hollywood, declined. After Fred Niblo replaced him on *The Temptress* (1925) he went to Paramount, where he directed *Hotel Imperial* (1926) and began work on *The Street of Sin* (1927) with Emil Jannings and an original Josef von Sternberg story. He abandoned this to return to Sweden—Lothar Mendes and Ludwig Berger completed it—and died in 1928, aged forty-five. "I have Mauritz Stiller to thank for everything in the world," Garbo said later.

Almost unnoticed, George K. Spoor, founder of the defunct Essanay, screened a programme of three-dimensional films, and also worked with P. John Berggren on the 70mm "Natural Vision" process using a screen seventy feet by thirty-four. Spoor agreed with the industry that the processes were probably "impractical and too expensive," but both struggled on, 3-D to have some minor feature use and "Natural Vision" to be the basis of M-G-M's "Grandeur" system. Like Fox with sound, it would take the logic of events to force an acceptance of their advances on an innately conservative Hollywood.

THE SALVATION HUNTERS. Academy Pictures/ United Artists. Directed and written by Josef von Sternberg. Photographed by Edward Gheller. Players: George K. Arthur (The Boy), Georgia Hale (The Girl), Bruce Guerin (The Child), Otto Matiesen (The Man), Nelly Bly Baker (The Woman), Olaf Hytten (The Brute), Stuart Holmes (The Gentleman).

Josef von Sternberg's first film was made under the conditions of artistic tension and straitened resources that were to haunt his professional life. As a skilful but enigmatic assistant director, living in one room at the corner of Hollywood Boulevard and Vine Street in an apartment so cramped that he had to sleep in a large bureau drawer, he had already, by his affectation of eccentric clothing—in imitation of his mentor von Stroheim—and manner of intellectual superiority, established a reputation as an inscrutable genius of the cinema. For *The Salvation Hunters* Sternberg (real name Jonas Sternberg; birthplace Vienna, though he came to America with his family as a child) persuaded English actor George K. Arthur to sink his money into an original script to star Arthur. The actor, who had wanted to make a comedy from his own story, reluctantly agreed, finding extra finance from among his relatives. Sternberg drew his cast from extras and minor players with whom he had

Paramount Studios at the corner of Sunset Boulevard
and Vine Street in the early 1920s.

worked, the sole "name" being Stuart Holmes, who agreed to play a minor role for $100, in advance.

Cutting corners with skill learned as an assistant, Sternberg shot the film in three weeks on exteriors at San Pedro, an industrial dock area, and in borrowed studios. Typically, *The Salvation Hunters* imitates Stroheim and *Greed* in its gloomy story of three slum dwellers struggling to escape their environment, a release achieved only at the last minute when The Boy rejects The Man's overtures for The Girl to enter a brothel, and walks with her into the sunset. As an often misquoted title ("This film is an attempt to photograph a thought") makes clear, Sternberg wished the film to show how human emotions affect behaviour, rejecting the often superficial melodramas of the time in favour of a psychological approach adapted from Stroheim and playwrights like Schnitzler. Critics of the time found the acting of Arthur and Hale wooden, but today we recognise that Sternberg hoped, in restricting mannerisms and trying to extract the "spiritual power" of his characters, was pioneering a technique Strasberg's Actors' Studio made popular.

After a disastrous *première*, Arthur, all of whose capital was in the film, tricked the United Artists hierarchy into seeing it, and was rewarded by instant interest from both Chaplin and Fairbanks, an enthusiasm so unaccountable that it was explained away by cynics as a Chaplin practical joke on the ease with which opinion could be manipulated. With UA paying $20,000 for a film that cost only $4,800 to make, its success and that of the principals was assured, and though Sternberg's invitation to direct a film for Mary Pickford and Georgia Hale's casting as the lead in Chaplin's *The Gold Rush* (1925) each led to disaster —Pickford disliked Sternberg's suggested realist drama and Hale, mediocre in the Chaplin film, had only a minor career thereafter—*The Salvation Hunters* established Sternberg as a name of interest, and was the cornerstone of his later distinguished but erratic career.

THE LOST WORLD. Director: Harry D. Hoyt. Willis O'Brien, who almost single-handed had pioneered the technique of model animation for twenty

Nelly Bly Baker, George K. Arthur, Bruce Guerin, George Hale and Otto Matiesen. *The Salvation Hunters.*

years, achieved deserved success in Hoyt's romance in which forty-nine miniature dinosaurs, carefully photographed in convincing small-scale sets, recreated the remote Amazonian plateau of Sir Arthur Conan Doyle's story. Unremarkable in its acting except for Wallace Beery's rowdy impersonation of the black-bearded Professor Challenger, aptly-named *enfant terrible* of science determined to prove the existence of prehistoric beasts even if, to do so, he must bring back a brontosaurus to ravage London and wreck Tower Bridge, *The Lost World* succeeds because of its magnificent special effects sequences which opened the way for the immortal *King Kong*.

THE BIG PARADE. Director: King Vidor. The most prestigious film of 1925 now has an inflated reputation as a classic pacifist work, even though the emphasis in Vidor's direction and the story by Laurence Stallings —whom M-G-M had hired after the success of "What Price Glory?" as play and film—is personal, romantic and, since Stallings, like his hero, lost a leg during

the war, one assumes also autobiographical. Dealing mainly with the recruitment of an impressionable young American patrician (John Gilbert) into the army, his integration into service life and an affair with a French girl, played with charm and precision by the short-lived Renée Adorée, it leaves actual war until the film is almost over, and the description, when it comes, is softened by Hollywood schmaltz. Stallings had written his story, originally called "The Return of a Soldier," as a down-beat criticism of flag-waving patriotism, but when famous "road show" film promoter J. J. McCarthy saw the film while visiting M-G-M to confer on the release of *Ben Hur,* he offered to invest $250,000 in its exploitation if the studio would add more romance to the beginning and end (via an imposed romantic conflict) and fatten the battle scenes. Since McCarthy had enjoyed phenomenal success in exhibiting and promoting Griffith's films, and Mayer wished to sustain John Gilbert's image as a romantic star, new material was shot and George Hill called in to direct some additional battle scenes. Vidor still manages some specific criticism of war fever—"What a thing is patriotism," a caption notes as the hero is led by a foot-tapping march to enlist. "We go for years not knowing that we love it." —but as a suggestion of war's horror and its effect on the youthful cannon-fodder, it falls far short of Pabst's *Westfront 1918* (1930) and other European productions whose principals instilled the sting of war into their work.

1926

Marcus Loew, founder of Loew's Inc. and of M-G-M, died quietly, almost unnoticed. By contrast, the death of Rudolph Valentino at the height of his fame created a sensation, and brought mobs into the streets to mourn him. Reaction to the two deaths suggested a growing alienation of Hollywood and its personalities from the real power behind the studios, men who remained anonymous, even secretive. With his ambitious US plans forestalled, Adolph Zukor expanded into Europe, hiring a number of continental stars and luring the German Ufa company's production manager Erich Pommer to Hollywood as controller of all Paramount's imported talent. The following year, when newspaper magnate Alfred Hugenberg bought control of the bankrupt Ufa, Zukor also gained an interest in it. M-G-M's European involvement had proved alarmingly unprofitable during the production of *Ben Hur* (Fred Niblo, 1926) on location in Italy: production difficulties, of the kind experienced later in 1963 by 20th Century-Fox on *Cleopatra,* made this film one of M-G-M's most expensive and frustrating.

This year saw the start of the sound revolution. In 1925, William Fox had become interested in a system designed by Theodore W. Case and Earl Sponable (see 1927) and installed it in six of his cinemas, only to remove the equipment when public reaction was negative. An alternative system developed by Bell and Victor was offered to various studios, including M-G-M, where Thalberg refused it, until Sam Warner saw the potential and persuaded the struggling Warner Brothers to explore its possibilities. On August 6, at the Manhattan Opera House, Warners presented John Barrymore and Mary Astor in *Don Juan* (Alan Crosland), the first feature with synchronised music and effects, and a spoken introduction by Will Hays lauding the new invention. Fox immediately retaliated with a series of sound shorts featuring opera or vaudeville stars. The battle was on.

MANTRAP. Paramount. Produced by Hector Turnbull and B. P. Schulberg. Directed by Victor Fleming. Script by Adelaide Heilbron and Ethel Doherty from a story by Sinclair Lewis. Titles by George Marion. Photographed by James (Wong) Howe. Players: Clara Bow (Alverna), Ernest Torrence (Joe Easter), Percy Marmont (Ralph Prescott), Tom Kennedy (Curly Evans), Josephine Crowell (Mrs. McGavity), William Orlamond (Mr. McGavity), Charles Stevens (Indian Guide), Miss Du Pont (Mrs. Marker).

Clara Bow, whose image is that of the Twenties' sexual ideal, an emancipated "sexy little girl" using her attraction to tease and exploit the male world, actually resists the categorisation imposed on her by *It* and *Hula,* the two 1927 sex comedies directed by Clarence Badger for which she is best known. Both

M-G-M's Culver City studios in the late 1920s.

Advertisement for *Flesh and the Devil.*

earlier, with the lively *Mantrap*, and later, in her penultimate film *Call Her Savage* (John Francis Dillon, 1932) she proved herself a skillful romantic actress able to display her physical appeal and girlish manner without hiding the woman beneath. Burdened in *Call Her Savage* with a plot contriving to be by turns a Western, society comedy, kitchen-sink drama and romance, she shines as the heiress afflicted by inherited eroticism and wilfulness. *Mantrap*, boasting a clever "Collier's" plot and direction by her current *fiancé*, allows her to express unhindered the humour and spirit too often inundated by Badger with mannerism. Lured from her Minneapolis manicurist job by the backwoods honesty of trader Joe Easter, Clara's Alverna appreciates the peace and affection of marriage to Joe without entirely escaping her flirtatious nature. The arrival of jaded divorce lawyer Ralph Prescott brings to the surface instincts she had thought gone, and, impatient with the tedium of life in the backwoods—which Fleming cleverly suggests in a party scene with the caption "At ten o'clock the orgy was at its height" and a cut to the minister twiddling his thumbs—she persuades Prescott to take her back to civilization ("You must look on me not as a man," he says cautiously, "but as a means of transportation"), only to return, charming and unrepentant, after her fling.

Fleming exploited his star with two English actors experienced enough to showcase her fragile gifts. Percy Marmont gives diffident elegance to Prescott, and the adaptable Ernest Torrence, who with equal skill played Peter in *The King of Kings,* Luke Hatburn in *Tol'able David* and an amiably crude scout in *The Covered Wagon* (James Cruze, 1923), is both amusing and real as the good-natured Joe. But the film is Clara Bow's, the authentic forest settings a foil to her girlish charm, the plot an opportunity for her to shine and provoke. Fleming's intent comes out strongest when the fugitive couple, hungry, exhausted and dishevelled, discover their essential liking for each other when their guide abandons them in the woods. "Seeing you like this has made me realise how strong and good you are," Prescott says, "and I'd thought you just a butterfly." One takes the director's implied point, and acknowledges that Bow, though never a major actress, was considerably more than the featherheaded flirt most believed her to be.

FLESH AND THE DEVIL. Director: Clarence Brown. The most thoughtful of American directors, whose films are created with an essayist's feel for balance, Clarence Brown made his debut at M-G-M with this adaptation of a Hermann Sudermann melodrama after having for some years been the sworn enemy of Irving Thalberg. The enmity, mainly on Thalberg's side, stemmed from the purchase by Brown, who was a shrewd businessman, of the rights to the story of "The Unholy Three," which M-G-M wished to use as a Lon Chaney vehicle, and their later expensive resale to the company. But Brown and William Daniels so superbly used Greta Garbo's icy charm in *Flesh and the Devil* that they became her regular team, charged with sustaining the image of distant sexuality that enchanted audiences. The affair between dashing officer John Gilbert and temptress Garbo, parallelled by their off-screen romance, still communicates its fire to audiences, just as Brown's meticulous judgment of tempo makes this one of the most watchable of silent dramas.

THE STRONG MAN. Director: Frank Capra. Frank Capra began his career as a Keystone gagman for the difficult Mack Sennett, and later graduated to being one of Harry Langdon's team and director of the first features that established the lugubrious pasty-faced actor as a major, if fleeting, comedy star. In *The Strong Man,* he is assistant to a European weight-lifter on tour in the US, a visit complicated by an elaborate sub-plot in which Harry finds the love of his life with whom he has lost contact because of the war. Although this complex additional story slows the film down, Capra shows his skill in the comic set-pieces: the struggle to extract the strong-man's belongings from Customs and the tension as to whether his most precious possession (a top hat presented to him by a royal admirer) will survive; Harry's attempted seduction and near-rape by a plotting female antagonist, which includes his desperate attempts to haul her unconscious figure up a flight of stairs, achieved at last by sitting with her on his lap and pushing himself up backwards step by step; and notably the climax in a Western town, where Capra's skill with crowds makes the human cannonball act, which finally brings the hall down around the ears of the brawling audience, a classic of violent humour. Langdon, increasingly egotistical, broke with Capra soon after, and while the director thrived on adversity, his old boss became one of Hollywood's least-lamented casualties of success.

1927

On October 6, Warner Brothers premiered in New York *The Jazz Singer* (Alan Crosland), the first feature film with synchronised dialogue and music. Essentially a silent with only the musical numbers in sound —the first song specifically written to be sung for the screen was "Mother, I Still Have You" (Louis Silvers/ Al Jolson) —*The Jazz Singer* brought to public attention a development inevitable from the time radio had interrupted an essentially visual culture pattern.

As early as 1887, Edison and W. K. L. Dickson, his assistant and the cinema's true inventor, had experimented with sound for films using the primitive acoustic method of amplification, but sound film really dates from the invention in 1906 of the "Audion Tube" by Dr. Lee de Forest, which also made possible the radio telephone and the gramophone. (De Forest later sued Fox for infringing his patents, but derived little benefit from the advance he began.) From his basic invention, two lines of development issued. One, mainly led by Victor and the Bell Telephone Company, aimed to exploit sound recorded on discs by linking the film projector mechanically to a gramophone—the basis of Warner Brothers' "Vitaphone." The Radio Corporation of America (RCA), a company formed to consolidate all major radio patents as the MPPC had consolidated those of the cinema, worked on an alternative and ultimately better method in which sound was recorded visually beside the film image as a "sound track." This system, to which the Case-Sponable patents were related, became Fox's "Movietone" and is the basis of modern optical sound reproduction.

These were far from being the only methods by which it was attempted to blend sound and image. From the earliest days, exhibitors had experimented with actors standing behind the screen reading their lines to the silent image, and in 1925, M-G-M stars Norma Shearer and Lew Cody had broadcast some of their dialogue for *A Slave of Fashion* (Hobart Henley) from a radio studio to the theatre. Douglas Shearer, Norma's brother, developed the idea, synchronising the film and a recorded talk by using punched tape and a gramophone; the film had a number of screenings in what was basically a variation on Vitaphone, and Shearer later returned to manage M-G-M's sound department, making many of the field's early advances.

The advantage in developing sound cinema was completely with William Fox, who had the necessary patents, the capital to buy and instal equipment and a chain of cinemas in which to put it. Warner Brothers, on the other hand, owned only one major theatre, relying on other chains that were often unwilling to spend the necessary $10,000–$30,000 a theatre for sound equipment. But the patent monopoly held by Fox and Warners enabled them to stave off bankruptcy, and by 1929 Warner Brothers was prosperous enough to buy the Stanley-First National theatre chain, which was weakened from its battle with Zukor, and establish itself as one of Hollywood's most important studios.

THE KING OF KINGS. Paramount. Produced and directed by Cecil B. DeMille. Script by Jeanie Macpherson adapted from the Four Gospels. (Uncredited script: Denison Clift, Clifford Howard and Jack Jungmeyer.) Photographed by J. Peverell Marley. Costumes by (Gilbert) Adrian, Gwen Wakeling and Earl Luick. Art direction by Anton Grot, Edward Jewel, Dan Groesbeck and Julian Harrison. Edited by Anne Bauchens and Harold McLernan. Players: H. B. Warner (Jesus Christ), Dorothy Cummings (Mary), Ernest Torrence (Peter), Joseph Schildkraut (Judas), James Neill (James), Joseph Striker (John), Robert Edeson (Matthew), Sidney D'Albrook (Thomas), David Imboden (Andrew), Charles Belcher (Philip), Clayton Packard (Bartholomew), Robert Ellsworth

Al Jolson in *The Jazz Singer*.

(Simon), Charles Requa (James the Less), John T. Prince (Thaddeus), Jacqueline Logan (Mary Magdalen), Rudolph Schildkraut (Caiaphas), Sam de Grasse (Pharisee), Casson Ferguson (Scribe), Victor Varconi (Pontius Pilate), Montagu Love (Centurion), William Boyd (Simon of Cyrene), George Siegmann (Barabbas), Kenneth Thompson (Lazarus), Alan Brooks (Satan), Viola Louie (Woman Taken in Adultery), Muriel McCormac (Blind Girl), Noble Johnson (Charioteer), Clarence Burton (Dismas), Sally Rand (Slave to Mary Magdalen), Josephine Norman (Mary of Bethany), Julia Faye (Martha of Bethany).

Among Cecil B. DeMille's many religious epics, *King of Kings* was the most successful, a lavish $2½ million drama that, under the guise of retelling the story of Christ as recounted in the New Testament, offered sex, violence and spectacle. DeMille shrewdly prefaced the production with an announcement that all its cast had signed a contract guaranteeing that their conduct during the shooting would be exemplary. H. B. Warner, who played Christ, not only ate alone, but while moving from one part of the studio to another was also always veiled or carried in a closed car, and when in costume could be spoken to only by DeMille. Every morning on location at Catalina Island, where much of the film was shot, a priest celebrated Mass, while the production began with a service comprising Protestant, Catholic, Jewish, Buddhist and Moslem prayers. The advertising, built around a series of hand-coloured stills from the film corresponding to famous Biblical illustrations, promised "a tale of the Christ," unsullied by commercialism, and credits were omitted from the film to emphasise its devotional character.

In fact, the film was one of DeMille's most calculatedly commercial productions, with the Bible used as a framework for a totally invented romance. A hand-

70

Advertisement for *The Jazz Singer.*

Musical Suggestions for
THE KING OF KINGS

By ROY ROBERTSON.

NOTE TO MUSICAL DIRECTORS.—We strongly advise all Musical Directors to obtain the Original Score for this Film, as it is *most* difficult to obtain correct synchronization without it.

		Music Suggested	Type of Music	Composer	Publisher
THEME	I—Christ	9/4 Section from Hunckback of Notre Dame	Broad Maestoso	Massenet	Lafleur
THEME	II—Mary Magdalen (before conversion)	Karma	Dram. March Maestoso	Herbert	Fischer
THEME	III—Blind Girl	6/8 Section of L'Arlesienne Suite No. 4	Semi-Lullaby	Bizet	Fischer
THEME	IV—Mary the Mother	6/8 Section from Hunchback of Notre Dame	Sad Flowing	Massenet	Lafleur
THEME	V—High Priest	Largo from Dalibor Sel	Mysterious Flowing	Smetana	Fischer
THEME	VI—Caiaphas	Crepuscule D'angoisse	Mysterious Dramatic	Fosse	Liber
THEME	VII—Christ Prayer	Les Perses, from 20	Mysterious Sad	Leroux	Leduc
THEME	VIII—Miracle Music	Symphonie in E Minor (Brass Muted)	Mysterious a la Hymn	Pierne	Liber
THEME	IX—Soldiers Mysterious	Cabal	Mysterious March	Kay	Forster
THEME	X—Judas	Lohengrin from 4/4	Dramatic Mysterious	Wagner-Potoker	Fischer

Titles and Action Cues	Music Suggested	Type of Music	Composer	Publisher
Overture	Grand March from Opera Cleopatra	March grand	Mancinelli	Hawkes
"This is the story"	THEME I			
"In Judea"	Persian Suite No. 2	Andante 4/4	Rubenstein	Liber
At C.U. of actor with mirror	Torchlight Dance from Feramors Ballet	Light 3/4 Moderato	Rubenstein	Fischer
"Mary I know"	Allegro Appassionata	Passionate	Curzon	Dix
As Mary grips actor's neck	Appassionata in A Minor from Major Sect.	Dramatic Agitato	Savino	Francis & Day
"Nay, 'twas no woman"	THEME I			
As Mary strikes gong	Two cymbal beats (loose)			
Segue	THEME II			
"Mary I will wager"	Dramatic Dialogue	Dramatic	Brusselmans	Liber
As chariot arrives	Emotional Agitato	Dramatic Agitato	Savino	Robins
"And it was"	Antar from Allegro, D Major	Dramatic Maestoso	Rimsky-Korsakow	Leduc
As blind girl appears	THEME III			
As blind girl exits	Antar from last 32 bars	Broad Dramatic	Rimsky-Korsakow	Leduc
As Mark is seen	Ariadne auf Nuxos	Light 4/4	Massenet	Leduc
Spies of the High Priests	THEME VI			
As Peter grabs crutch	Sous les Tenailles	Dramatic Heavy	Fosse	Yves
As Peter goes to Mark	Les Pheniciennes	Maestoso Light	Massenet	Lafleur
As blind girl is seen	THEME III			
"And gathered in the House"	D'Albert Suite No. 1	Flowing	Becce	Liber
At Mary the Mother spinning	THEME IV			
As horn is blown	Trumpet Call (horn if any). Watch screen	Neutral		
Segue	Deluge	Drama Largo	Urbine	Liber
At C.U. of Mary the Mother	THEME IV			
As blind girl kneels	L'Arlesienne Suite No. 1 from Poco Lentamente	Sad	Bizet	Fischer
As light appears	Lead Kindly Light	Hymn		
Segue	THEME VIII			
At face of Christ	Tannhauser 6/4 Section	Calm	Wagner	Bosworth
As girl stretches out hands	THEME III			
At Chariot scene	Minor Agitato	Hurry	Berge	Robbins
"Where is this vagabond?"	THEME II			
As Mary approaches	Restart THEME II *ff*			
As Christ gazes at Mary	THEME I			
As vision appears	Romantic Suite, Verstorf	Moderato 4/4 Weird	Erdman	Liber
After Mary is cleansed	Extase	Moderato Sad	Bizet	Liber
As Mary kneels	Adagio	Adagio	Rubenstein	Liber
"But the High Priest"	THEME VI			
As Simeon appears	THEME V			
As Caiaphas touches money	Kinothek I A No. 5 *pp*	Dramatic Myst.	Becce	de Wolfe
"And then they watched"	Novellettes (from Piano Solo)	March—flowing	Schumann	Augener

One page of the elaborate music-suggestion sheet issued with all major features of the late silent period.

THE BIG SHOT

BEN HECHT & CHARLES MacARTHUR

They wrote the outstanding Broadway success "Front Page"

Ben Hecht

Charles MacArthur

Based on the life of one of New York's most sensational personalities, this is a startling and accurate picture of the underworld and its rackets. It reveals a man, merciless and powerful, whose lawlessness wins him millions, but whose happiness is strangled in the net he weaves about himself.

Will also be made "Silent"

"Will also be made Silent," reads a note on this display for Ben Hecht-Charles MacArthur biography of gambler Arnold Rothstein, eventually released as *Street of Chance* (John Cromwell, 1930).

The King of Kings. H. B. Warner as Christ.

Cecil B. DeMille, screenwriter Jeanie McPherson and exhibitor Sid Grauman considering the advertising display for *The King of Kings*.

some young aristocrat with political ambitions, Judas Iscariot sees Christ as the next king. Support, he reasons, will result in high office when Christ comes to power. Piqued by Judas's non-attendance at her elegant *soirées,* his mistress, the prostitute Mary of Magdala, with an imperious "Harness my zebras!", goes in search of him, is dazzled by Christ 'and becomes a convert. Judas meanwhile urges kingship on his candidate, personally offering the crown to Christ and denigrating his efforts to heal the sick or entertain his followers unless some direct political gain can be made from it. The invitation "Suffer little children to come unto me" (shot in DeMille's own garden) is greeted by Judas with a gesture of irritation, while he argues against the raising of Lazarus on the grounds that the man has no money which he might in gratitude contribute to the campaign fund. Played in high style by Schildkraut with Jacqueline Logan a fetching Mary

Magdalen, the lovers overshadow Warner's wan charm, as does a skilful supporting cast, including fan-dancer Sally Rand as Mary's slave and William "Hopalong Cassidy" Boyd as Simon of Cyrene.

No opportunity is missed to give *The King of Kings* DeMille's characteristic production values. First seen reclining in a brief costume among her admirers and caressing a tame leopard, Mary Magdalen is no uncertain symbol of sex, and when in the course of her instant conversion the phantoms of the Seven Deadly Sins arise to tear at her—including Lust, who points out reasonably "With me you have enslaved kings"—the effect is strongly erotic. Even the Woman Taken in Adultery shows a generous sweep of thigh, while the relish of the crowd that prepares to stone her—one man, in a sly touch, weighing two stones in his hands and choosing the heavier—has the sadistic edge typical of the director's work. DeMille the showman reveals

74

himself in many sequences: in the Raising of Lazarus, with the shrouded figure rising in the shadows, bandages falling first from his blank, haunted eyes; in Pilate brooding before an enormous bronze eagle while Caiaphas introduces hitherto unsuspected politico-economic dimensions to Christ's death; and even in so small a scene as the temptation by Satan, a suave black-cloaked figure like an Aubrey Beardsley grandee sliding from behind a white-pillared colonnade, DeMille's taste for the romantic is clear. Predictably the disturbances following Christ's death cannot pass unmarked, and DeMille calls up a lavish earthquake, ending with Judas's hanging corpse sucked into the abyss, while the Resurrection is handled in a final reel of two-colour Technicolor, rosy dawn leading to visitations from some hygienic-looking angels. All the contradictions of DeMille's personality are apparent in this film, a work at once sacred and profane, entertaining to millions for its prurience and drama, but to some a genuinely moving religious experience, a commercial success in which DeMille declined to share, donating his profits to charity. It may be an index to the importance he placed in this film that a set of iron gates used in it later appeared barring the entrance to his huge Tijunga Canyon estate, which he called "Paradise."

1928

Warner Brothers produced the first all-talking feature film, *The Lights of New York* (Bryan Foy) in July amid an industry thrown into confusion by the unanticipated popularity of sound films. Most companies cautiously announced that a few features would be produced with sound, while others promised both silent and talking versions of their productions. The companies holding sound patents, Fox and Warners, saw opportunities for speculation, and both began stock raids on the weakest major studio, M-G-M, its administration confused by Loew's death and commercial prospects impaired by a failure to anticipate the swing to sound. The Rockefeller-owned RCA also exploited its advantage by buying the ailing Film Booking Office studio and Keith-Albee-Orpheum vaudeville theatre chain to form Radio-Keith-Orpheum, soon as RKO to be a major studio with New York's Radio City Musical Hall as its figurehead (see 1932).

"Photoplay" magazine named Hollywood's top stars as John Gilbert, Emil Jannings, George Bancroft, Richard Barthelmess, Betty Compson, Gary Cooper, Joan Crawford, Marion Davies, Louise Dresser, Greta Garbo, Janet Gaynor, Jean Hersholt, Thomas Meighan, William Powell and Fay Wray. A year later, the careers of Gilbert, Barthelmess, Compson, Dresser, Meighan and (at least in the US) Jannings had declined almost to nothing. Hollywood's response to the artistic problems of sound film was as inept as its perception of the industrial possibilities two years earlier. Automatically assuming that nothing of the silent cinema had value, its visual beauty and subtle acting were discarded in favour of ideas and personalities from the stage. Broadway actors were imported in quantity to appear in clumsy imitation revues and drawing-room comedies, romantic stars like Blanche Sweet, Mae Murray and Alice White grimly miscast in musicals the failure of which ended their careers, as those of action specialists like serial queen Allene Ray and Western hero Art Acord were terminated (the latter in suicide) when, for no logical reason, they were called upon to deliver slabs of dialogue often into crude machines unable to record accurately even the best voice. Booming stage projection registered best on such primitive devices, but paradoxically it was these artificial voices that proved least suitable for film recording as techniques improved. The most famous example of a career ruined by sound is also the least authentic. M-G-M star John Gilbert was signed to a new contract in March 1929 without anyone thinking a voice test necessary, and it was not until the influential "Photoplay" published an article called "Is John Gilbert Through?" describing his voice, inaccurately, as "shrill, almost piping," (at most, this was true only when he was nervous or excited) that rumours of unfitness began. Despite success in *Queen Christina* (Rouben Mamoulian, 1933) Gilbert worked little after sound, and died in 1936, rich but prematurely aged through drink.

In 1910 a competition run by Essanay to rename the motion picture had produced "photoplay"; nineteen years later, "Photoplay" magazine launched another such quest, selecting "Phonoplay" as a fitting description for sound film. (Other suggestions were "Alluretone," "Sayshow," "Speakeasy," "Sonopingo," "Smotion picture," "Parlandociné.") Less concerned with names, Hollywood studios were struggling with the technical problems of sound. Since sound could best be recorded at twenty-four frames per second, as compared with silent film's sixteen to twenty-two f.p.s., sets had to be more brightly lit, and were therefore hotter. Microphones were non-directional, and as many as a dozen were placed around the set, hidden by convenient props or incorporated into telephones or light-fittings; direction came to consist of moving actors from one hidden microphone to another, timing dia-

John Gilbert at the height of his popularity, shortly before shooting began on his first sound feature, *Redemption* (Fred Niblo). (M-G-M photo by Ruth Harriet Louise)

Lighting for early sound films. M-G-M's *The March of Time*.

logue so that it was directed at the appropriate prop. To cut out the noise of the drive mechanism, cameras were installed in massive glass-fronted boxes, often cruelly cramped and hot for the operator, and after each take actors and crew trooped into the next room for a playback before going on.

Inside a camera booth before cinematography had its mobility restored.

Without adequate mixing or dubbing facilities, all sound was recorded at the time of shooting. One engineer recalled adding a dripping tap to a dialogue scene by crouching on a ladder near the ceiling microphone and duplicating the drip with a wetted finger on his own hand. The sound of a girl's stockings rubbing together as she walked, or of her knees knocking, was enough to lose her a role, and when costumes and props proved too noisy, such ruses as rubber jewellery were tried. Inventive film-makers quickly broke the more absurd rules. Various directors, among them Lionel Barrymore and Ernst Lubitsch, are credited with replacing a score of fixed microphones with one suspended from a pole which could be moved from actor to actor—the origin of the modern boom—while Michael Curtiz and Rouben Mamoulian, the former aided by inventive cameraman Lee Garmes, fitted wheels to the camera box, restoring its mobility. Hungarian Paul Fejos, faced with the necessity of making

sense of the imitation revues then popular in Hollywood, developed the camera crane for *Broadway* (1929) * allowing him to soar above a dance formation and show its geometrical logic, the precursor not only of Busby Berkeley's musical numbers but also the fluid style of Hollywood's Thirties camerawork.

HANGMAN'S HOUSE. Director: John Ford. From being a director of action films like *The Iron Horse* (1924) and *Three Bad Men* (1926) which, though already invested with the subtle consciousness of landscape's symbolic value that was to make his classic films so stimulating, were in essence Westerns with limited thematic material, John Ford graduated at Fox to become a master of melodrama, often using glamorous locations or plots of a complexity other directors would have found daunting. *Hangman's House*, though set in Ford's beloved Ireland and starring Victor McLaglen, an actor whose character, Ford later revealed, recalled that of his father, begins in a Foreign Legion outpost, and uses a revenge plot—McLaglen, exiled from Ireland for his political activities, returns in disguise to murder the man responsible for the death of his sister—whose convolutions inspire one's admiration of Ford's control. Scenes suggestive of Nineteenth century fantasy make Ireland seem a land of mystery, and disguise the fact that the whole film, except for brief exterior scenes like the horse race, is shot on a set. McLaglen, disguised as a monk, passes unseen through the countryside, to find the home of his antagonist, the cursed "Hangman's House," a Gothic mansion squatting by a lake like the traditional moated grange. Although, like much of Ford's best work, the core of *Hangman's House* is a complex discussion of moral and religious issues, his stylistic vitality is seen at its best in the horse race, a lively event in which Ford captures the ebullience of the Irish and their complete involvement in all that they do. (Among the crowd collapsing to the ground when a fence gives way may be seen John Wayne in an early uncredited appearance when he was Ford's assistant and occasional extra.)

THE DOCKS OF NEW YORK. Director: Josef von Sternberg. One of von Sternberg's finest melodramas marks the peak of his silent career, after which he declined as a Hollywood star director until his association with Marlene Dietrich elevated him to his previous eminence. Again exploring the hermetically-sealed world of the urban tenderloin, extracting from George Bancroft's ship stoker and Betty Compson's prostitute the power of their personalities, he shows their casual affair to contain the substance of great love, Bancroft saving the suicidal girl from drowning, intending to abandon her later after a fake marriage, but returning at last to save her and himself.

* Primitive "cranes" with the camera bolted to one end of a beam had been used, but Fejos invented the continually extensible variety.

Recording the famous M-G-M lion emblem.

Olga Baclanova's arrest, one of Sternberg's superb crane shots from *The Docks of New York*.

1929

When the Wall Street crash came, America had more movie theatres than banks, 9,000 of them alone fitted with sound. 110,000,000 admissions were sold a week, the highest figure Hollywood was ever to reach. Two years later there were fewer banks, but the number of sound cinemas had grown to 13,000, suggesting the relative ease with which the film industry weathered a storm that crushed others. Many individuals, however, suffered. Mack Sennett, who had just built new studios in the San Fernando Valley, was bankrupted, and William Fox's attempt to acquire M-G-M collapsed when, after overextending himself to buy secret control of its shares from Nicholas Schenck and the Loew family, the crash wrecked his financial empire and he was forced to sell out. Countless small producers on the Sunset Boulevard/Gower Street "Poverty Row," where independents ground out low-budget quickies for state-by-state distribution, were put out of business. When James Cruze closed his studio in February 1930 "Poverty Row" virtually ceased to exist, though a few individuals continued by joining forces. The hardiest survivors were the Cohn brothers, Jack and Harry, and Joe Brandt, who consolidated their holdings first as CBC Films, and then as Columbia Pictures. Always a poor studio—Twenties success was built on hiring stars for a few days and shooting scenes for two or three films in that time, leaving the supporting cast to fill in the rest later—Columbia became one of the Forties' most inventive companies without losing its low-budget orientation. Its emblem, Columbia holding aloft a torch—actress Evelyn Venable played the role—became famous.

Two great silent stars, Mabel Normand and Lon Chaney, died. Interrupting a production of *Anna Karenina* for Thalberg at M-G-M, Erich Pommer was recalled to Ufa. In 1927, the Academy of Motion Picture Arts and Sciences had been formed, and on May 16, 1929, it met to present its first awards. *Wings* (Wil-

liam Wellman, 1927) was the best film and Emil Jannings and Janet Gaynor received prizes for the best performances of the preceding two years. It is ironic that Jannings was not there to receive his award, having accompanied Pommer back to Germany, his Hollywood career terminated by the coming of sound. With Josef von Sternberg, he was returning to Berlin to make his first sound film, *The Blue Angel*. With Prohibition strictly enforced, reformers turned to the cinema for employment, and the Rev. William Sheafe Chase earned instant fame by organising the Federal Motion Picture Council of America which lobbied Congress in 1928-9 to introduce stringent censorship. Hollywood, as usual, responded with a promise of voluntary control. Trade publisher Martin Quigley and drama teacher Daniel A. Lord drew up a 4,000-word Production Code covering correct language, morality, costume and social attitudes for the movies, an ominous document soon to be the cause of some of Hollywood's greatest absurdities.

HALLELUJAH! M-G-M. Story and direction by King Vidor. Script by Wanda Tuchock. Dialogue by Ransom Rideout. Titles by Marian Ainslee. Treatment by Richard Schayer. Photographed by Gordon Avil. Art direction by Cedric Gibbons. Edited by Hugh Wynn and Anson Stevenson. Costumes by Henrietta Frazer. Songs: "Swanee Shuffle" and "Waiting at the End of the Road" by Irving Berlin. Players: Daniel L. Haynes (Zeke), Nina Mae McKinney (Chick), William E. Fountaine (Hot Shot), Harry Gray (Parson), Fannie Belle De Night (Mammy), Everett McGarrity (Spunk), Victoria Spivey (Missy Rose), Milton Dickerson, Robert Couch, Walter Tait (Johnson kids), Dixie Jubilee Singers.

While sound film shattered the reputations of many routine film craftsmen, directors of proven ability seldom found adaptation difficult. New arrivals like

**Lon Chaney in a publicity shot for *The Unholy Three*
(1930), his last film. (M-G-M photo by Hurrell)**

A Jenny strafes a German staff car in Wellman's historic *Wings*.

Rouben Mamoulian with *Applause* (1929) combined stage visual and dramatic conventions with an almost surreal use of sound to create arresting if uncomfortable hybrids, but Hollywood's best directors saw instantly the new form's cinematic potential. King Vidor

Josef von Sternberg and Emil Jannings on the set of *The Blue Angel*.

resourcefully used the stage as a departure point for his first sound film, *Hallelujah!*, its then-fashionable all-Negro cast exploiting the popularity of black revues like "Blackbirds of 1928" (his star, Nina Mae McKinney, came from its chorus line) and of Paul Robeson (Daniel Haynes was Robeson's "Show Boat" understudy) but in his treatment of the story Vidor relied on his cinematic sense. Recognising that, to shoot the film around his childhood home in Memphis, Tennessee, and Arkanas would make sound recording difficult, Vidor planned the drama on almost operatic lines. Songs frequently further the story, or underline the impact of sequences like the mass baptism, and much of the synchronised dialogue and effects were recorded later in Hollywood. Like Mamoulian, Vidor saw that "synthetic" sound could create a more effective mood than accurate location recording, a lesson later forgotten in Hollywood's search for verisimilitude.

Hallelujah's simplistic story is of a confused young Negro preacher who fights his carnal impulses with only limited success until the flight of his wife with a lover sends him out into the swamps in pursuit—to cause his wife's death in a fall from their carriage and then to strangle the lover. Claiming to present a picture of "the real Negro," Vidor instead perpetuates most of the specious myths of black emotionalism, shiftlessness and vulnerability to superficial religious observance, but his background is harshly moving. Early scenes of a riverboat loading up with cotton from wagons lined up beside the wide river are accurate enough to be used today as documentary material, and the brawling vitality of bars and dance halls where much of the action takes place has seldom been more effectively achieved. The plumply inviting Nina Mae McKinney, well used in some noisy dance sequences and songs, gives a spirited performance, while Vidor's visual flair transforms the massed baptism and the final swamp chase amid the predatory sucking of mud and the shrieks of water-birds into unique screen poetry.

ALL QUIET ON THE WESTERN FRONT. Director: Lewis Milestone. Universal's adaptation of Erich Maria Remarque's anti-war novel of life in the German trenches was the most successful product of Carl Laemmle Jnr.'s brief tenure as Production Manager of his father's company. Originally to have been directed by Herbert Brenon, whose skill with ambitious realist epics had been proved on *Daughter of the Gods* (1916) and other features, the film eventually went to the young Lewis Milestone when Brenon's price of $125,000 seemed too high. Paid on a weekly basis, however, Milestone eventually received $130,000, as the film took nine months to complete. Although some of Remarque's pacifist fervour was brought over in the film, with Lew Ayres and his friends conveying not only the brutality of war but also its comradeship and affirmation of humanity, nevertheless, as in *The Big Parade*, the narrowing of focus to comply with Hollywood's obsession with the hopeful leads to a softening of the point. Even Ayres's furious repudiation of patriotic myths when he addresses his old classmates and his vigil beside the bed of a dying friend have a sentimental romanticism that impairs their force, as does Milestone's improvised conclusion where, to convey Remarque's downbeat ending, he shot a scene of the boy's hand reaching to catch a butterfly, then falling to the ground as a sniper's bullet found him. (The hand is Milestone's own, and though the film itself was shot by Arthur Edeson, this particular scene, done long after the main shooting, used new arrival Karl Freund on camera.)

1930

To the five thousand actors out of work on Broadway in 1929, even the shaky prospects of Hollywood employment were tempting, and the film industry found its need for sound picture performers filled by Broadway's unemployed. Most Hollywood producers, including Irving Thalberg whose scepticism about sound film never quite faded, visualised speaking cinema as a series of lush but simplified screen stage plays. M-G-M achieved considerable *kudos* with a film of Frederick Lonsdale's 1925 stage success *The Last of Mrs. Cheney* (1929), and Thalberg set out to lure Broadway's top stars Alfred Lunt and Lynne Fontanne to Hollywood, a difficult task accomplished when they appeared in a stiff but historically interesting version of Ferenc Molnar's *The Guardsman* (Sidney Franklin, 1931). Both productions had the reverent theatricality Thalberg made a trademark of his personal films, and in which Sidney Franklin specialised. His *Private Lives* in 1931 with Norma Shearer and Robert Montgomery is the best of the series that reached a peak of prodigality in 1936 with George Cukor's *Romeo and Juliet,* another vehicle for Miss Shearer, Thalberg's wife, and Leslie Howard, with lush designs by Oliver Messel. Franklin scored a further success with his reverent version of Rudolf Besier's *The Barretts of Wimpole Street* (1934), Miss Shearer playing the role Katherine Cornell had created on Broadway. Miss Cornell never came to Hollywood, though one of Fritz Lang's first American projects in the mid-thirties was a script for her that was never filmed. Nor did many of Broadway's established names, except for a brief uncomfortable experiment. Hollywood's prime acquisition from Broadway was a *corps* of talented actors who, quickly typed in character roles, surrendered their minor star status for long and remunerative careers in which they propped up less skilled but more popular colleagues: Dudley Digges, Aline McMahon, Morris Carnovsky, Henry Hull, Will Geer, Dean Jagger, Lee Tracy,

Lionel Atwill and others give a texture and style to Thirties cinema which stars like Claudette Colbert, James Cagney and Franchot Tone, often *ingénues* or understudies on Broadway, could not hope to attain.

Playwrights willingly disposed of film rights to their work, but those who chose to write in Hollywood even part-time, like Sidney Howard or Laurence Stallings, were exceptional. The 1933–4 Broadway season contained, as usual, a dozen plays that were later filmed, Howard's "Yellow Jack," Maxwell Anderson's "Mary of Scotland," Jerome Kern's "Roberta," Eugene O'Neill's "Ah, Wilderness!" and Jack Kirkland's "Tobacco Road" (from Erskine Caldwell's novel) among them, but in no case did the writer have any hand in the screenplay. The phrase "sold for the movies" was in common use, suggesting that the play, like a car sold for scrap, had no hope of retaining its personality. As a source of technicians, Broadway proved even less valuable to Hollywood; designers deplored rigid studio styles and the committee design system, in which a head of art direction like Cedric Gibbons of M-G-M supervised a team of specialists. George Cukor was one of the few directors imported as "dialogue directors" in the early Thirties to prevail in the new medium, and Rouben Mamoulian transferred his reputation for stylish and *outré* productions intact. The rest, like Arthur Hopkins and George Abbott, are largely forgotten.

HELL'S ANGELS. Caddo Company/United Artists. Produced and directed by Howard Hughes. Dialogue directed by James Whale. Script by Harry Behn and Howard Estabrook from story by Marshall Neilan. Dialogue by Joseph Moncure March. Photographed by Gaetano Gaudio (ground) and Harry Perry (aerial), plus twenty-eight cameramen. Art direction by Julian Boone Fleming and Carroll Clark. Edited by Douglas Biggs. Music by Hugo Riesenfeld. Players:

One of the many Broadway stars to work in Hollywood during the early sound period was Tallulah Bankhead.

Ben Lyon (Monte Rutledge), James Hall (Roy Rutledge), Jean Harlow (Helen), John Darrow, (Karl Armstedt), Lucien Prival (Baron von Krantz), Frank Clark (Lt. von Brauen), Roy Wilson ("Baldy"), Douglas Gilmore (Capt. Redfield), Jane Winton (Baroness von Krantz), Evelyn Hall (Lady Randolph), William B. Davidson (Staff Major), Wyndham Standing (RFC Squadron Commander), Lena Malena (Gretchen), Carl von Hartmann (Zeppelin commander), Stephen Carr (Elliott), Hans Joby (von Schieben), Pat Somerset (Marryat), Marilyn Morgan (Girl Selling Kisses), F. Schumann-Heink (1st. Officer of Zeppelin), William von Brinken (von Richter).

Determined to produce the greatest air war-film ever made, Howard Hughes, neophyte film-maker and aircraft engineering tycoon, spent most of 1928 scouting Europe for intact World War One aircraft and assembling a cast of both expert barnstorming pilots and promising young actors who would not impede what was, to him, a technological extravaganza. Swedish actress Greta Nissen was hired to play the female lead, an emancipated English aristocrat, and romantic comedian Ben Lyon borrowed from First National to star. (Initially required for only a few weeks, Lyon finally worked 104 weeks on the film, returning to find himself forgotten and his career drastically impaired.) Hughes leased or built airfields all around the Los Angeles area to accommodate his forty planes and the seventy-eight pilots and thirty cameramen hired to fly them, and contracted with Luther Reed, a Paramount director whose main qualification for the job was having been aviation editor of the "New York Herald," to make the film. Marshall Neilan, veteran director on whose *Everybody's Acting* (1926) Hughes, then twenty-one, had gained his first production experience, suggested the idea of *Hell's Angels,* and was hired to develop a script in collaboration with poet Joseph Moncure March, whose epic narrative verses were to be the source of films like *The Set-Up* (Robert Wise, 1949).

Much of the film, including its flying sequences, had been shot when sound came in, and Hughes abruptly decided to remake it with dialogue, a relatively simple process for such a large film since the air footage, which composed more than half the story, could have effects dubbed in. Greta Nissen's accent made her inappropriate for the role of an English girl, and Ben Lyon was responsible for nominating a minor extra, Jean Harlow, for the role after seeing her dancing in a party scene at the Christie lot. Her performance in what is almost a cameo part sets the tone of the highly naturalistic and sexually frank first section (directed by English newcomer James Whale) in which the elder and more responsible of two brothers, played by James Hall, falls in love with the beautiful, unconventional Helen, who propositions his brother Monte, more attractive and amoral, in one of the film's most famous scenes, culminating in the much-quoted "Do you mind if I put on something more comfortable?" Her frank seduction of Monte, her casual dismissal of elder brother Roy with the remark "He'd be horrified if he knew what I was really like," set a style for screen sex that persisted until the conservatism of the mid-Thirties and Roosevelt's puritan administration. As Monte, Lyon gives a relaxed, natural performance that contrasts with the stiff Hall, whose booming voice and obvious style typify Hollywood's less successful stage imports of the time.

Hell's Angels's aerial sequences are impressive even today, and have been re-used often, notably in *Crimson Romance* (David Howard, 1934), and *British Intelligence* (Terry Morse, 1940). Four men died in their completion, two in an aerial crash over San Francisco Bay during the dog-fight, another ferrying a plane across country when he hit telegraph wires, and a fourth when pilot Al Wilson bailed out after executing the difficult stall and spin of the Gotha bomber, leaving a mechanic inside the fuselage controlling smoke pots, unaware that the plane was pilotless. Even on the Zeppelin raid sequence, in which a twenty-eight foot model was used, careful attention to detail created an air of realism, reinforced by Hughes's meticulous shooting. 103 takes were demanded of a zeppelin observation car, with Karl Armstedt inside, being cut loose, and dozens for relatively simple images of machinery. Hughes finally spent $4 million on the film, but retrieved most of this on its first distribution. It has since grossed a much larger amount, and gained endorsement as a unique work of action cinema. Often discarded as irrelevant, the framing dialogue sequences are in fact of a high quality, directed by newcomer Whale (Lewis Milestone also alleges he directed certain portions himself), then seeking film experience before embarking on the film of "Journey's End," R. C. Sherriff's play which he directed on the London stage. A duel scene silhouetted against the dawn sky, Roy's murder of Monte to prevent him revealing the plans, and the stylish ballroom sequence, shot in colour, show Whale's talent at its best.

1931

Contrary to 1941 claims made on behalf of Orson Welles, 1931 saw the first appearance of ceilings in Hollywood film sets, laying the foundation for a more realistic style of set design and allowing cinematographers to develop techniques that would later enable them to shoot on actual interior locations. *Transatlantic* (William K. Howard), photographed by James Wong Howe at Fox, *The Mad Genius* (Michael Curtiz) and *Svengali* (Archie Mayo), both shot by Barney McGill and designed by Anton Grot at Warner Brothers, used stretched muslin for ceilings, after Grot discovered that action could be illuminated with lamps above the cloth without destroying the illusion of solidity. At the Goldwyn studios, Gregg Toland was also experimenting with the style he was to make famous on *Dead End* (William Wyler, 1937), *Citizen Kane* and other films. He pioneered much of modern camera technique: coated lenses, high speed stock, Waterhouse Stops (thin metal slips drilled with differing apertures and placed in a lens to alter focus beyond its normal optical properties, the precursor of "deep focus" style) were all introduced as a result of his experiments. Toland also developed a sound-deadening camera "blimp" with an external attachment for focus-pulling, and was one of the first cinematographers to use a photo-electric exposure meter.

Toland owed his freedom to Sam Goldwyn, who kept him on staff as his top cameraman with ample time and funds for research. Although not himself creative, Goldwyn recognised talent in others and fostered it. For his studio's first sound film he chose the popular Ziegfeld musical *Whoopee!* (Thornton Freeland, 1931), importing star Eddie Cantor to appear in it, and Florenz Ziegfeld himself to supervise the production. (Ziegfeld was so impressed with the starlets, among them Virginia Bruce and Paulette Goddard, in the "Goldwyn Girls" chorus line that he hired them for his own Broadway shows.) Goldwyn also brought to Hollywood the show's dance director, Busby Berkeley, starting a notable trend in the film musical. After four musicals for Goldwyn, *Whoopee!, Palmy Days* (Edward Sutherland, 1931), *The Kid From Spain* (Leo McCarey, 1932), and *Roman Scandals* (Frank Tuttle, 1933), Berkeley went to Warner Brothers, where his kaleidoscopic patterns of semi-naked chorus girls, his elaborate filmlets of sexual misbehaviour and dizzying *mélange* of tracking and crane shots became synonymous with the best of Hollywood's Thirties musicals. Predictably, his favourite number was "Lullaby of Broadway" from *Golddiggers of 1935* (also directed), a clever film miniature in which Dick Powell and Wini Shaw act out the song's dusk-to-dawn round of New York clubs before a shocking climax in which the girl tumbles to her death from a skyscraper. Berkeley's prodigality was notorious; crew and stars would sit about playing cards for days before ideas came to the director, and an elaborate process of working out shots and camera movements followed. Vincente Minnelli had his first break in Hollywood when, sent to provide ideas for a Berkeley number, he glimpsed a bowl of fruit on the table and suggested a routine with this *motif*. It became "The Lady in the Tutti-Frutti Hat" in Carmen Miranda's vehicle *The Girl He left Behind/The Gang's All Here* (1943). In the late Forties, Berkeley was much in demand to enliven musicals by adding additional dance numbers. André Previn recalls attending a conference with Berkeley on M-G-M's *Two Weeks with Love* (Roy Rowland, 1950) where the master began roughing out his concept of a new sequence for Jane Powell, but stopped to enquire of Previn: "Before we go on, tell me one thing. Can you get me forty trained eagles?" These were to have swooped into the scene and carried the star away. Not surprisingly, it was never filmed.

While Goldwyn was exploiting American talent, Carl Laemmle at Universal, a company tottering as a result of ambitious sociological dramas like *All Quiet on the Western Front* (Lewis Milestone, 1929), financed by Carl Laemmle Jnr. during his tenure as Production Manager of his father's studio, saved it by returning to the foreign importations and cheap films on which its reputation was based. James Whale, Karl Freund, Peter Lorre and other European talents were accumulated, and Laemmle Snr. embarked on a programme of low-budget horror films of high imagination which quickly reestablished Universal as the most viable of the lesser studios.

FRANKENSTEIN. Universal. Presented by Carl Laemmle. Associate producer: E. M. Asher. Directed by James Whale. Based on the composition by John L. Balderston from the novel by Mrs. Percy B. Shelley. Adapted from the play by Peggy Webling (uncredited additional material: Robert Florey). Screenplay by Garrett Fort, Francis Edwards Faragoh. Scenario editor: Richard Schayer. Photographed by Arthur Edeson. Edited by Maurice Pivar, Clarence Kloster. Art direction by Charles D. Hall. Make-up by Jack Pierce (uncredited). Players: Colin Clive (Henry Frankenstein), Mae Clarke (Elizabeth), John Boles (Victor Moritz), Boris Karloff (The Monster), Edward van Sloan (Dr. Waldeman), Dwight Frye (Fritz), Frederick Kerr (Baron Frankenstein), Lionel Belmore (Burgomaster), Michael Marsh (Peasant Father), Marilyn Harris (Little Maria).

After the success of R. C. Sherriff's war play "Journey's End," James Whale, who had directed the London, Broadway and Hollywood versions, was offered thirty stories, choosing Mary Shelley's metaphysical horror/romance because of its "strong meat" and the fact that "it would be amusing to try and make what everybody knows is a physical impossibility seem believable in sixty minutes." ("Films in Review," May 1962) Robert Florey, originally chosen to direct, was replaced. Casting was a major problem. Laemmle wanted Leslie Howard, but later decided on Bela Lugosi with his success in *Dracula* (Tod Browning, 1931) in mind, and Whale, with Paul Ivano as camera-

Science's Monster Terror!
"FRANKENSTEIN"
Starring
BORIS KARLOFF
X Cert.
ADULTS ONLY

Frankenstein. **Boris Karloff and Colin Clive.**

Noah's Ark—Zanuck's folly. Michael Curtiz, 1929.

man, shot twenty minutes of tests. Soon afterwards, however, Whale met and recommended for the part character actor Karloff, and Lugosi was dropped. Whale's skill in subtle lighting and design (he was trained as a stage designer and artist) counterbalances the story's horror, so that the inky shadows and lowering menace of the Germanic horror film are replaced by patterns of light streaming along the walls, lightning flaring above Frankenstein's hill-top mill as he animates the composite body he has assembled. Brilliantly chosen visual and aural symbols complement the story: a distant tolling bell in the opening cemetery scene as the doctor and his crippled helper exhume a coffin; the jiggling skeleton that observes Fritz as he creeps into the medical school to steal a brain for the monster, and whose almost comic clattering causes him to drop the chosen brain and replace it with that of a madman. Added to the story by Robert Florey, this idea ingeniously rendered the mystical basis of the novel acceptable to American audiences by explaining the monster's madness in quasi-medical terms, and the last minute "happy" ending, with the doctor rescued from his burning mill, allowed, against Whale's will, a string of usually inferior sequels.

Despite the humour of *Frankenstein*, it has the quirky poetry of which Whale was a master, seen at its best in the "Old Man River" montage of *Showboat* (1936) and the sharply witty *The Bride of Frankenstein* (1935); but here, in scenes like the doctor's almost loving caress of the exhumed coffin as he says of its corpse, "He's just resting, waiting for a new life to come," and in the superb image of the monster groping with both hands for the light, a symbol of reason and grace from which he is forever barred, the humour is conveyed with a deeply moving poetic judgment.

THE PUBLIC ENEMY. Warner Brothers. Produced by Darryl F. Zanuck. Directed by William A. Wellman. Script by Harvey Thew from a story by Kubec

Glasmon and John Bright. Photographed by Dev Jennings. Edited by Ed McCormick. Art direction by Max Parker. Costumes by Earl Luick. Players: James Cagney (Tom Powers), Jean Harlow (Gwen), Edward Woods (Matt Doyle), Joan Blondell (Mamie), Beryl Mercer (Mrs. Powers), Donald Cook (Mike Powers), Mae Clarke (Kitty), Mia Marvin (Jane), Leslie Fenton (Nails Nathan), Robert Emmett O'Connor (Paddy Ryan).

When he joined Warner Brothers in 1928 after having been a writer for Lewis Milestone and scenarist on films featuring the wonder dog Rin-Tin-Tin, Darryl Zanuck's ambitions outran his capacity. Offering to produce "the greatest picture ever made," he tied up the company's newest European import Michael Curtiz and most of its resources in the lavish but disastrous *Noah's Ark* (1929). As Production Manager, he was less prodigal, and by 1931, basing all films on "spot news" and cutting costs to the bone, he had brought Warners to a precarious profitability. It was to Zanuck that director William Wellman showed "Beer and Blood," an original story by two Chicago druggists and would-be scenarists, Kubec Glasmon and John Bright. "I said, 'This is the greatest story I ever read,'" Wellman recalls, "(Zanuck) read it and said, 'Look, I can't take a chance. I've just made *Doorway to Hell* (Archie Mayo, 1930), and I don't want to make another underworld picture. You give me one reason why you think you can do it and make a great picture out of it.' And I said, 'I'll make it the toughest picture of them all.' And he said, 'You've got it.'"

True to his word, Wellman made *The Public Enemy* (the Hays office disliked the word "blood"), a film unprecedented at the time in its physical and sexual violence. James Cagney, then still a minor actor close to his beginnings as a Broadway dancer, became the vehicle for a savage fantasy of wish-fulfilment in which slum kid Tom Powers blasts his way from obscurity to a position of power, only to be killed treacherously after cutting down his enemies. Wellman attributed the film's success totally to Cagney and the boyish innocence he gave to a role others would have made a routine criminal portrait. "You're my bashful boy," his girlfriend Gwen says. But she recognises the brutality beneath. "You know what you want and you take it. Other men—and I've known dozens of them—are polite and gentle, but you're different." She takes him on her knee like a child, and a gramophone murmurs "I Surrender, Dear." Even the brutal climax has contradictory elements. After blasting his way into a rival gang's headquarters, the wounded Tom staggers into a rainstorm and with a muttered "I ain't so tough" collapses into the gutter. Kidnapped from hospital, he is delivered to the home of his upright family, his brother opening the door to have Tom's bandaged body sway like a hideous mummy before him and then thump to the floor. Upstairs, his mother sings cheerfully, making the bed for her son, and a record of "I'm Forever Blowing Bubbles" on the turntable quavers to a stop.

Much of the story is based on fact. Details of Tom Powers's life coincide with those of Hymie Weiss, Chicago gangster murdered in 1926, while the "rubbing out" of a horse by henchmen after he has thrown their boss recalls a similar execution by the "Nails" Nolan mob when he was killed in a riding accident. (Wellman has also revealed that the scene in which Cagney squashes a grapefruit into Mae Clarke's face reflected his own ambition to do this to his estranged wife.) But in telling the story, Wellman adopts a characteristically original style. Consistent use of low angles—at one point he even put the camera into a pit to get a shot of the car moving over it, revealing as it clears the frame a midget spy lurking in a doorway at the rear of the frame—gives one a sense of the underworld from which Powers and his men look up at reality. Out of hiding, they are vulnerable and exposed, starting in terror at the rattle of coals in a chute. Significantly they are trapped in a bright, sunlit street, the rival gang cutting them down with a machine gun hidden in an upstairs window. For the bashful boy and his playmates, the game becomes too real for them to survive it.

1932

As unemployment spread under Hoover's slack administration and New York banks struggled to maintain their stability, the Hollywood studios that had turned so eagerly to East Coast finance ten years before found the supply of new capital and the renewal of vital loans more and more complicated. The once-strong Paramount, depleted by Government insistence that Zukor split his holdings, went into receivership, and was kept going almost entirely by the occasional spectacular success, such as its Mae West films (e.g. *Night After Night,* Archie Mayo, 1932; *She Done Him Wrong,* Lowell Sherman; *I'm No Angel,* Wesley Ruggles, 1933), and Fox by Shirley Temple and Will Rogers. RKO was bankrupt, and its brilliant production manager David O. Selznick, taking with him the studio's best director, George Cukor, left to join M-G-M, to whose management he was now connected by marriage, having married Louis B. Mayer's daughter Irene in March 1930. The quip "The son-in-law also rises" had great currency. A necessity for more and better products to stave off financial ruin kept film-makers working at white heat. Completing *State Fair* at Fox late in 1932, Henry King spent thirty-six consecutive hours in a recording studio, taking naps while sound engineers prepared the next reel.

The crash made Hollywood aware for the first time of reality, and Darryl Zanuck at Warner Brothers built a new style of film on what he called "spot news." One of his most successful productions was *I Am a Fugitive from a Chain Gang* (Mervyn LeRoy, 1932) based on the true story of William Burns, the Georgia convict whom New Jersey refused to extradite back into imprisonment. M-G-M also had a taste of realism when members of the Russian aristocracy sued for defamation in Richard Boleslawski's *Rasputin and the Empress* (1932), a confused melodrama in which

I Am a Fugitive from a Chain Gang. Paul Muni.

Lionel, John and Ethel Barrymore appeared together (for the first and last time), as Rasputin, his killer and the Empress Alexandra. Prince Youssoupov sued over the suggestion that Rasputin had raped his wife, and Prince and Princess Chegodiev, three years later, for errors in John Barrymore's performance as Chegodiev in the film. M-G-M's official historian estimates that $750,000 was paid on these suits, plus $380,000 costs. From then on, every M-G-M film carried the statement that the characters were intended to bear no resemblance to real people living or dead, a practice which shortly became universal.

At the Fox studios the last film of Erich von Stroheim, Hollywood's most corrosive realist, was released, mutilated and partly re-shot, as *Walking down Broadway* (also *Hello Sister*). Though Stroheim had a long career after this as an actor, and contributed uncred-

Advertisement for *Walking Down Broadway.*

ited "business" to most of the films in which he appeared, he never again directed. At a fabulously inappropriate time, considering Hollywood's struggles to survive, RKO opened New York's Radio City Music Hall, flagship of its theatre chain. The cinema's high cost and lavish amenities made profit almost impossible, and further large amounts were spent on maintaining a permanent orchestra, a chorus line (The Rockettes), and in presenting ambitious stage shows to accompany the weekly change of programme. Among the artists who designed these shows was the young Vincente Minnelli.

IF I HAD A MILLION. Paramount. Directed by Ernst Lubitsch (Laughton sequence), Norman Taurog (Fields sequence), Stephen Roberts (Ruggles sequence), Norman Z .McLeod (Raft sequence), James Cruze (Wynne Gibson and May Robson sequences), William A. Seiter (Cooper sequence), H. Bruce Humberstone (Gene Raymond sequence). Scripts by Claude Binyon, Whitney Bolton, Malcolm Stuart Boyland, John Bright, Sidney Buchman, Lester Cole, Isabel Dawn, Boyce DeGaw, Walter De Leon, Oliver H. P. Garrett, Harvey Gates, Grover Jones, Ernst Lubitsch, Lawton Mackall, Joseph L. Mankiewicz, William Slavens McNutt, Seton I. Miller, Tiffany Thayer from a story of Robert D. Andrews. Players: Gary Cooper (Steven Gallagher), George Raft (Eddie Jackson), Wynne Gibson (Violet Smith), Charles Laughton (Phineas Lambert), Jack Oakie (Mulligan), Frances Dee (Mary Wallace), Charlie Ruggles (Henry Peabody), Alison Skipworth (Emily La Rue), W. C. Fields (Rollo), Mary Boland (Mrs. Peabody), Roscoe Karns (O'Brien), May Robson (Mrs. Walker), Gene Raymond (John Wallace), Lucien Littlefield (Zeb), Richard Bennett (John Glidden).

The sketch film, growing out of early sound experiments like *King of Jazz* (John Murray Anderson, 1930) and *Paramount on Parade* (various directors, 1930) to imitate the successful Broadway revue format, had its finest flowering in this showcase for some new Paramount stage acquisitions. Eccentric millionaire John Glidden, vexed by greedy relatives waiting for him to die, chooses eight people from the city directory and gives each a certified million dollar cheque. Sensing the depression mood, Paramount's scenarists showed all the receipiants using the money to assert themselves as individuals in a society oppressed by the unequal distribution of wealth. Some fulfil a long-time ambition. Porcelain salesman Henry Peabody wrecks the shop where he worked; prostitute Violet Smith takes the best room in an expensive hotel and goes to bed, luxuriously alone; Phineas Lambert ascends countless steps from a soulless office to deliver a rousing raspberry at the company president; retired vaudevillians Emily and Rollo set out in a car convoy to destroy the city's road-hogs; Mrs. Walker metamorphoses the old folks' home and her fellow inmates, reconstituting it as a cooperative club (while prudently retaining the old staff on high salaries merely to sit and rock, avoiding the charge that she contributes to unemployment). Only the improvident fail to benefit from the gift. Forger Eddie Jackson's paper-hanging is so well known that only a flop-house owner will redeem his cheque, for 10¢— he promptly turns Jackson into the police and burns it. Marine Gallagher disposes of what he thinks an April Fool joke prop to an illiterate cafe owner for $10, and convicted killer John Wallace is dragged to the electric chair, the money coming too late to hire the smart lawyer who would have pleaded extenuating circumstances and saved his life. Least stylish of all the episodes, this harshly stated fragment focuses the film's social criticism. "I didn't know what a gun was," the victim whines. "You can't think when you're hungry." Despite delightful comic images like Charlie Ruggles entering his old place of torment in impeccable morning dress with a white rabbit on a leash or Fields's anticipatory "Can you furnish us with some strong, brave drivers?" before reducing Los Angeles's roads to chaos, Gene Raymond's brief appearance has the most lasting impact.

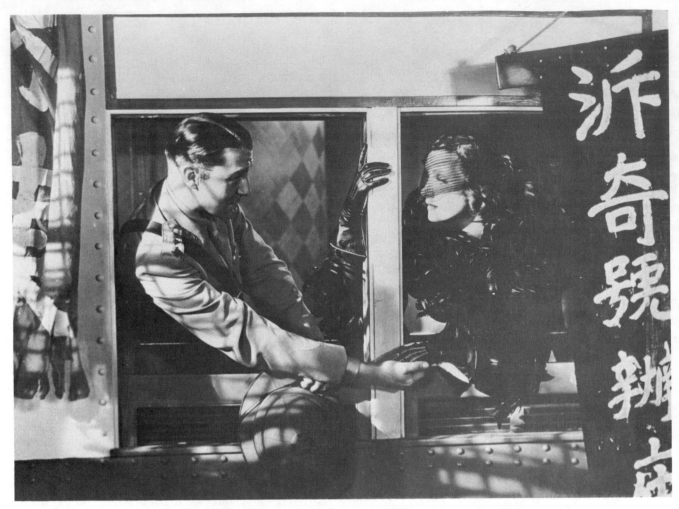

"It took more than one man to change my name to Shanghai Lily." Clive Brook and Marlene Dietrich in *Shanghai Express.*

SHANGHAI EXPRESS. Paramount. Directed by Josef von Sternberg. Script by Jules Furthman from an original story by Harry Hervey. Photographed by Lee Garmes. Art direction by Hans Dreier. Costumes by Travis Banton. Players: Marlene Dietrich (Shanghai Lily), Clive Brook (Donald "Doc" Harvey), Anna May Wong (Hue Fei), Warner Oland (Henry Chang), Eugene Pallette (Sam Salt), Lawrence Grant (Rev. Carmichael), Louise Closser Hale (Mrs. Haggerty), Gustav von Seyffertitz (Baum), Emile Chautard (Major Lenard).

Josef von Sternberg's richest excursion into his obsession, the destructive power of love, and the finest of his eight films starring his *protégée* Marlene Dietrich, *Shanghai Express* is the pivotal work of this director's uneven career. Even more successful than the same team's *Morocco* (1930), *Express* earned $3 million, as well as an Oscar for cinematographer Lee Garmes and nominations for both film and director—tributes to Sternberg's concentration at a time when

his recently divorced first wife was suing Dietrich for defamation of character and alienation of his affections. The film's success encouraged both director and star into attempts at independence the Paramount regime would not permit: Sternberg's failure to impose on the studio his original story for *Blonde Venus* (1932), a mistimed 1933 attempt to begin independent production in Germany with his star, and extravagant use of resources in his last two films with Dietrich, *The Scarlet Empress* (1934) and *The Devil is a Woman* (1935), led to the termination of his association with Dietrich and Paramount, twin blows from which he never fully recovered professionally.

Like many of Sternberg's films, *Express* follows the evolution of a sexual obsession, in this case the revival of an extinguished affair between elegant doctor Donald Harvey and the woman, known only as Magdalen, whose love he lost some years previously after a disastrous though unspecified test of faith. Now she is "Shanghai Lily, the notorious White Flower of

Mata Hari. Greta Garbo and Lewis Stone.

China," *en route* to Peking on the Shanghai Express which, unknown to all on board, will be the scene of their downfall as an *incognito* bandit leader discovers their weaknesses, which he exploits to rob them of both dignity and self-esteem. Only the lovers remain untouched, united by a bond of mutual need for immolation, and as the train arrives, Lily, in a suggestive and incomparably subtle scene of presenting her lover with a watch and taking in return his whip and gloves, signals that the all-powerful woman has won. The man is now her abject slave and possession.

A technical achievement of impressive stature, the film was managed by Sternberg with inspired generalship. Not, as he claimed, the creator of either sets, script or camerawork, he nevertheless made suggestions for each, moulding the contributions of his talented collaborators into a coherent whole. Dreier was instructed to build city sets so claustrophobically close to the train that on some occasions the carriages threatened to pull them down, Furthman to explore the multiple deceptions that lie at the core of personality, Garmes to extract from Dietrich the "spiritual power" which to Sternberg was the essence of art. A thousand Chinese extras were accumulated, a spur of the Santa Fé railroad closed off, and the San Bernardino and Chatsworth stations converted to Chinese terminals for the express. A train was painted, to Sternberg's specifications, in white and odd camouflage patterns, and miles of trackside country scoured of every un-Chinese building, sign or feature in preparation for a running battle between two trains that was never included in the film. As in all his work, Sternberg created a world merely to set off the beauty and charisma of his star, one in which, surrounded by enigmatic Chinese ideographs and clad in black plumes quivering constantly from the train's vibration, she reigns supreme, the imperturbable spirit of love and its concomitant, the desire to destroy.*

---

* The plot of *Shanghai Express* and some of its footage, as well as excerpts from *The General Died at Dawn* (see 1936), were used in *Peking Express,* a 1951 remake directed by William Dieterle.

MATA HARI. Director: George Fitzmaurice. Greta Garbo's appeal defied analysis even by Clarence Brown and William Daniels, her regular director and cameraman, who recorded her angular charm without understanding its elements. Although popular, Garbo appealed mainly to the female audience and to European film-goers; the decline of both markets during the Second World War was a powerful influence on her decision to retire (see 1942). In *Mata Hari,* a story one doubts the urbane Brown would have accepted, Garbo lopes through an absurd dance before a gaping idol, seducing Russian courier Ramon Navarro from fear of suave spymaster Lewis Stone and his club-footed helper, and finally betrays herself through love. As in many of her films, the seduction scenes most effectively use Garbo's physical intensity. Alone with her victim in his apartment, she responds to his advances, but the room is too light. . . Flames are extinguished until only one remains, a candle burning before an icon, but even this, kept as part of a promise to his mother, must be snuffed, the eclipse of the tiny light symbolizing the collapse of his resistance to her unconquerable erotic force.

1933

The year in which silent cinema and the old Hollywood finally expired. Lewis J. Selznick, pioneer independent producer, died, as did Roscoe "Fatty" Arbuckle (see 1922). One of many film-makers ruined in the crash, Mack Sennett filed a petition in voluntary bankruptcy, after allegedly losing $5 million; his new studio in the San Fernando Valley became the Republic lot. As the depression bit deep, a third of America's 16,000 cinemas closed, and after Roosevelt's bank moratorium, Eastern finance houses applied pressure on Hollywood, demanding a cut in costs. Some studios, notably Universal, responded by suspending all contracts, and all companies, with the agreement of the Academy of Motion Picture Arts and Sciences (a decision that brought accusations from the Directors' Guild and other organizations that the Academy had become a tool of the studios), instituted a general 50% pay cut.

People recall Louis B. Mayer breaking into tears as he asked his staff to accept the reduction in salary: only later was it discovered that the one salary not cut was his own. At Warner Brothers, Jack L. Warner promised Production Manager Darryl F. Zanuck that cuts would be restored within a few weeks, and on Zanuck's personal guarantee stars like Cagney reluctantly agreed. When Warner refused to honour his promise, Zanuck left (Hal Wallis replaced him) to set up his own company, 20th Century Pictures, with Joseph Schenck and William Goetz as partners. $1½ million to form the company came from Louis B. Mayer, Goetz's father-in-law, and Nick Schenck, brother of Joseph. Zanuck adopted his Warners "spot news" system, beginning with Raoul Walsh's *The Bowery* (starring Wallace Beery, George Raft) and Rowland Brown's *Blood Money*, but as the vogue for film realism had passed the films did not have the success they deserved, and in 1935 20th Century merged with the ailing Fox to create one of the Thirties' most important studios.

BLOOD MONEY. 20th Century. Produced by Darryl F. Zanuck. Associate producers: William Goetz, Raymond Griffith. Directed by Rowland Brown. Script and adaptation by Rowland Brown and Hal Long. Photographed by James van Trees. Edited by Lloyd Nosler. Art direction by Al D'Agostino. Music by Alfred Newman. Players: George Bancroft (Bill Bailey), Judith Anderson (Ruby Darling), Frances Dee (Elaine Talbert), Chick Chandler (Drury Darling), Blossom Seeley, Etienne Giradot, George Regas, Theresa Harris, Kathryn Williams, John Bleifer, Ann Brody, Henry Lewis Jr., Sandra Shaw, Henry Kolker, Bradley Page.

Among the properties Zanuck took with him from Warners was the original story of *Blood Money* by Rowland Brown. An extraordinary talent of the early Thirties, writer/director Brown created in a brief career three of the period's most inventive underworld dramas, of which *Blood Money* is the best. Starring George Bancroft as an ambitious bail bondsman and Judith Anderson, then a stage actress new to Hollywood, as the sophisticated night club owner who loves and protects him, *Blood Money* has that intimate knowledge of the real underworld and instinctive grasp of its morality displayed by Brown in his remaining films as director (*Quick Millions*, 1931, *Hell's Highway*, 1932, and *The Devil Is a Sissy*, 1936), as well as in the classics, including Michael Curtiz's *Angels with Dirty Faces* (1938), for which Brown supplied original stories. Brown's care with the rhythm of dialogue, his concern for the exactly appropriate gesture, gives to all his films an impressive poetry. The artist who in *Quick Millions* can take time off in a party scene to insert a sinuous and graceful dance solo for George Raft, then best known as a Broadway hoofer only recently introduced to dramatic roles, or who

Blood Money. George Bancroft.

can be troubled to dig up a boy with a genuine six-toed foot to dazzle the slum kinds of *The Devil Is a Sissy,* unconcernedly introduces into *Blood Money* a girl in male evening dress and monocle to score a point on the then-notorious Marlene Dietrich, Paramount's "Woman all women want to see." Bancroft, after an astonished glance, retires laughing uproariously to Anderson's office.

Brown genuinely attempts to render human behaviour in terms other than those of pulp fiction. Bancroft's ambitous semi-gangster frankly acknowledges the futility of his obsession with the rich, spoiled Elaine, just as both he and her father, with whom he forms a believable *entente,* accept philosophically her kleptomania and sexual masochism. Frances Dee is convincing as the corrupt heiress, putting sullen delight into her "You've hurt my lip" after thief Drury Darling has kissed her with the brutality she invites; "I'd do anything for the man who'd beat me," she says longingly to Bailey, but the irony of their relationship is that he loves her too much to oblige. Brown cunningly develops this situation with detail that, while avoiding censorship, has a tingling erotic charge.

Her frank admiration at her father's *luau* of the hula girls, whose dance she imitates with movements all the more explicitly erotic since she, unlike the dancers, is fully clothed, leads to the film's wry final shot where Elaine, cast off by Bailey after having double-crossed him with the obliging Drury, meets a dishevelled girl in the lobby of the office building. As she explains that her visit to an artist upstairs in search of a job posing for "art studies" led to a violent rape attempt, Elaine grabs the paper and, pausing only to ask "What did you say his name was?", heads for the stairs.

Brown's determination to give the women in his films believable motivations applies also to Judith Anderson's role. Although the gangsters see that she is motivated by jealousy and unrequited love, they obey her injunction to ruin Bailey, accepting without question her charge that he is the cause of her brother's arrest. When she discovers this to be untrue and tries to call them off, they are equally understanding, but reasonably point out that the feud, once started, cannot be stopped. Morality, tradition and "face" are evoked without any suggestion of motives lower than those of other men. Brown's only concession to conventional drama occurs in the climax, with Ruby racing to head off an attempt to murder Bailey with a billiard ball filled with nitro-glycerine, but even this is enlivened with comedy, the cab's swooping passage through peak-hour crowds intercut with the tension of Bailey's frequent near-misses of the fatal eight-ball. The skill of *Blood Money* makes all the more tragic Brown's failure to exploit his own talent. After graduating from being Reginald Denny's gagman on films like *Skinner's Dress Suit* (William A. Seiter, 1926) to a contract director at Fox and RKO, only his first feature, *Quick Millions*, was released in its approved form. *Hell's Highway* suffered a change of star before production, and John Cromwell, against Brown's wishes and those of star Richard Dix, was called in to insert extra close-ups. Zanuck altered the continuity of *Blood Money* and dictated the inclusion of a song for Mae West-imitator Blossom Seeley. Finally, while making *The Devil Is a Sissy* for M-G-M, Brown punched a producer and was dismissed*; W. S. Van Dyke completed the film and took credit. Except as writer of original stories for *Angels With Dirty Faces*, *Nocturne* (1947) and *Kansas City Confidential* (1952) he did not work in Hollywood again.

Golddiggers of 1933. **The visual style Busby Berkeley was to make famous.**

42nd STREET. Director: Lloyd Bacon.
FOOTLIGHT PARADE. Director: Lloyd Bacon.

Golddiggers of 1933. **"We're in the Money."**

GOLDDIGGERS OF 1933. Director: Mervyn LeRoy.

Perhaps the musical's greatest year, 1933 saw Warner Brothers' estimation of public taste vindicated by three classics, all sustained by sharp comedy playing and direction from a seasoned studio team, but spiced by the unique talent of Busby Berkeley. The films derived from Ziegfeld's shows in their stage pyrotechnics, massed sexuality and forgettable tunes, but were enlivened by Berkeley, Lloyd Bacon and Mervyn LeRoy, comedy technicians of skill. Pitched at the stalls, all the Warners musicals discarded jewels for tinsel, style for vitality, high life for low. *42nd Street's* showgirls scuffle for position, Ruby Keeler ascending the heap with the help of bankrupt producer Warner Baxter and star Bebe Daniels, who conveniently breaks her ankle and gives up the stage for George Brent. In *Golddiggers* the eccentric millionaire composer (Dick Powell) not only writes, finances and stars in the show, but marries its leading lady. Perhaps the most effective, in *Footlight Parade* James Cagney produces prologues for the movies (see 1923), appearing as an agile dancer—he began with Texas Guinan's troupe on Broadway—in "Shanghai Lil," one of Berkeley's most inspired mini-films, foreshadowing his later eminence as a feature director. Musicals were to become lusher as M-G-M recognised their potential, and more stylish as Paramount's Mamoulian and Lubitsch exploited the form, but Warner's backstage romances remain indelibly fresh.

---

* Some sources suggest that Brown's assault may have been on David Selznick during the production of *A Star Is Born* (1937, qv.).

Two posed shots from *Footlight Parade*. a) "Honey-moon Hotel." b) "Shanghai Lil," with James Cagney.

a

b

1934

As admissions climbed to seventy million and the previous year's slump passed, most studios boosted their production, and the average cost of a feature rose to $250,000. M-G-M announced profits twice those of 1933, and Warners acquired as an affiliate Cosmopolitan Pictures, a company formed by William Randolph Hearst to showcase his mistress Marion Davies. In return for producing Davies vehicles with its own stars, the company taking Cosmopolitan under its wing gained generous free publicity and advertising privileges in Hearst papers, but endured difficulties like Hearst's interference and Miss Davies's insistence on having her large bungalow on the lot, which was dismantled and moved with her when she went from studio to studio. A minor but talented comedienne, Miss Davies had a worthwhile career at Warners until the company, in a time of declining profits, severed the relationship.

In an attempt to regain his lost supremacy, William Fox acquired European patents on two technical devices perfected by Tri-Ergon in Germany, as he had earlier bought the German Klang sound system, and sued most Hollywood studios then using the techniques of which he claimed ownership—a flywheel integral to sound reproduction and a method of printing soundtrack and image on film simultaneously. The studios fought Fox in the courts, but though he won cases in the first instance, the Supreme Court in 1935 ruled his patents invalid.

The National League of Decency was formed, promoted by the Catholic church, with Joseph I. Breen appointed as the MPPDA's Production Code authority with power to licence films for exhibition and deny screening to films transgressing the Code (first promulgated in 1930 but since then largely ignored by film-makers). The MPPDA undertook not to show any film without a Breen certificate, and fines of up to $25,000 were levied for infractions. Even films already released, like John Ford's *Arrowsmith* (1931), were subject to the Code if re-shown, and studio cuts in the Ford film removed the now-forbidden infidelity theme by excising Myrna Loy's entire role. Breen and his successors laid a dead hand on Hollywood films with their prohibition of even the vaguest reference to sexual or social problems, any alleged blasphemy or the suggestion that American government was not all it should be. In 1935, when Michael Curtiz's mining drama *Black Fury* had its anti-management messages removed by the Code authority, star Paul Muni contemptuously suggested the film should be re-titled, in line with its bland new story, *Coaldiggers of 1935*. Code power continued until the post-war years, when

Jack Warner (left) with two acquisitions: German producer Max Reinhardt (centre) imported to direct *A Midsummer Night's Dream* (Reinhardt, William Dieterle, 1935) and William Randolph Hearst.

Murder at the Vanities. "The Human Powder Box" number.

the destruction of studio-theatre links made enforcement impossible and changing morality rendered its strictures obsolete.

MURDER AT THE VANITIES. Paramount. Directed by Mitchell Leisen. Script by Carey Wilson and Joseph Gollomb based on the play by Earl Carroll and Rufus King. Dialogue by Sam Hellman. Art direction by Hans Dreier and Ernst Fegté. Photographed by Leo Tover. Music by Arthur Johnston. Lyrics by Sam Coslow. Dances by Larry Ceballos and LeRoy Prinz. Players: Carl Brisson (Eric Lander), Victor McLaglen (Bill Murdock), Jack Oakie (Jack Ellery), Kitty Carlisle (Ann Ware). Dorothy Stickney (Norma Watson), Gertrude Michael (Rita Ross), Jessie Ralph (Mrs. Helene Smith), Charles Middleton (Homer Boothby), Gail Patrick (Sadie Evans), Donald Meek (Dr. Saunders), Otto Hoffman (Walsh), Charles McAvoy (Ben), Beryl Wallace (Beryl), Bar-

bara Fritchie (Vivien), Toby Wing (Nancy), Lona Andre (Lona), Colin Tapley (Stage Manager), Clara Lou Sheridan (Lou), Gwenllian Gill (Gwen).

An inspired costume designed for DeMille, notably for *Male and Female* (see 1919), *The Volga Boatman* (1926) and *The Sign of the Cross* (1932), Mitchell Leisen became Paramount's expert in the spikey, suggestive comedies in which it specialised during the Thirties. All his films parody the conventional male/female relationship, showing women as assertive, arrogant mistresses of their weak men, a style that made his association with Billy Wilder on *Midnight* (1939) one which produced the Thirties' most acid comedy. Although an early work, *Murder at the Vanities* shows a familiar bitterness, as well as the polish and opulence that characterised Paramount's European-oriented style.

"Earl Carroll's Vanities" was a popular girl show of the time, presenting an undressed version of Ziegfeld's "Follies." Justifying his motto "Through These Doors Pass the Most Beautiful Girls in the World," which Leisen parodies in an opening scene with a raddled charwoman dragging her bucket under the sign, Carroll packed his film with displays of nudity extensive even by today's standards. Besides a number of dressing-room scenes, there are extensive set-pieces, including "The Human Powder Box" (huge compacts opening to reveal girls cuddling on giant powder-puffs) and an odd South Seas number in which a semi-naked Kitty Carlisle sings a duet with husband Carl Brisson, German star of Hitchcock's *The Ring*, while similarly undressed showgirls with feather fans imitate the surf. Later, in an even more bizarre scene, a line of girls dressed as flowers, nude except for cupped petals around their waists, line the back of the stage. One of them, posing stiffly, screams as blood dribbles down her breasts from the corpse of a murdered detective hidden above.

Typically for Leisen the detective is female and her body is sprawled under the ropes that operate the curtain, an eerily interesting spot with cables disap-pearing in the shadows and making a complex net over the slumped corpse. There are extended close-ups of the cadaver's white face, and McLaglen has great fun by bringing suspects into the manager's office, pulling back the sheet and demanding "Have you seen her before?". The interpenetration of sex and death has its apotheosis in "Marahuana," an ambitious production number with Duke Ellington's band (the film also premiered his popular "Cocktails For Two" and "Ebony Rhapsody"). Against a backdrop of crudely painted phallic cacti and accompanied by a crowd of girls dressed as Mexican peons, Gertrude Michael wails a torchy tune intimating that, when her lover is absent, she gains peace with "sweet Mara-huana" and entertains him in her drugged fantasies. After a few choruses, a man with a machine gun enters and massacres them all. The curtain falls, and Michael lurches off, shot to death under cover of the fake execution. Notwithstanding Leisen's later more sophisticated work, this remains one of his most arresting films.

It Happened One Night. Clark Gable and Claudette Colbert.

IT HAPPENED ONE NIGHT. Director: Frank Capra. "Bus stories" were a Hollywood commonplace, and Capra received little encouragement from Harry Cohn when he put forward Robert Riskin's script from "Night Bus" by Samuel Hopkins Adams. Having been loaned to M-G-M on Thalberg's request to make a major film, then sent back to impoverished Columbia by Louis B. Mayer when Thalberg's departure for Europe because of illness allowed Mayer to interfere with Thalberg's personal M-G-M unit, Capra insisted that he be allowed to make a film with Clark Gable, the M-G-M star lent to Columbia for one film as part of the same deal. Myrna Loy, Margaret Sullavan and Miriam Hopkins all turned down the part of the runaway heiress whom ruthless newsman Gable befriends on a bus trip, first to gain an exclusive on her story, then because he loves her, and Claudette Colbert only accepted it on condition that her scenes be disposed of in four weeks. The result shows none of this strain, its simple, unforced action giving Riskin's humanist comedy a chance to expand. In what was perhaps an excessive recognition of its merit, the film won four Oscars, and remains a Hollywood classic.

BELLE OF THE NINETIES. Director: Leo McCarey. Although Paramount struggled out of bankruptcy in 1934 when negotiations with major creditors reduced its liability to a huge but at least bearable $50 million, its fortunes were still precarious, and it had reason to be grateful for the foresight that had led its scouts to choose Broadway comedienne/writer Mae West as one of its acquisitions from the stage during the early sound period. Her films were a key factor in sustaining the image of Paramount as a working studio, and their profits subsidised many more productions. Taming her suggestive dialogue, Paramount softened her sexual assault by casting her in period pictures where her hourglass figure and opulent looks could be excused as expressions of an Edwardian society. *Belle of the Nineties,* directed by the Catholic and reactionary McCarey, subdued the West attack with lavish costumes, additional songs and a melodrama plot with the star involved in an accidental murder, none of which showed her to advantage; she was happier the following year when, with the company fortunes less precarious, her talent for suggestive dialogue and bizarre characterisation was allowed its full scope in *Goin' to Town* (Alexander Hall), one of her least restricted works.

1935

Zanuck's 20th Century Pictures merged with Fox to create 20th Century-Fox of which Zanuck remained Production Manager until 1956. (The company's famous fanfare was written by Alfred Newman, who later added its subsidiary Cinemascope flourish.) M-G-M's brilliant producer David O. Selznick also broke away from father-in-law Mayer to form Selznick International, encouraged by producer Merian Cooper and financier John Hay Whitney, who had both invested large sums in the Technicolor Corporation but found themselves overextended after the commercial failure of early colour features (see *Colour*). In a year of technical expansion when, after development work by Joseph Walker and other cinematographers, crude zoom lenses first appeared, in *Private Worlds* (Gregory La Cava) and *Dante's Inferno* (Harry Lachman), colour was the most impressive advance.

Selznick's first independent film was a M-G-M-style literary adaptation, *Little Lord Fauntleroy* (John Cromwell, 1936). English novelist Hugh Walpole began the script from Frances Hodgson Burnett's book; he was soon joined by Sarah Mason and Victor Heerman (who wrote *Little Women*, George Cukor, 1935, for Selznick at M-G-M), Marshall Neilan, John V. A. Weaver and three other writers, all working largely in ignorance of one another, while Selznick also made his own contributions. Finally Walpole got sole credit. In the years that followed, Selznick's committee writing system became standard Hollywood practice, and as all scenarists knew, writing credit came to depend on being assigned to the film late enough to be working on it when production ceased.

Under pressure from Electrical Research Products Inc., the marketing arm of Western Electric that had gained control of many sound patents and made a fortune when studios slow to see the trend towards sound signed "suicide" contracts for Western Electric equipment, William Fox went into court to protect himself against anti-trust charges and attempts by ERPI to gain control of his sound patents. As a result of a 1935 Supreme Court decision, Fox was forced to hand control of his patents to Western Electric, and to sell his Fox voting stock for $18 million.* Western Electric, with RCA, went on to dominate the Hollywood sound world, with RCA slowly gaining the ascendancy in the late Thirties.

COLOUR.

Colour film existed from the beginning of the cinema, but in a multitude of systems, most depending on hand-colouring individual frames, the mechanical application of colour by stencil, or "tinting and toning," by which the celluloid stock and/or emulsion were coloured by immersion in chemical baths. This last process, capable of great subtleties, gives late silent films a remarkable beauty. In 1917, Herbert T. Kalmus formed the Technicolor Company to investigate a more precise process, and developed "Two-colour Technicolor," a system involving two negatives exposed in the same camera at the same time—a prism divided the image—but differing in that each was shot through a filter so as to record separate parts of the spectrum. In the laboratory two prints were made, dyed in the basic tones of pink/orange (magenta) and blue/green (cyan), and sandwiched together. Though the process lacked subtlety, it did render colours with relation to their original tones and not, as in the case of tinting, in shades arbitrarily chosen by an artist. Two-colour Technicolor's bilious skies and shrimp-pink complexions modulating to brick red

---

* In 1935, Carl Laemmle also sold his Universal stock, for $5.5 million, leaving no major Hollywood studio still in its founder's hands.

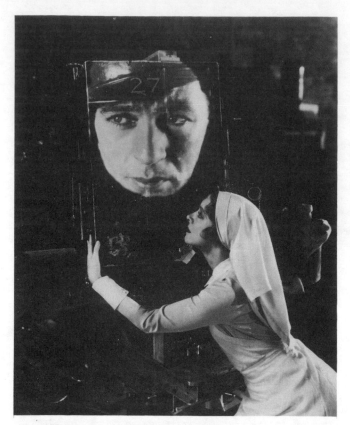

This publicity still, suggested by a scene in *A Farewell to Arms*, 1932, in which Frank Borzage directed Helen Hayes to "make love" to the camera as if it were co-star Gary Cooper, shows the bulky Technicolor camera.

were common in films of the Twenties, often enlivening the last reel of early musicals and epics. *King of Jazz* (John Murray Anderson, 1930) exploited the process to its limit, offering fifteen shades of cyan, all nasty, in its "Rhapsody in Blue" sequence with Paul Whiteman.

Kalmus meanwhile perfected his three-colour Technicolor, a refinement in which red, blue and yellow could be shown by sandwiching another colour-sensitive layer on the film's reverse side and perfecting the light-splitting mechanism to handle three levels of the spectrum. He joined with Merian Cooper and John Hay Whitney to form the Technicolor Corporation. Exclusivity was guaranteed by retaining all patents and developing the technique in complete secrecy. Technicolor not only supplied stock and processed the film, but also provided cameras and cameramen. In 1933, the Disney studios made the colour cartoons *Flowers and Trees* and *The Three Little Pigs,* the latter so successful that Disney began planning his first feature, *Snow White and the Seven Dwarfs.* Technicolor also imported Broadway designer Robert Edmond Jones for a showpiece short, *La Cucaracha* (Lloyd Corrigan, 1934). Despite Jones's imaginative

use of colour—he argued against conventional lighting and used coloured filters to give a three-dimensional quality few later designers achieved—the film's $80,000 budget was not repaid in studio interest. Cooper then persuaded David O. Selznick of the system's future, and Whitney offered to back Selznick in his own company if he would exploit Technicolor in his productions.

Paramount was also licensed to produce a colour feature (with Jones again designing) but *Becky Sharp* (1935), an adaptation of Thackeray's "Vanity Fair" based on a successful Broadway play version, was dogged by misfortune. Director Lowell Sherman died after two weeks' shooting, and Rouben Mamoulian took over. During sound mixing, the vital ballroom reel burst into flame, and had to be reconstructed from the cutter's notes. In addition, the film was a box-office failure, and independent producer Walter Wanger's *The Trail of the Lonesome Pine* (Henry Hathaway, 1936) became the first commercially successful colour film, its popularity encouraging the cautious Hollywood establishment to adopt the system. As colour became commonplace, Technicolor Corporation flourished, though its monopoly of the process led to a restriction of technical development in both film stock and cameras that was not totally broken until the Fifties when Eastman-Kodak developed Eastmancolor—an offshoot of research material obtained from German companies as part of war reparations. Eastmancolor's ability to apply all emulsion layers to one strip of celluloid and to control tones accurately made colour cameras light, and developments in sensitivity removed the necessity for highly-lit studio shooting. The last three-colour Technicolor feature was *The Glenn Miller Story* (Anthony Mann, 1953), and in the years that followed Technicolor's role deteriorated until it became merely the best and most respected of Hollywood's processing laboratories.

THE INFORMER. RKO. Associate Producer: Cliff Reid. Directed by John Ford. Script by Dudley Nichols from Liam O'Flaherty's novel (uncredited: John Ford, James Kevin MacGuinness). Photographed by Joseph August. Music by Max Steiner. Art direction by Van Nest Polglase and Charles Kirk. Set decorations by Julia Heron. Costumes by Walter Plunkett. Edited by George Hively. Players: Victor McLaglen (Gypo Nolan), Margot Grahame (Katie Madden), Heather Angel (Mary McPhillip), Wallace Ford (Frankie McPhillip), Preston Foster (Dan Gallagher), Una O'Connor (Mrs. McPhillip), J. M. Kerrigan (Terry), Joseph Sawyer (Barney Mulholland).

Academy Awards went to Ford, McLaglen, Nichols and Steiner, and John Ford's critical reputation was made by this gloomy drama set in the fog-bound streets of Dublin during the 1922 Irish Rebellion. A public that had looked on Ford as an action director recognised in his sure grasp of theatrical drama and powerful religious sense the mark of a major talent. Stories

The Informer. Victor McLaglen and Margot Grahame.

of the film's production vary. Ford discussed the project with Nichols and MacGuinness as early as 1931, but they found the book was owned in part by an English film company. Fox, where all were working, refused to buy the property, but when Ford and Nichols moved to RKO-Radio, MacGuinness having joined M-G-M, the RKO studio manager, J. R. McDonough, approved its production (Ford suggests at the instigation of Joseph Kennedy, who then owned the studio). Although B. B. Kahane, RKO Production Chief, called it "a criminal waste of money," the company bought the film rights for $5,000, Ford cleverly waiving his salary in lieu of a share of the profits. The project was given a low budget and the most meagre facilities, forcing cameraman Joseph August to disguise the canvas flats and tatty properties by a low-key, almost Germanic camera style which agreed with Ford's view of Dublin as a symbolic representation of his hero's mental confusion. Ford finished the film in three weeks at a cost of $218,000—$50,000 under budget—and despite desultory promotion it became a major financial and critical success.

However much one may object to Nichols' emasculation of the story's politics in which he discards the Communist affiliations of Gypo and "The Party," *The Informer* is a Hollywood classic, capturing deep feeling for Ireland's problems and Gypo Nolan, one of Ford's best self-sacrificing heroes. ("Physically and mentally he *was* the informer," Ford said at the time. Then added "Just make that physically," implying that McLaglen relied on Ford's control and vision of the character.) Ford emphasises Gypo's physical characteristics. Lumbering along the street, his head hits a swinging sign, establishing his size and stupidity, but suggesting too that he wanders in a world for which he is out of proportion both in mind and body. Later, low lighting in the police station accentuates the Neanderthal crudity of his skull, emphasising his rough, animalistic nature. The foggy streets and lancing light, linking, as Ford often did, a silhouette with death, convey his sense of guilt and exclusion from society, while Ireland's political chaos has never been more beautifully conveyed than in the scene where police search a boy (Dennis O'Day) singing on a street corner to his friend's scratchy violin. Still singing "The Minstrel Boy," that most defiant of traditional airs, he rotates once as they check him for weapons, takes with his upraised hand the coin one offers and, in the same movement, flings it contemptuously away.

DANGEROUS. Warner Brothers. Produced by Harry Joe Brown. Directed by Alfred E. Green. Script and story by Laird Doyle. Photographed by Ernest Haller. Art direction by Hugh Reticker. Players: Bette Davis (Joyce Heath), Franchot Tone (Dan Bellows), Margaret Lindsay (Gail Armitage), Alison Skipworth (Housekeeper), John Eldridge (Gordon Heath).

After some crackling melodramas for Warners, Bette Davis was recognised by John Cromwell in *Cabin in the Cotton* (Michael Curtiz, 1932) as a major talent and, when no other actress could be found for the part, cast her as Somerset Maugham's wanly provocative shop-girl in *Of Human Bondage* (1934). The Oscar most people felt to be rightfully hers went to Claudette Colbert for *It Happened One Night* (Frank Capra), but she received one the following year for *Dangerous*, a film she despises. The award, she and her fans suggest, was a retrospective consolation prize. Nevertheless, *Dangerous* is a minor masterpiece of acting, with Davis a jinxed alcoholic actress, based on Jeanne Eagels. Her career ruined, she is picked up in a bar by admiring architect Dan Bellows and rehabilitated at his country home. As their friendship metamorphoses to romance, her husband returns and, in a curious piece of Russian Roulette, she drives their car into a tree, believing the death of one or both will solve their problem. Inconveniently, both survive, the husband a cripple; and Joyce, after some soul-searching and advice from Bellows' omniscient housekeeper, sacrifices her happiness to care for the invalid, giving her life the meaning it has not until then possessed.

Miss Davis transforms the unpromising story with her superbly accomplished physical acting style. Initially morose, slumped over a drink in a dingy bar, she exudes despondency and an almost suicidal despair. Her revival by Bellows and slow return to life that culminates in her moral rebirth is reflected in her manner and voice, sustained by low-key sequences in which she discusses her problems with Alison Skipworth's quietly positive housekeeper or with Bellows in an ingenious confrontation where, pretending to read from a play, she implies he should leave her before the jinx begins to work on him. The peak is a brief scene in which, to escape a storm, she and Bellows run to a barn stacked with bales of hay. Rain and lightning enhancing the aphrodisiac effect of their exertions, they face each other in the damp, electric air. Joyce moves her arms in a gesture of seductive negligence, offers a mockingly companionable half smile, and we understand instantly the combination of sexual desire and malicious contempt for men that is both her mood at the moment and the key to her life.

THE LIVES OF A BENGAL LANCER. Paramount. Produced by Louis D. Lighton. Directed by Henry Hathaway. Script by Waldemar Young and John Balderston, from an adaptation by William Slavens McNutt, Grover Jones and Achmed Abdullah of Francis Yeats-Brown's novel. Photographed by Charles Lang. Art direction by Hans Dreier and Roland Anderson. Edited by Ellsworth Hoagland. Music by Milan Roder. Second unit direction of Indian location footage: Ernest B. Schoedsack. Players: Gary Cooper (Lt. McGregor), Franchot Tone (Lt. Forsythe), Richard Cromwell (Lt. Stone), Sir Guy Standing (Colonel Stone), C. Aubrey Smith (Major Hamilton), Monte Blue (Hamzulla Khan), Douglass

Dumbrille (Mohammed Khan), Kathleen Burke (Tania), Colin Tapley, Akim Tamiroff, Jameson Thomas, Noble Johnson, Rollo Lloyd, J. Carol Naish, Lumsden Hare, Charles Stevens, Leonid Kinskey, Eddie Das, James Warwick, Boswan Singh, James Bell, General Konnikoff, F. A. Armenta, Abdul Hassan, Clive Morgan, George Regas, Maj. Sam Harris, Carli Taylor, Ram Singh, Claude King, Reginald Sheffield, Lya Lys.

Few films are remembered with more affection than this stylish Indian romance, based on a novel that outdid Kipling in quiet heroics and evocation of India in the 1890s. With more money at its disposal than Curtiz had on *The Charge of the Light Brigade* (1936), the Crimean War epic to which Warner Brothers grafted a long Indian sub-plot in order to exploit *Bengal Lancer*'s success, Paramount spent it not on elaborate cavalry manoeuvres but in the careful re-creation of military life and atmosphere.* The Lancers' barracks have a whitewashed neatness that is immediately convincing, while out in the harsh sun an ox plods wearily in its yoked wheel, a muezzin calls at dusk, and the bored officers compete at tent-pegging with their lances. Cromwell sets up an amusing rivalry between Scottish-Canadian Cooper and elegant English career officer Tone, with an untried Richard Cromwell, son of Sir Guy Standing's commander, an admiring auxiliary, a relationship emphasised when all three are captured by the Oxford-educated Emir, played by Douglass Dumbrille with the sly corruption that was to make the classic line "We have ways of making men talk" all his own. Whereas the young officer gives in as the lighted bamboo slivers are forced under his nails—his snapped response, "Leave me alone!", when they ask whether he gace information betraying the fact that he has succumbed to the torture—his companions respond with wisecracks and cool bravado, declining to acknowledge their mangled hands but remarking "This is the worst torture ever invented: put us in a bug-infested cell and fix it so we can't scratch." The final shoot-up seems vulgar by comparison with what is mainly a witty and intimate study of a relationship between two fighting men, and

Advertisement for *The Lives of a Bengal Lancer*.

on balance one prefers scenes like the reception at the Emir's palace, a vast black-floored edifice of which the elegantly-uniformed Cooper comments with studied understatement "Quite a teepee!".

* As an assistant director at M-G-M in the early Thirties, Hathaway had taken a nine-month research trip to India collecting material for a possible feature documentary on pilgrimages, a project that died with its producer, Paul Bern. Since this production had been inspired by Ernest B. Schoedsack's documentary *Grass*, it is appropriate that Schoedsack should have supplied the authentic Indian background footage.

1936

Unionism, a growing force in Hollywood despite efforts by conservatives like Cecil B. DeMille to head it off, finally took hold, and from 1936 the studios comprised a "closed shop" with guilds and unions exerting a control that in times of underemployment would strangle the industry. In an exhibition market plagued by block-booking, cinema-owners turned to the double feature and "bank nights." (Prizes were given to seat-holders on the basis of the seat they held the previous week, an encouragement to attend regularly, as was the popular practice of giving sets of dishes to patrons at the rate of one dish a week). As weekly admissions reached eighty million, Hollywood struggled to provide audiences with the material they wanted, mostly light-hearted escapist musicals and comedies. At the end of 1935 Shirley Temple topped the "Motion Picture Herald" popularity poll. Fred Astaire had zoomed from 121st. and Ginger Rogers from 34th. to share 4th. place after *Flying down to Rio* (Thornton Freeland, 1933), *Roberta* (William A. Seiter, 1934) and *The Gay Divorcee* (Mark Sandrich, 1934) made them the musical's greatest team.

Such popularity, combined with the growth of a double-feature market, forced Hollywood into far greater production, and pressure on actors increased, particularly at Warner Brothers, whose thriller/musical/working-class comedy output was preferred in suburban and rural areas. James Cagney, who shot from 20th. to 10th. in the "Motion Picture Herald" poll, protested that fourteen films in a contract for twenty features originally to have been made over a period of five years had been done in slightly more than two years between 1933 and 1936. He demanded time off to accept the $100,000 offer of another studio for one film. Warners refused and suspended him as an example to Ann Dvorak, Edward G. Robinson, Dick Powell, Bette Davis and Mervyn LeRoy, all of whom protested at the inhuman efforts required under an "exclusive personal services" contract. Bette Davis, incensed by Warners' habit of lending stars like herself to General Electric, a large shareholder, for dishwasher commercials and personal appearance tours to advertise new appliances, fled to Europe where she tried unsuccessfully to overturn her contract in the English courts.

Most studios worked from 9 a.m. to 5 p.m. six days a week, and occasionally on Sunday as well. Ben Lyon recalls working twenty-six consecutive hours at Warner Brothers. Frank McHugh completed his scenes for *The Mystery of the Wax Museum* (Michael Curtiz, 1933) one Saturday, slept overnight at the studio and began *Grand Slam* (William Dieterle) Sunday morning. (Equity forced an obligatory twelve-hour break which ended this practice, though Saturday work continued until 1956.) A star was bound not only while under contract: Loretta Young went nine months without work in 1936 when Zanuck black-listed her after she refused to renew her contract with 20th. Century-Fox. Her agent, Myron Selznick, eventually placed her at Columbia with a 50% salary cut; perhaps understandably, Selznick became a pioneer of actors' production companies and the "package deal."

"For Cohens, in this haughty small berg/Bow but to God, who's cut by Thalberg." The legendary career of the man about whom Dorothy Parker wrote this couplet ended in September, when he died at the age of thirty-seven, his health at least partly depleted by his now-open conflict with Louis B. Mayer, who promptly dismantled Thalberg's elaborate production machinery and team of expert writers and producers. Perhaps not before time, the school of literary, elegant, stylishly performed films of which he was a master and which Metro-Goldwyn-Mayer had made its speciality, died with him.

SWING TIME. RKO-Radio. Produced by Pandro S.

Berman. Directed by George Stevens. Script by Howard Lindsay, Allan Scott and Erwin Gelsey. Photographed by David Abel. Music by Jerome Kern. Lyrics by Dorothy Fields. Choreography by Hermes Pan. Art direction by Van Nest Polglase. Players: Fred Astaire (Lucky), Ginger Rogers (Penny), Victor Moore (Pop), Helen Broderick (Mabel), Eric Blore (Gordon), Betty Furness (Margaret), George Metaxa (Romero), John Harrington (Raymond), Landers Stevens (Judge Watson), Pierre Watkin (Simpson), Abe Reynolds, Floyd Shackleford, Ferdinand Munier, Frank Jenks, Jack Good, Donald Kerr, Ted O'Shea, Frank Edmunds, Bill Brand.

Arguably the most integrated and attractive of the Astaire/Rogers musicals for RKO, *Swing Time*, their sixth together, boasts the direction of George Stevens, later to make his mark with *A Place in the Sun* (1951) and *Giant* (1956), a witty and poignant score from Jerome Kern and Dorothy Fields, including an Oscar-winning "The Way You Look Tonight," agile choreography from Hermes Pan and one of the most lavish black glass-and-chrome set designs Van Nest Polglase ever created. The script too has more substance and humour than many films in the series. Fred is a layabout gambler challenged by his prospective parents-in-law to earn $25,000 as the price of their agreement to his marriage. Hopping a freight with his valet Pop he arrives in New York without luggage and becomes involved with dancing teacher Penny (Ginger), whom he eventually marries after some problems from the unctuous band-leader Romero for whose orchestra they become a specialty dancing act. Along the way, the couple manage all the set-pieces fans had come to expect: an eccentric solo for Astaire with the narcissistic dancing-with-myself twist common to all his films, in this case "Bojangles of Harlem," a tribute to "Bojangles" Robinson in which he dances with three enormous silhouettes of himself; a fast duo with comic overtones, here supplied when Lucky crashes the dancing school where Penny works, makes a pass and, when they are caught by proprietor Gordon, dash off a dazzling "Pick Yourself Up" in which Lucky seemingly progresses from stumbling tyro to fleet-footed expert under Penny's tutelage; and a high-style "mood" number, in this case Kern's touching and complex "Never Gonna Dance," with its shifting time-signatures and tricky lyrics. This last song gives backing to some of the team's best dancing: set in a deserted night-club, first on a black floor backed with mirrors, then on a curving metal staircase, it takes them through a ballet of seduction, Lucky appearing through a mirrored wall, asking Penny for forgiveness, then luring her into a graceful walk that blends imperceptibly into dance. As in all their musicals, however, the film's essential tone is comic, and Astaire manages some nices touches, notably forestalling Penny's wedding to the fashion-conscious bandleader Romero by drawing cuffs on the trousers in a current issue of "Esquire" which sends him out to have his

altered. Serenading an absent Penny with "The Way You Look Tonight," Lucky does not see her emerge from the bathroom where she has been washing her hair. Sensing the presence of an enthralled girl behind him, he finishes the song with a flourish and turns on the attenuated last note to stop dead at the sight of the foam-covered head which both, charmed by the song, have forgotten. Stevens's ironic comment, far from destroying the illusion of the music, merely makes it more charming by stressing the human feeling it embodies.

THE GENERAL DIED AT DAWN. Paramount. Produced by William Le Baron. Directed by Lewis Milestone. Script by Clifford Odets from a story by Charles G. Booth. Photographed by Victor Milner. Edited by Eda Warren. Art direction by Hans Dreier and Ernst Fegté. Music by Werner Janssen. Special Effects by Gordon Jennings and Art Smith. Players: Gary Cooper (O'Hara), Madeleine Carroll (Judy Perrie), Akim Tamiroff (General Yang), Dudley Digges (Mister Wu), Porter Hall (Peter Perrie), J. M. Kerrigan (Leach), William Frawley, Philip Ahn.

"They're refugees," an American explains as the Chinese pour past them down the street. "They wouldn't pay their taxes. But General Yang fixed them. They understand pain well enough." His wife nods in agreement. Then a tall man with a marmoset on his shoulder steps from the crowd and asks the man for a light. "Sorry, I don't smoke." The tall man frowns and knocks him to the ground. "Refuse me a light, would you?" "I told you," the man expostulates, "I don't smoke!". "And those people didn't have the pennies to pay General Yang," the tall man says. The marmoset twitters and he melts back into the crowd. This next-to-opening scene sets both the background and tone of Lewis Milestone's film, and establishes in one quick sketch the character and preoccupations of Cooper's O'Hara, who in this film as in many others plays the tough guy with a conscience, the gentleman adventurer who, when the chips are down, sells his services only to the side that is in the right. The difference in this case is that he is thrown against a lady adventurer who, contrary to the conventions of the code, is neither tough nor ambitious but a nervous, lost girl drawn against her will into a violent situation that terrifies and sickens her.

Madeleine Carroll is the dominant force in a film distinctive for its superior acting. From her first appearance as the silent, bitter third partner in a billiard game between her father and the Chinese agent of the General, her hard and emotionless face becomes a *motif* that, changing subtly from scene to scene, indicates the drama's course. The thin pencilled eyebrows, tight turned-down mouth and blonde hair, its waves as smooth as metal, are vital parts of her characterisation. Porter Hall's consumptive Peter Perrie, Tamiroff's brilliantly egomaniacal Yang and Cooper as the rigorously cavalier O'Hara make their contribution, but it

Swing Time. Fred Astaire and Ginger Rogers in "Pick Yourself Up."

The General Died at Dawn. Madeleine Carroll, Gary Cooper.

is Carroll who holds the film in her hand. Odets has worked out a script with more than usually sophisticated motivations. A leftist whose play about union racketeering "Waiting for Lefty" in a 1935 Group Theatre production had galvanised Broadway, Odets disparaged the charge that he had "sold out" to Hollywood by writing a script in which character and political reality are ingeniously integrated. Judy Perrie's lines reflect a life so full of bitterness that it is not too surprising she should offer it almost casually in return for O'Hara's. "Some day there'll be a law to abolish the blues," she says to her father. "Something big, like an amendment to the Constitution, for all of us." And later: "You've played me for a sucker for as many years as I'm old." Delivered with a weariness that never descends to the vulgarity of Hollywood "realism," lines like these are touching and believable, though it takes a simple Milestone action—like, while sitting in the train thinking out her plan to betray O'Hara, flicking from the window-sill one by one the half-smoked cigarettes she has lined up—to encapsulate her disenchantment with the world. "I'm one of the nameless legion that always gets stuck"—but she says it without rancour, as a simple statement of fact.

Judy's essential sensitivity is the key to her character, and Milestone plays on it to expand her part in the action. Persuaded to betray O'Hara so that her father can die in the peace of an American home, she takes each step in the plan with the agony of a person trapped between two fires. When she and O'Hara meet, she is unable to resist his easy charm, and his implied appeal for help ("There are things on the ground that don't like me") moves her to respond to his advances until, as he bends to kiss her, she realises this is the man she is to send to his death and her head twists away in pain, her face turned, as if from the light, down to the floor. The death of Peter Perrie, shot by

O'Hara only after he has tried to murder him—in a bravura image, O'Hara shoots him through the lighted crack between the hinges of a half-open door—provides an even more revealing scene. Horrified at the corpse slumped over the telephone, Judy cringes away, reaches unthinkingly for the phone, then draws back, unable to look as O'Hara drags the body away and hides it in a chest. Pain and disbelief are reflected in every line of her body as she leans against the wall, eyes averted. Her horror of death and violence is again stressed when, in a particularly grisly touch, the General has the body of a tortured Chinese brought in to join the others at dinner. She betrays no reaction when the corpse is put down, but when Yang leaves she shrinks slowly away and says quietly, "Would someone please be good enough to hide Mr. Chen's face?".

Her affair with O'Hara has the beauty of complete inevitability. "We could have made wonderful music together," he says. "We could have made a circle of light and warmth," words that evoke just the world she wants, an uncomplicated place of things others take for granted. The financial courier O'Hara, with his stern democratic principles, seems an undesirable match, not unalike in character to Yang, who emerges as O'Hara's Fascist equivalent. The final scene, where O'Hara plays for his life by promising to tell the world of Yang's last hours and the heroic suicide of his personal guards, can be seen as a shrewd move to trade on the general's ego, but it is equally possible that his stated admiration for the General's *ethos* is at least partly sincere. Judy, we sense, will remain, even after the last fade-out, a lost soul.

Though Carroll and Cooper dominate the film, other performances, mostly by newly-recruited Broadway actors, are memorable: J. M. Kerrigan's predatory blackmailer, aptly named Leach; Dudley Digges' effete and finally subtly weak Mr. Wu; Porter Hall as the consumptive and worthless Peter Perrie, childishly devoted to the idea of dying at home; and William Frawley's drunken gunrunner, cheerfully soused in a hideously Victorian Shanghai hotel, singing to the stuffed moose head "I'll Be Glad When You're Dead, You Rascal You." Akim Tamiroff gives a rounded portrait of a strong, flawed character; "He was a talented man," Wu says, "but very, very corrupt." Yet he does not seem as corrupt as Wu himself, who is prepared to let Judy give her life for O'Hara's. Yang's childish delight in the devotion of his personal guards, all of whom are prepared to die for him, is not corrupt, merely egotistical. All his tricks—the slow smile, his affectation of "You betcha life!", the laborious English interrupted by occasional rapped requests for translations of individual words always supplied by his reptilian lieutenant—lend to his characterisation a conviction, even likeability. O'Hara is an enemy, but not an implacable one. "I don't like your politics," he says. "I don't like your friends. I don't like your hat." And this, we sense, is as far as it goes.

Milestone's direction is, as one expects from the man

who created *All Quiet on the Western Front*, excellent. The first shot, a long pan over a hilltop that seems to bear soldiers like the field of dragon's teeth, is the first memorable image. Odd pieces of bravura like a dissolve from billiard ball to door knob, or the use of process swords to divide the screen into five, each section showing a different action, are less artistically justifiable than the prowling tracks in the final sequence, shot in a cluttered junk at sea. One remembers best the train raid, with O'Hara jumping out of the carriage, only to be driven back by a ring of bayonets and forced into the dining car which he finds empty except for Peter Perrie drinking his tea, Carroll sitting white-faced at her table and Yang seated like a potentate at the end. The interview over and the money now in Yang's hands, O'Hara pauses by Judy's table and calmly slaps the upturned face. Yang and Perrie turn away; the face, more rigid and mask-like than ever, can no more be looked at than the sun. In this moment, Madeleine Carroll achieves, as much as in any Hollywood film, the true dimensions of tragedy.

THE CHARGE OF THE LIGHT BRIGADE. Director: Michael Curtiz. One of the most lavish of Warner Brothers' Thirties spectaculars, this film established Errol Flynn as the studio's most profitable star, a position to which he was helped inestimably by Michael Curtiz, who badgered, terrorised and coaxed the young and inexperienced actor into performances that concealed both his unconvincing style and limited physical dexterity. Taking a year to make, and involving some of the most elaborate direction of spectacle ever attempted, *The Charge of the Light Brigade* is deservedly a classic. Tennyson's poem underwent substantial revision to provide the basis for a two-hour epic. The Light Brigade now charges into the valley of death not because of military stupidity but as a result of Flynn having forged a directive in order to have his men avenge a previous massacre perpetrated in India by a man now on the enemy side. The historical inaccuracy is undeniable, and students of military history discovered such additional deviations as the habit of flying the Union Jack upside down. But this seems irrelevant beside the tightening spiral of action into which Curtiz winds the story, building up through a superbly directed Chakoti massacre to the last charge. The editing by George Amy is often almost subliminal, the relentless pace created by long tracks and sweeping panoramas, and the thundering synthesis of sound and image showing Hollywood at its peak. It is also, however, Hollywood at its most prodigal. The charge, a classic piece of second unit direction, was handled by 150 stunt riders under B. Reeves "Breezy" Eason, who also created the chariot race of the 1926 *Ben Hur,* but watching the remarkable stunts, one seldom realises the suffering entailed. Horses executed spectacular falls by the "Running W" method, a brutally simple system in which one end of a wire was tied to a stake and the other to the legs of a horse. The animal was then galloped until the wire went taut, guaranteeing a realistic fall. Many horses died from such falls and from riding into the gun-pits. Eason and three assistants were brought to trial by the Society for Prevention of Cruelty to Animals, which charged that at least three horses had died painfully in stunts. Each man was fined $5.

1937

As admissions hovered on an average weekly eighty millon, the highest since sound, some expansiveness was evident in Hollywood's outlook. David O. Selznick had bought the film rights to Margaret Mitchell's "Gone With the Wind" for $50,000 and was seeking an unknown to play the plum role of Scarlett O'Hara, a stunt disguising the fact that his chosen male lead, M-G-M's Clark Gable, would not be available for another two years because of distribution agreements between Selznick and United Artists, Louis B. Mayer refusing to lend Gable for a film not released through Loew's Inc. Mayer announced his salary for the year as $1,296,503, highest of any individual in the US, and perhaps in the world, but nobody was really surprised.

In France, Henri Chrétien demonstrated a new use for his spherical "hypergonar" lens, developed during the First World War as a viewing device for tank observers. The hypergonar squeezed a wide horizontal field of vision into a small distorted image, which another lens then reversed to the original proportions. Applying this to cinema, he photographed scenes through his squeezing lens, then projected them through another lens to give pictures of extreme width. By using two projectors and blurring the division, he created a panoramic picture more impressive than those achieved by Abel Gance in his triptych screen sections of *Napoléon* (1927). Chrétien's invention was the basis for both Cinemascope and Cinerama.

Among the technical Oscars awarded in 1937 was one to the Walt Disney organisation for the multiplane camera, which freed animation from its reliance on a two-dimensional background with figures moving before it. With backgrounds placed at varying distances from a camera that moved in three dimensions, artists could achieve true perspective. Disney's longtime collaborator Ub Iwerks developed the camera, Disney financing the research even though the men had ceased to be friends. Iwerks' multiplane had its first use in a Disney short, *The Old Mill,* which also received a 1937 Oscar, and its success, combined with that of his color cartoon *The Three Little Pigs* (see 1935), suggested to Disney a feature-length colour cartoon using the multiplane and Frank Churchill's music; his "Who's Afraid of the Big Bad Wolf?" had been the hit of 1933. The result was *Snow White and the Seven Dwarfs* (1937).

In June, a girl died of kidney disease in the Los Angeles Good Samaritan Hospital. Her body was anonymously voluptuous, but her hair above the oxygen mask was a metallic white some inspired PR man had dubbed "platinum." Jean Harlow, the Blonde Bombshell whose frank sexuality epitomised the Thirties erotic ideal, went to an end the unprofessionalism of which she deplored—her last film, the racing drama *Saratoga* (Jack Conway, 1937), unfinished.

THE PRISONER OF ZENDA. Selznick International/United Artists. Produced by David O. Selznick. Associate producer: William H. Wright. Directed by John Cromwell. Script by John L. Balderston from novel by Anthony Hope and play by John L. Balderston, adapted by Wells Root. Additional dialogue by Donald Ogden Stewart. Photographed by James Wong Howe. Art direction by Lyle Wheeler. Edited by James E. Newton. Music by Alfred Newman. Players: Ronald Colman (Rudolf Rassendyll/King Rudolf V), Madeleine Carroll (Princess Flavia), Douglas Fairbanks Jr. (Rupert of Hentzau), Mary Astor (Antoinette de Mauban), C. Aubrey Smith (Colonel Zapt), Raymond Massey (Black Michael), David Niven (Fritz von Tarlenheim), Lawrence Grant (Marshal Strakencz), Ian Maclaren (Cardinal), Byron Foulger (Johann), Howard Lang (Josef), Ralph Faulkner (Bersonin), Montague Love (Detchard), William von Brincken (Krafstein), Philip Sloeman (Lauengram),

Snow White and the Seven Dwarfs.

Alexander D'Arcy (De Gautet), Ben Webster (British Ambassador), Evelyn Beresford (British Ambassador's Wife), Boyd Erwin (Master of Ceremonies).

Anthony's Hope's 1896 Ruritanian romance had been three films and a play, all of which David O. Selznick was determined to ignore in his lush 1937 adaptation. Elements of parody that crept into the story through its many incarnations were rigorously controlled by Selznick, who demanded that at least a third of the scenes be re-shot when it seemed to him its stars had not captured the right spirit. Emphasis in John Cromwell's direction—he had been an actor—and in the sets and photography is on characters and their dramatic situation, rather than on action and humour. The huge, shadowy hall of Rupert's castle was designed around the climactic sword battle between Rupert (played with mocking humour and charm by Douglas Fairbanks Jr.) and Ronald Colman's gentlemanly Rudolf Rassendyll rather than the battle, with its non-stop sardonic verbal duel, around the set. Even the white ballroom with its gleaming floor and huge flight of steps reflects the growing affection between Rudolf and Flavia, with the guests staring in astonishment as the notoriously weak and disdainful king romances his startled *fiancée*.

Ronald Colman, playing Rudolf Rassendyll, the distant cousin who replaces the Ruritanian king when his enemies, led by his brother Black Michael, drug and kidnap him on the eve of his coronation, gets top billing, but so carefully is the film cast that none of its male characters is truly the star. Even C. Aubrey Smith as the solemn chamberlain Zapt and David Niven's boyish von Tarlenheim occasionally threaten to steal the spotlight from more melodramatic figures. "We must trust in Providence" Zapt remarks portentously at one point, and von Tarlenheim quips "You'll never get Providence interested in this enterprise." Against such competition, Douglas Fairbanks Jr. recalls, Raymond Massey as Black Michael had trouble getting the range of his part. Asked for advice, the veteran—and deaf—C. Aubrey Smith switched on his hearing aid, listened thoughtfully to Massey's appeal, and said, "Ray, in my time I've played every part in *Zenda* except Flavia, and I've always had trouble with Black Michael." He then switched off his hearing aid and returned to reading the "Times." Fairbanks' Hentzau, given some of the best lines, is one of the Thirties' most engaging rogues. "You and I are the only ones worth saving out of this business," he says eagerly to Rassendyll, but later he is equally receptive to Michael's suggestion of a way to solve the confusion with multiple murders, including that of Rassendyll. "There are times in the presence of your Majesty," he says with respect, "when I feel myself an amateur." Doubtful about taking what is ostensibly a supporting role, Fairbanks was advised to do so by his father, who considered it "actor-proof. Even Lassie the dog could get good notices with it." Fairbanks also accepted his father's advice in the matter of costume,

and designed his own simple black uniform, on which cameraman Howe capitalised by placing him in slanting backlight—giving the impression of a shadow come to life, a slim black figure moving against blackness. Such a rash of costume pictures followed *Zenda* that the field became glutted, and even M-G-M's 1952 remake by Richard Thorpe—with Stewart Granger and James Mason, the same music score speeded up, many of the same shots and the same script with Donald Ogden Stewart's name removed (see 1942)—could not recapture the original's popularity. The Selznick/Cromwell *Zenda* remains the supreme costume romance of its time.

LOST HORIZON. Columbia. Produced and directed by Frank Capra. Script by Robert Riskin from James Hilton's novel. Photographed by Joseph Walker. Music by Dmitri Tiomkin. Art direction by Stephen Goosson. Costumes by Ernest Dryden. Edited by Gene Havlick. Aerial photography by Elmer Dyer. Technical advisor: Harrison Forman. Players: Ronald Colman (Robert Conway), Jane Wyatt (Sondra Bizet), John Howard (George Conway), Edward Everett Horton (Lovett), Isabel Jewell (Gloria Stone), H. B. Warner (Chang), Margo (Maria), Thomas Mitchell (Barnard), Sam Jaffe (High Lama), David Torrance (Prime Minister), Hugh Buckler (Lord Gattsford), Val Durand (Talu), Milton Owen (Fenner), Willie Fung (Bandit Leader), Victor Wong (Bandit), John Burton, John Miltern, Dennis D'Auburn (Englishmen).

One of the few American directors to combine a political conscience with box-office success, Frank Capra, even in his first feature *The Strong Man* (1926) with Harry Langdon, by-passed Hollywood rules to entertain and influence his audience. The five-Oscar-winning *It Happened One Night* (1934) went beyond simple comedy to press the essential point of all Capra's films, the dignity and worth of ordinary Americans and their society, a creed argued energetically in *Mr. Deeds Goes to Town* (1934) but displayed with greatest force in *Mr. Smith Goes to Washington* (1939), a film which most powerfully states Capra's simplistically sincere philosophy. While *Mr. Smith* is Capra's manifesto, *Lost Horizon* crystallises the philosophical and emotional structure of his belief. Using Hilton's visionary novel as a starting point, he explores the promise and implication of perfect existence with a depth and poetry the original never achieved.

Uncharacteristic of Capra in that the pace is relaxed, the style formal and the action lacking crowd scenes and evocations of mass movement so common in his other films, *Lost Horizon* can be, for a sympathetic audience, a touching work, though its oversimplified ideas, expressed by hopeful diplomat Conway in the prediction "When the strong have devoured one another, the Christian ethic will again take over, and the meek shall inherit the earth" falls flat. The Tibetan empire of Shangri-La, to which Conway and his friends are whisked while fleeing from a Chinese revolution, has the same unreality: calm, reflecting pools; white walls wreathed in gnarled vines; noble staircases and plazas that recall, disturbingly, the corrupted Bauhaus architecture adopted by Hitler as his ideal. The Lama's doves circle overhead, a curious tone whistling from flutes tied to their legs. Conway's puritan ethic is untouched by the promise of eternal life the valley offers to those who decide to stay within its mountain walls—"A prolonged future doesn't interest me. It must have some point," he explains—but he is tempted by the charmingly boyish Sondra who, with horse-rides through a suspiciously Californian forest and glimpses of nude bathing (explicit for the time), manages to divert his attention from the problems of escape. Finally influenced to go by his friends, he returns after a long-time valley resident has withered before their eyes to an ancient crone and the rest are killed. His black-hooded figure staggers through an impossible landscape of icefields and crevasses to find his paradise again, a visionary drop-out escaping, as many American wished, into a detached and untroubled world.

Capra's management of this project is expert in the extreme, and for his 117 shooting days and $2 million budget he returns a work of great technical skill. China's high wind-swept plateaux and jagged mountains were superbly evoked by the Sierras, and snow scenes shot in a Los Angeles cold storage warehouse. Lacking Tibetan extras and rejecting the conventional Japanese or Chinese substitutes, Capra chose instead a tribe of Pala Indians from an Oceanside, California, reservation, men who, as enigmatic Mongolians refuelling the kidnap plane during its trip to Shangri-La, convincingly suggest an alien culture in their impassive, staring faces. Stephen Goosson's vast sets, complete with real grass and flowers, show remarkable imagination—a complete Tibetan village was also built at Sherwood, forty miles from Hollywood—but

Lost Horizon. Ronald Colman, Jane Wyatt. Sets by Stephen Goosson.

it is the atmospheric lighting and Capra's use of bare white walls to emphasise mood that give *Lost Horizon* its memorable style. Casting also contributes, Capra having spent months choosing appropriate players. The central role of the Grand Lama caused most problems. Two venerable actors, including Henry B. Walthall, star of *Birth of a Nation,* were chosen, but both died before filming began. After his success in *The Good Earth* (Sidney Franklin, 1937) Walter Connolly was tested, but Capra finally chose thirty-eight-year-old Sam Jaffe who convincingly impersonated the two-hundred-year-old sage (H. B. Warner, Christ in *The King of Kings* (1927), played his deputy). It is Capra's use of people like Jaffe, notably in the Lama's death, a foreground candle flickering out to sink the room and its slumped figure into darkness, that makes *Lost Horizon* a film difficult to forget.

1938

With more than eleven thousand independent theatres operating in the United States, the problems of exhibitors who had to compete with the large studio-tied chains for product were brought forcibly to federal government attention in a series of suits alleging restraint of trade, block-booking and other offences against the Taft-Hartley anti-trust act. Independent producers also alleged that studios had bought up their films in order to restrict competition, releasing them in inferior theatres where they played at a disadvantage to studio product. These came to a head when the government instituted lawsuits against seven major Hollywood companies charging that they had actively denied to independent producers and exhibitors the rights given them under anti-monopoly legislation. The government demanded, as well as correction of studio attitudes to independents, a divorce between the film making and film distribution activities of all studios. Block-booking, though not outlawed, was limited to groups of five films, all of which the exhibitor could demand to preview.

Following the Spanish Civil War, which dramatised to many American intellectuals the growing threat of Fascism, a number of anti-Fascist groups were founded in both California and New York, designed to counteract pro-Nazi propaganda distributed through active American Fascist organisations. "Films for Democracy" and the Hollywood Anti-Nazi League had a large membership of active liberals, including Fredric March, his wife Florence Eldridge, and many writers, notably Donald Ogden Stewart and Ben Hecht. Some others, more politically oriented, joined the Communist Party or related groups. The activities of leftists, though not in any real sense Communist, marked Hollywood as a possible source of Socialist activity, and the first murmurs of political resistance were apparent, accelerated by films like Walter Wanger's Spanish Civil War production *Blockade* (William Dieterle, 1938, written by John Howard Lawson) which was to be a prime target for anti-Communist attacks on Hollywood.

The growing traffic in screen stories slowed abruptly when abuses of the screen-writing system became public. Plays and novels were usually bought on the basis of a synopsis prepared by a Screen Story Analyst or "reader," and retailed verbally to a producer. The trick, as seasoned scenarists knew, was to cultivate the reader and discover her interpretation of the property, since it was on this basis that it had been bought. Most Hollywood films used only a book's title and skeleton plot, discarding the substance or replacing it with material from other sources. Plagiarism, intended or accidental, became widespread* leading to a racket whereby unscrupulous authors circulated their work to studios, then later charged that company writers had stolen plots or themes for use in another film. Most companies preferred to pay off such claims rather than become involved in court actions. R. C. Sherriff's famous anti-war play "Journey's End" (filmed in 1930 by James Whale at Universal) was one of many properties thus affected. In 1938, when M-G-M lost a suit charging that portions of *Letty Lynton* (Clarence Brown, 1932) were taken from the play "Dishonored Lady," the tide turned against indiscriminate acquisition of screen properties. The pre-purchase of screen rights while a novel was in proof form, as Selznick did with "Gone with the Wind," or the commissioning of original screenplays replaced the old system, establishing a Hollywood tradition.

---

* F. Scott Fitzgerald's "Pat Hobby" stories and S. P. Perelman's essay "And Did You Once See Irving Plain" record the anomalies of screen-writing with humour and, in Fitzgerald's case, with compassion.

BRINGING UP BABY. RKO-Radio. Produced by Cliff Reid. Directed by Howard Hawks. Script by Dudley Nichols, Hager Wilde from a story by Hager Wilde. Photographed by Russell Metty. Art direction by Van Nest Polglase and Perry Ferguson. Edited by George Hively. Music by Roy Webb. Players: Cary Grant (David Huxley), Katharine Hepburn (Susan), Charlie Ruggles (Major Applegate), May Robson (Aunt Elizabeth), Barry Fitzgerald (Gogarty), Walter Catlett (Slocum), Fritz Feld (Dr. Lehman), Lana Roberts (Mrs. Gogarty), George Irving (Peabody).

The term "screwball comedy" had wide currency in the Thirties and early Forties, initially used to describe the comedy of illogic and eccentricity, but widened to include the violent farces Preston Sturges perfected and directors of the late Forties brought to their nadir with Red Skelton vehicles. True screwball comedy depended on scriptwriting of colloquial sharpness and performers who embodied the monomania of a mind wavering between carefree disregard for logic and pure insanity. Not surprisingly, the best directors of such films were action specialists, Howard Hawks (*Twentieth Century*, 1934; *Ball of Fire*, 1941), William Wellman (*Nothing Sacred*, 1937; *Roxie Hart*, 1942) and Jack Conway (*Libeled Lady*, 1936) all making eccentric comedy of high quality, filled with the violence and sexual competitiveness typical of their dramas. No film shows this combination more effectively than Howard Hawks's nihilistic *Bringing up Baby*.

Belying the tranquil title, "Baby" is a leopard which an unworldly palaeontologist finds himself helping a screwball character to mind until her brother returns from the Amazon. The obedient beast is pacified by "I Can't Give You Anything but Love, Baby" which Cary Grant's David and Katharine Hepburn's Susan sing almost constantly, occasionally carrying on conversations in tune, like operatic recitative. David feels his *amour propre* slipping with every minute of his relationship with the eccentric Susan. In the early scenes, he is concerned only to get an "intercostal clavicle" to complete the dinosaur skeleton whose reconstruction is his life's work. Eschewing "domestic entanglements of any kind" and assuring himself that "privately I feel I have some dignity," he is a victim ripe for slaughter, a word adequately describing the ruin Susan works on his personality. At dinner, she causes him to sit on his top hat. "You're silly in your hat," she comments with mild interest. "I know it," he acknowledges glumly. Later, when she grabs his clothing as he is walking away and rips something, her "Oh, you've torn your coat" has the same detachment. Such illogic finally conveys itself to David, who remarks distractedly, "In moments of calm I'm quite drawn to you, Susan, but there have been no moments of calm."

Though the film's final third is more conventional in its comedy, big-game hunter Charlie Ruggles imitating the mating call of the leopard in Susan's aunt's staid country home and being transfixed by a replying howl, the tone remains that of logic crumbling under the onslaught of a monomania which seems to carry its own logic with it. When David's dinosaur collapses around him at the climax, it is not only a life's work that had disappeared but a devotion to the concept of that work which Susan has made irrelevant. The maniacs have taken over the asylum, and, as in all screwball comedy, nobody notices.

JEZEBEL. Warner Brothers. Produced by Hal B. Wallis. Associate Producer: Henry Blanke. Directed by William Wyler. Script by Clements Ripley, Abem Finkel and John Huston from the play by Owen Davis Jr. Additional material by Robert Bruckner. Photographed by Ernest Haller. Art direction by Robert Haas. Edited by Warren Low. Music by Max Steiner. Costumes by Orry-Kelly. Players: Bette Davis (Julie Marston), Henry Fonda (Preston Dillard), George Brent (Buck Cantrell), Margaret Lindsay (Amy), Donald Crisp (Dr. Livingstone), Fay Bainter (Aunt Belle), Richard Cromwell (Ted Dillard), Henry O'Neill (General Bogardus), John Litel (Jean La Cour), Gordon Oliver (Dick Allan), Janet Shaw (Molly Allen), Theresa Harris (Zette), Margaret Early (Stephanie Kendrick), Irving Pichel (Huger), Eddie Anderson (Gros Bat), Symie Beard (Ti Bat), Lou Payton (Uncle Cato), George Revenant (De Lautruc).

Bette Davis' consolation prize for not being invited to play Scarlett O'Hara in *Gone with the Wind* was stardom in *Jezebel*, Warner's "answer" to Selznick and her most accomplished portrayal in the grand manner, earning her second Oscar. Making a characteristic entrance from the back of a huge horse, hooking up her train with her crop and sweeping in among the goggling guests at her mother's party, Miss Davis, from her first scene, dominates a film built to accommodate her talent. More changes are rung on the spoiled Southern belle stereotype than the directing committee of *GWTW* permitted Vivien Leigh, and greater depth achieved in the relationship between Julie and her upright lover Pres; also perhaps because of black-and-white photography and the relatively restricted budget, a mood more evocative of personal drama is introduced into this story of the Southern aristocracy in full flower. Max Steiner's score, its waltz *motif* as unforgettable as his "Tara's Theme" for the Selznick film, smoothly sustains the film's texture precisely in tune with Wyler's unobtrusive direction, only being overdone when a carefully placed accent marks Pres' fatal mosquito bite. The dialogue has typical Huston bite. A tradition of coquetry and gentlemanly passion is evoked in opposition to Pres' almost Yankee pragmatism, Crisp's Dr. Livingstone recalling that his contemporaries, to quell a woman of Julie's independent spirit, "cut a hickory, beat the daylights out of her, helped put lard on her welts and bought her a diamond bracelet." But Miss Davis in a memorable

Bringing up Baby. Katharine Hepburn and the dinosaur.

scene shows that no man has her measure. Demurely strolling into the Prescott bank, a sacrosanct male institution, she extracts her lover from a board meeting, charms away his irritation with her fidgetting girlishness, and leaves with a casual "Good day, Mr. Dillard. I'm sorry to have troubled you," knowing he cannot stand against her.

1939

As part of a rationalisation of studio/employee relations, the companies, after a long fight in which directors had threatened a strike and the Academy of Motion Picture Arts and Sciences, reversing its usual pro-studio bias, agreed to cancel the annual Oscar Awards, now valuable for publicity purposes, if negotiations were not opened, the Actors' Guild (affiliated with Equity in 1934 to become the sole performers' union), Screen Writers' Guild and Directors' Guild were recognised as official bargainers for screen artists. The battle, led respectively by presidents Ronald Reagan, John Howard Lawson and King Vidor, with Frank Capra as Academy President, at last met the studios with power equal to their own.

Having ignored the growing influence of Fascism in Europe and penalised those producers and directors who dared to criticise totalitarianism, Hollywood was shocked when Mussolini ordered an embargo on all foreign film-making and distribution, ejecting American companies from Italy; Britain, also, faced with war, slapped a 50% restriction on the funds taken out of the country by American firms. US audiences remained indifferent to politics, and Carl Laemmle, who died in 1939, went to his grave happy in the knowledge that Universal, which had sagged after his sale in 1935/6, was booming with a series of saccharine musicals produced by Joe Pasternak, directed by Henry Koster and starring a plump young soprano named Deanna Durbin.

At the New York World's Fair, a film exhibit designed by engineer Fred Waller drew wide attention. Developed into a commercial presentation, Waller's panoramic screen and stereophonic sound, similar to that planned by Disney for *Fantasia* (see 1940) but never used, was recognised by a 1942 Oscar as a technique of interest, though full exploitation was delayed until 1953, when it emerged as Cinerama. Meanwhile, the Technicolor Corporation announced that the first film to be shot on its improved high-speed colour stock would be David O. Selznick's epic *Gone with the Wind*.

THE WOMEN. M-G-M. Produced by Hunt Stromberg. Directed by George Cukor. Script by Jane Murfin and Anita Loos from the play by Clare Boothe. Photographed by Joseph Ruttenberg (colour sequence only) and Oliver T. Marsh. Art direction by Cedric Gibbons and Wade B. Rubottom. Edited by Robert J. Kern. Costumes by Adrian. Music by Edward Ward and David Snell. Players: Norma Shearer (Mrs. Stephen Haines), Joan Crawford (Crystal Allen), Rosalind Russell (Mrs. Howard Fowler), Mary Boland (Countess De Lave), Paulette Goddard (Miriam Aarons), Phyllis Povah (Mrs. Phelps Potter), Joan Fontaine (Mrs. John Day), Virginia Weidler (Little Mary), Lucile Watson (Mrs. Moorehead), Marjorie Main (Lucy), Virginia Grey, Ruth Hussey, Muriel Hutchison, Hedda Hopper, Florence Nash, Cora Witherspoon, Ann Morriss, Dennie Moore, Mary Cecil, Mary Beth Hughes.

Even after Thalberg's death, the tradition he established of glossy, high society comedy with a stage orientation remained strong at M-G-M, sustained less by policy than by the roster of popular female stars the company had built up in the preceding years. In retrospect, this adaptation of Clare Boothe's Broadway comedy in which the entire cast, even to the pets, is female, can be seen as the company's last fling with its Thirties queens before they dispersed in the harsher Hollywood of the Forties. Norma Shearer, Thalberg's widow and essentially a Thirties star out of place even in this *recherché* film, worked little after its completion; Joan Crawford later abandoned her sultry image to join Warner Brothers and reforge her career with Michael Curtiz's Germanic *Mildred Pierce* (1945); while both Joan Fontaine and Rosalind Rus-

The Women. Joan Fontaine, Norma Shearer.

sell went on to starring roles on the strength of their success in *The Women.* Even George Cukor's style hardened in the years that followed, and Mayer dispersed the *coterie* of distinguished writers Thalberg had built up, men whose skill makes this a film of enduring interest.

At least nine scenarists worked on adapting the difficult and, for Hollywood, excessively outspoken play, including at one point the failing F. Scott Fitzgerald, who was assigned, with Donald Ogden Stewart, to work on it but whose material was never used. The allocation of sole credit to Anita Loos and Jane Murfin suggests that consistency to the all-female image of the production may have dictated the removal of all other names. Producer Hunt Stromberg, a no-nonsense sportsman who underlined his image with much manly spitting and exercise on his leg with a riding crop, used "a dumb Scranton miner" as his basic imaginary audience, rather as "New Yorker" magazine pitched its material at "a little old lady in Dubuque." Since the Scranton miner might not appreciate Miss Boothe's bedroom politics, the film's base was broadened with some lively scuffles among its cast of society matrons, and a good deal of broad innuendo about the off-screen romance of Stephen Haines with rapacious perfume salesgirl Crystal Allen, an affair Mrs. Haines's friends do their best first to advertise, then end by encouraging her to get a divorce. The background is the New York cocktail set, with confidences passed at the hairdresser's by a gossipy manicurist, wife facing mistress in the changing room of a fashionable *couturier,* and friends exchanging intelligence at the slimming studio, fashion show and afternoon tea party. The society depicted had as little relation to reality as the fanciful hats and costumes worn by its members, but to Stromberg's miner *The Women* offered an acceptable image of New York society to which his wife at least could respond with enthusiasm.

Norma Shearer's bland niceness smothers her scenes and those with her daughter, but the more astringent Rosalind Russell, arch-gossip, with her bizarre clothes, gawky walk and shrill insistent dialogue, and Joan Crawford's Crystal, greedy, ambitious and cynical, soon divert attention from her. Crystal's wheedling phone call to her lover, keeping her tone casually pleading while expression, movements and asides show the calculation of her plan, is a *tour de force* on a level with Luise Rainer's famous telephone scene in *The Great Ziegfeld* (Robert Z. Leonard, 1936), for which she won an Oscar, and her whole performance is one of delightful bitchiness, permeated with a sense of sexual availability that makes one understand her appeal over the wan Mary Haines. "Take my advice and don't wear that," the latter says of the playsuit Crystal tries on during their fitting room confrontation. "Stephen dislikes anything so obvious." "If Stephen dislikes anything I'm wearing," Crystal snaps with deadly accuracy, "I take it off." Joan Crawford is the film's true star, but in such a production it is bound to be the supporting cast that attract most attention. One relishes Mary Boland's blowsy countess on her way to Reno for her fourth divorce, celebrating the occasion with champagne and reminiscences; Joan Fontaine, engagingly scatter-brained and innocent; the credits, in which major players are identified with animals, Fontaine represented as a lamb; Paulette Goddard as the wisecracking chorus girl, and Marjorie Main as the Reno ranch owner whose honest acceptance of marriage's pleasures and problems is in contrast to the weakness of the spoilt women she advises.

GONE WITH THE WIND. Director: Victor Fleming. David Selznick's masterwork needs no further elaboration here, since its merits and faults have already been analysed in books both on Selznick and the film itself. Industrially, its importance was substantial, Selznick cutting across the strictly compartmented Hollywood establishment to create the film he visualised. The style is essentially that of M-G-M, with which Selznick had been intimately associated, but the literary basis of the film, its length and the meticulous detail its producer brought to the production are personal Selznick trademarks, shortly to be incorporated into general usage. *Gone with the Wind* marked the beginning of true producer-dominated Hollywood production. Previously, producers had been "supervisors," keeping schedules and managing the purse-strings, but Selznick, with Goldwyn and a handful of other pioneers, established the producer's cinema over the performer's cinema of the Twenties and Thirties, a state of affairs to remain unchanged for twenty years.

The machinations of *Gone with the Wind*'s production—George Cukor's replacement by Victor Fleming, who in turn gave way to Sam Wood; the relays of writers, with Sidney Howard's script resurrected after his death and its merit recognised with an Oscar; Selznick's much publicised talent search ending when his brother produced Vivien Leigh to play Scarlett—are less examples of confusion and Hollywood prodigality than signs of a typical Selznick film. Outwardly, all may have been chaos, but inside Selznick's mind the form and point of *Gone with the Wind* were from the outset quite clear. One senses this in the coherent visual and dramatic style, in which the contributions of a dozen major artists are drawn together into a colourful fabric: from production designer William Cameron Menzies to art director Lyle Wheeler, and from cameramen Ernest Haller, Joseph Ruttenberg, Lee Garmes (uncredited), Ray Rennahan and Wilfrid Cline (the latter men supplied from Technicolor's staff to supervise colour shooting) to George Cukor's own tasteful additions to the performances he supervised. By 1970, when it was given a new life by a 70mm reissue (ineptly done by lab. technicians from the shrunken negative), *Gone with the Wind* had made $200 million and gained a unique eminence as the greatest triumph of Hollywood production.

Advertisement for *Gone with the Wind*.

Gone with the Wind. Vivien Leigh, Clark Gable.

1940

Despite war in Europe, Hollywood entered the Forties dominating world entertainment. A $100 million industry in the US alone, with weekly national audiences of eighty-five million, the cinema could boast an influence extending into every area of life. According to a *couturier*, "Every costume picture starts a ripple on the surface of style" (even *Snow White and the Seven Dwarfs*—"Dopey Caps" were a brief fad). War in Europe only briefly disturbed Hollywood's faith in its role as a crystalliser of national ideals. Confronted with the paradox, Loretta Young announced: "The turning of ten million homely women into beauties is a lot more important to the well-being of this country than the building of one medium sized battleship, and wouldn't cost as much."

Nevertheless, the outer world was intruding. In August, national radio commentator Martin Dies accused forty-two Hollywood personalities of Communist sympathies, including Fredric March, Humphrey Bogart, James Cagney, Lester Cole, Abner Biberman, Bud Schulberg, Lionel Stander, Franchot Tone, Fritz Lang, Sam Ornitz and Frank and Tania Tuttle. A furious response from those charged, some—though not all—of whom merely supported anti-Fascist protest groups like the Hollywood Anti-Nazi League, caused Dies to withdraw his allegations, which had been based on the evidence of "reformed" party member John R. Leech, but concern grew over political views in the cinema, and many of those named were later victims of the 1947 HUAC investigations and the notorious blacklist.

1940 also saw the climax of the federal campaign to declare illegal Hollywood's monopolistic activities. By a "Consent Decree" announced in July, all companies had two years to curtail "block booking," and a tribunal was appointed to hear exhibitors' complaints about its use. Of all the studios, only the poorly-financed United Artists, Universal and Columbia announced an intention to appeal: the larger companies accepted the ruling and began work on dismantling their empires. Meanwhile, changes were apparent in the structure of Hollywood recruitment as forces gathered that were to create a unique cinema style typical of the decade. With Broadway in the doldrums, casting agents looked to the magazine world, and models like Lauren Bacall, whose haughty glamour hinted at the films to come. The RCA-owned RKO, casting about for a new approach, began hiring radio people for Hollywood, including Irving Reis, Norman Corwin, Frank Woodruff and the young Orson Welles.

FANTASIA. Walt Disney Studios/RKO. Produced by Walt Disney. Production supervisor: Ben Sharpsteen. Story direction: Joe Grant, Dick Huemer. Film editor: Stephen Csillag. Musical director: Edward H. Plumb. Music by the Philadelphia Orchestra conducted by Leopold Stokowski. Narrative introductions by Deems Taylor. Sequences: Bach: Toccata and Fugue in D minor (Directed by Samuel Armstrong). Tchaikovsky: The Nutcracker Suite (Directed by Samuel Armstrong). Dukas: The Sorcerer's Apprentice (Directed by James Algar). Stravinsky: The Rite of Spring (Directed by Bill Roberts, Paul Sattersfield). Beethoven: Symphony No. 6, "The Pastoral" (Directed by Hamilton Luske, Jim Handley, Ford Beebe). Ponchielli: Dance of the Hours from La Gioconda (Directed by T. Hee and Norm Ferguson). Mussorgsky: Night on a Bare Mountain/Schubert: Ave Maria (Directed by Wilfred Jackson).

The Walt Disney studio's most intriguing and ambitious work comes from a period of deep internal dissension. Shortly after *Fantasia*'s release, Disney animators went on strike against repressive management and an unequal pay structure, while its box-office failure—some years passed before its $2.3 million cost was returned—was a major factor in the decision of the company, long a family-controlled concern, to "go public." An attempt by Disney to revive the failing character of Mickey Mouse with a short based on Dukas's "The Sorcerer's Apprentice" plus a meeting with conductor Stokowski sparked the idea of an animated feature using popular classical music selections. Disney and Stokowski, with critic Deems Taylor, then well known as a music populariser, chose eight pieces, supplied each with a "programme" that usually ran counter to the composer's intention (rescoring and editing of complex works like "The Rite of Spring" aided this) and linked them with a serio-comic narration in which Taylor introduced the audience to Stokowski and his orchestra, as well as to the mechanics of optical sound reproduction ("Ladies and Gentlemen, the Sound Track!") and an alleged propensity on the part of orchestral musicians to improvise Dixieland jazz during breaks in rehearsal.

Fantasia's most artistically ambitious section is also its most disappointing; an abstract rendering of Stokowski's own orchestral transcription of Bach merely extends the Disney taste for anthropomorphosis—high notes are shown as bright shapes in the "sky," low notes as dark rolling ground-swells in compositions that employ the conventionalised shapes of musical instruments. The Tchaikovsky and Ponchielli sections suffer from an attempt to express too much, though the former's sensuous "Arabian Dance" with its odalisque tropical fish—pale-faced, big-eyed evocations of Forties "glamour"— and the *pas de deux* of the latter, where a coquettish hippo in vestigial tutu dances with a straining alligator, show a powerful visual imagination. Ruined by brutal adaptation, "The Rite of Spring" still provides vivid backing to scenes of the world's creation and the extinction of the dinosaurs, though the images finally triumph. Beethoven's "Pastoral" is a romp for a chubby and lovable Greek pantheon, showing a considered cuteness equally apparent, though in a more sombre key, in the Mussorgsky, where his *totentanz* evokes a witches' sabbath in the lap of a bat-winged demon whose metamorphosis from a mountain crag is a moment of solemn horror. (The use of Schubert's "Ave Maria" to accompany a religious procession that ends both this sequence and the film is a device to demonstrate the virtuosity of Ub Iwerks' multiplane camera—see 1937).

It is perhaps to be expected that the film's most effective sequence is its cornerstone, "The Sorcerer's Apprentice," where a sinister cat-eyed magician conjures up a quivering bat spirit from a skull and changes it to a butterfly (the creative act in visual shorthand), when leaves his helper Mickey Mouse to create havoc when a broom, casually hexed to carry water, engulfs the laboratory and almost the world. Though Disney had long since ceased to participate in his films except as producer and in the conception of story and ideas, his influence—simplistic, vulgar but showmanlike to a remarkable degree—is every-

Fantasia. **The Sorcerer's Apprentice.**

where in this historic work. The refusal of backers to finance the original panoramic screen and stereophonic sound presentation envisaged may have contributed to *Fantasia*'s failure, but the success-oriented Disney turned abruptly from "cultural" projects towards the slick depersonalised product for which his studio became famous.

THE RETURN OF FRANK JAMES. 20th Century-Fox. Produced by Kenneth MacGowan. Directed by Fritz Lang. Script by Sam Hellman. Photographed by George Barnes and William V. Skall. Players: Henry Fonda (Frank James), Gene Tierney (Eleanor Stone), Jackie Cooper (Clem), Henry Hull (Maj. Rufus Todd), John Carradine (Bob Ford), J. Edward Bromberg (George Runyan), Donald Meek (McCoy), Eddie Collins (Station Agent), George Barbier (Judge), Ernest Whitman (Pinky), Charles Tannen (Charlie Ford), Lloyd Corrigan (Randolph Stone), Russell Hicks (Prosecutor), Victor Kilian (Preacher), Edward McWade (Colonel Jackson), George Chandler (Roy).

Fritz Lang's encounter with the Western is a bizarre one, even for Hollywood, but Lang briefly suspended his Germanic precision in *The Return of Frank James, Western Union* (both 1940) and *Rancho Notorious* (1951) to make some characteristically bitter comments on American mythology. All three are extravagantly visual, exploring the colours (*Frank James* was Lang's first colour film) and shapes of the Western landscape with obvious delight. For *Western Union,* he found a Utah location where red and blue mountains provided a fantastic backdrop; in *Frank James* a chase is shot among mountain crags with the rock shattered into grotesque pinnacles; and in *Rancho Notorious,* Altar Keene's hidden valley hideout "Chuck-a-luck" evokes the "Nibelungenlied." Lang is at his most witty in his Westerns. Interviewed as a prospective cook in *Western Union,* Slim Summerville lists the methods he knows for cooking beef, but the telegraph-line labourers only want reassurance that he doesn't cook it "with the hair on." The news that he does not is greeted by a ragged cheer. In *Frank James,* after the Ford brothers have murdered Jesse James, newsman Henry Hull predicts the revenge of brother Frank, whom they thought dead. Ordering two whiskies at the bar, the Fords review their plans. "What are you gonna do?" Charlie asks. "Thought I might go visit some friends on out West." Bob suggests. "When?" Ford pauses reflectively, downs his whisky and replies, "Now."

But the essence of *Frank James* is less humour than eccentricity: conventional Western characterisation is sacrificed to a revenge *motif* of European subtlety, with details, like those in all Lang Westerns, evoking the spirit and not the truth of the real West. The atmosphere, as in his Dr. Mabuse thrillers, is more that of Twenties German newspaper serials and the fanciful pulp Westerns of those days: Frank James, calm and precise, pursues the killers across the rural West with the relaxed persistence of Death in *Der milde Tod,* implacable and omnipresent. When he robs a train to gain more funds for his quest, even this act is an honourable one, since the St. Louis Midland

Railway offered the reward which brought about Jesse's death, and the visual approach is stylishly picaresque, the thief leaping aboard the train at night and creeping along the roof, his figure outlined against a flaring sunset sky. And during a performance by the Fords of a burlesque representing their gallant murder of Jesse, they swagger on stage to "rescue" a cringing maiden from Jesse's fiendish clutches, only to see Frank watching with polite interest from a box. More than a *coup de théâtre,* the scene makes incisive comment on the Western, implying a form in which even the truth connives at the construction of a more satisfying myth, a Langian insight of typical perception and one which this and his other Westerns embody.

THE BANK DICK. Director: Eddie Cline. For all his unique talent, W. C. Fields deserves at most a footnote to Hollywood history; his comedy, vaudeville-oriented and often using routines developed when he was mainly known as a juggler of genius, contributed nothing to the cinema except its own eccentric charm which regrettably died with its creator. *The Bank Dick* contains the fullest measure of Fields's humour. He

W. C. Fields as *The Bank Dick.*

is Egbert Sousé, again the inept and inactive small-town character, afflicted by shrewish wife and indifferent family. His brief moment of glory, in which he accidentally foils a bank hold-up and is rewarded by employment as a guard, is fleeting, and he again sinks into his niche on the bottom, muttering imprecations against the idiot establishment. One sees much of Fields's resigned acceptance of life's assaults in a classic gag where, after draining a slug from the proffered jug of whisky, his hosts discover embarrassedly that what he has drunk is not liquor but roach killer. The real whisky is produced and tasted, after which Fields pushes the whisky away and reaches again for the roach killer.

1941

In two sensational court cases, noted Hollywood figures went to jail. William Fox, who had long been involved in litigation to save a financial empire damaged by moves to buy control of the industry (see 1928), was convicted by a Federal Court of having conspired with others to obstruct justice by attempting to bribe a judge hearing his bankruptcy case. He was sentenced to one year in prison and a $3,000 fine, and, despite appeals, served nearly six months in the Northeastern Penitentiary at Lewisburg. Released in May 1943, Fox was no longer bankrupt, but imprisonment, combined with changes within the industry, terminated his Hollywood career, during which he had established new standards for ruthlessness.

Another 20th Century-Fox officer, Joseph Schenck, served four months of a one-year sentence for perjury in connection with extortion charges brought by the Federal Government against two leaders of the International Alliance of Theatrical and Stage Employees, William Bioff and George Browne, who had offered to guarantee studios freedom from strikes in return for personal bribes. Schenck at first denied involvement, but it was proved that he and his brother Nick had both paid an annual $50,000 to Bioff as protection money, and Joseph Schenck was jailed for perjury in connection with income tax claims made in respect of the bribes, a further charge of tax evasion being dropped in return for Schenck's co-operation. He was later pardoned and his citizenship restored by President Truman.

Another major career ended when Greta Garbo's last film, *Two-Faced Woman* (George Cukor) suffered the twin blows of box-office failure and critical attack. The Legion of Decency condemned its relatively mild story in which Garbo, in an ill-conceived double role, played twin sisters of contrasting temperament and morality, and Garbo resolved to make no more films, a pledge she has kept religiously, to the distress of her admirers.

An industry that had suffered major blows in 1940 from the government ruling on theatre chains and the closure of European markets, and which had responded with austerity measures and studio lay-offs, now cautiously adapted to the new conditions. Carmen Miranda, hired almost as an afterthought following a Broadway success, was featured by Warner Brothers in musicals to exploit her popularity in her native Brazil and other South American countries—Hollywood's nearest major market with Europe gone. Pearl Harbour in December meant war, with resulting restrictions on material and staff, but it also provided an unpleasant taste of reality from which Hollywood was ready to offer the public diversions.

CITIZEN KANE. RKO-Radio. Directed by Orson Welles. Script by Herman J. Mankiewicz and Orson Welles. Photographed by Gregg Toland. Art direction by Van Nest Polglase and Perry Ferguson. Décors by Darrell Silvera. Costumes by Edward Stevenson. Special effects by Vernon L. Walker. Music by Bernard Herrmann. Edited by Robert Wise and Mark Robson (uncredited). Players: Orson Welles (Charles Foster Kane), Dorothy Comingore (Susan Alexander Kane), Joseph Cotten (Jedediah Leland), Everett Sloane (Bernstein), George Coulouris (Walter Parks Thatcher), Ray Collins (Jim W. Gettys), Ruth Warrick (Emily Norton Kane), Erskine Sanford (Carter), William Alland (Thompson/Newsreel Narrator), Agnes Moorehead (Mrs. Kane), Richard Baer (Hillman), Paul Stewart (Raymond), Fortunio Bonanova (Matiste), Joan Blair (Georgia), Buddy Swan (Kane, at eight), Harry Shannon (Kane Snr.), Sonny Bupp (Kane III), Charles Bennett, Edith Evanson, Richard Wilson, Georgia Backus, Alan Ladd.

The wedding of Charles Foster Kane (Orson Welles)
and Emily Norton (Ruth Warrick) in *Citizen Kane*.

Shortly after completing *Citizen Kane* Welles began his next feature, *The Magnificent Ambersons*, photographed by Stanley Cortez (r).

"Rosebud"—and a legend begins. Welles's thickly disguised portrait of William Randolph Hearst as the ideal of American capitalist success damned by the narrowness of his aspirations follows naturally from the Thirties social dramas, where the theme and approach had been presaged in such films as *I Loved a Woman* (Alfred E. Green, 1933) and *The Power and the Glory* (William K. Howard, 1933), while the style, as in the case of Griffith's *The Birth of a Nation*, was an anthology of developments which had been going on for ten years (see 1931) both in the studios and in workshops of men like cinematographer Gregg Toland. *Citizen Kane*'s enduring force lies mostly in its compassion, Welles abandoning the logic of his structure to examine by-ways of experience, and to mark the film as the work of a feeling human being rather than the monstrous virtuoso exercise it sometimes seems. Perhaps its most touching moment, when Bernstein muses about the girl with a white parasol he saw on a ferry fifty years ago ("She didn't see me at all, but I'll bet a month hasn't gone by since, that I haven't thought of that girl"), proves more memorable than all the glamorous technical wizardry with which Welles surrounds himself and his story.

FLAME OF NEW ORLEANS. Universal. Produced by Joe Pasternak. Directed by René Clair. Script by Norman Krasna. Photographed by Rudolph Maté. Edited by Frank Gross. Costumes by René Hubert. Music by Frank Skinner. Songs by Charles Previn. Players: Marlene Dietrich (Claire), Bruce Cabot (Robert Latour), Roland Young (Charles Giraud), Teresa Harris (Clementine), Melville Cooper (Giraud's Brother-in-law), Anne Revere (Giraud's Sister), Laura Hope Crews (Giraud's Aunt), Mischa Auer (Zolatov), Franklin Pangborn (Zolatov's Friend), Andy Devine (Andrew), Frank Jenks, Eddie Quillan (Crew), Clarence Muse (Samuel, the Coachman), Bob Evans (William), Dorothy Adams (A Cousin), Gitta Alpar, Anthony Marlowe (Opera Singers).

The most distinguished *émigré* to linger in Hollywood after the fall of France, René Clair expected during his stay to work with light comedians like Henry Fonda, whose style he admired. Initially he suggested to Universal a costume film to star W. C. Fields and Deanna Durbin ("both were eerie, of another world") but received instead an invitation to direct Marlene Dietrich, then a declining star name. Determined not to be dominated by her known assurance about the style of her films, inherited from von Sternberg, nor by her aura of heavy glamour, and admiring Norman Krasna's original script (Clair and Krasna became close friends), he created a light, elegant comedy not without, as he now admits, an element of parody. Lavishly photographed and costumed by Maté and Hubert, old Clair colleagues who happened also to be under Universal contract, Dietrich plays the Countess Claire, a European *demi-mondaine* hoping to hide her disreputable past from New Orleans society long enough to marry wealthy but decrepit banker Giraud. To cover up various indiscretions, including her romance with sea captain Robert Latour and the untimely arrival of a Russian *roué* who knew her in St. Petersburg ("Well, I didn't know her—I knew *stories* about her"), she invents (and impersonates) a tearaway cousin, a deception that collapses on her wedding day, by which time it has become irrelevant. She leaves Giraud to sail off with Latour, her wedding dress trailing from a porthole of his boat to float off down the Mississippi.

Clair's New Orleans has the Nineteenth century charm and elegance of his France, a world of liveried servants and backstairs gossip, of lavish *soirées* and sexual innuendo. Noting the coins her maid Clementine shakes from her bodice after having supplied Giraud with information about her mistress, the countess asks idly, "Where did you get *those*, in the daytime?"; approached by coachman Samuel one night, with the gambit "Afraid of the dark?", Clementine says seductively "You ain't so dark." Clair's amusement with bourgeoise pretension has full play. The cocky but nervous Giraud plans elaborate deceptions to gain the countess' interest, plots defeated by his own class distinction: a servant primed to pick a fight, then flee to Giraud's credit, struggles with the unfamiliar situation, raising only a feeble "Do you care to make something of it . . . sir?" Mischa Auer, perfectly attuned to this subtle material, exploits the randy Russian's delightful mannerisms and lines: recognising the countess, his delight in finding a known and proven partner, his confusion at her detachment, and an uncontrollable urge to tell his friend about her, leads to the film's best sight gag as the anecdote, overheard by a relative, passes across the room in

Rene Clair directing Marlene Dietrich in *The Flame of New Orleans.*

the course of her song under Claire's horrified gaze until it comes to the ear of her devastated *fiancé*. Lavishly dressed in black plumes and veils, and lit with Maté's sensuous flair, Dietrich nevertheless manages excellent comic timing, while a lazy, self-indulgent sexiness mocks her Sternberg image—a tone audiences found offensive and which led to the film's box-office collapse. Clair went on to create a few more average comedies, hampered always by studio uneasiness, and only the delightful *I Married a Witch* (1942) is a total success. But with its visual style and clever script, a unique blend of French and American expertise, *Flame of New Orleans* remains his major Hollywood work.

THE MALTESE FALCON. Director: John Huston. One of Warner's most talented screen-writers, John Huston prevailed on the company to let him direct

his adaptation of Dashiell Hammett's famous private-eye thriller, already made twice before, once in 1931, by Roy Del Ruth (renamed *Dangerous Female* after the Huston film), and a second time in 1936 by William Dieterle as *Satan Met a Lady,* an alarmingly eccentric version with Warren William and Bette Davis which loses touch with logic for most of its length. Del Ruth's film has more of the authentic Hammett than Huston's, the latter replacing a slick, wisecracking gangster thriller with an exploration of tensions between those involved in a greedy pursuit of wealth. Like the time in which it was made, *The Maltese Falcon* is nervous, uneasy, afflicted by doubt; only Bogart as Sam Spade, a man for sale but incorruptibly loyal to a curiously outmoded conception of friendship, stands against the erosion of values, for which he is rewarded with loneliness and despair.

1942

After covert negotiations by Hollywood, Brigadier-General Hershey announced that he proposed to declare the film industry a restricted occupation and exempt its members from military service, but sensing public resistance to such a move, the Screen Actors' Guild led film unions in demanding that Hollywood face its responsibilities: actors were advised to discard the glamour image, ride on buses, and where they were ineligible for the draft, involve themselves in volunteer war work. The Hollywood Canteen movement, in which stars gave their time free to serve in servicemen's clubs on both coasts, was a shrewd publicity move and a valuable contribution to morale, as were the barn-storming tours on one of which, in 1942, Carole Lombard died in a plane crash.

The draft and power restrictions cut into film exhibition more than production, with blackouts and practice air-raids interrupting screenings, machinery proving difficult to repair and staff being drained into the forces. Censorship began, and though it was mainly apparent in a switch by studios from escapism to films designed to stiffen war-time morale, some sections of the industry were substantially affected. Documentarists particularly found the depiction of real events inconsistent with national policy. Louis de Rochemont, editor of "Time/Life"'s popular *March of Time*, rushed an anti-Nazi feature, *The Ramparts We Watch*, into production during 1941, using footage from the Germans' famous documentary of the Polish invasion, *Baptism of Fire*, to show the horrors of the *blitzkrieg* from which America was defending itself. So effective was the German material—confiscated, like much "captured enemy footage," from German flying boats at Bermuda, the main terminal for Europe-US traffic— that *The Ramparts We Watch* was withdrawn by government edict and its more dramatic moments edited out on the grounds that they would alarm audiences.

CASABLANCA. Warner Brothers. Produced by Hal B. Wallis. Directed by Michael Curtiz. Script by Julius J. and Philip G. Epstein and Howard Koch from the play "Everybody Goes to Rick's" by Murray Burnett and Joan Alison. Art direction by Carl Jules Weyl. Photographed by Arthur Edeson. Edited by Owen Marks. Music by Max Steiner. Players: Humphrey Bogart (Rick), Ingrid Bergman (Ilsa Lund), Paul Henried (Victor Laszlo), Claude Rains (Capt. Renault), Conrad Veidt (Maj. Strasser), Sidney Greenstreet (Ferrari), Peter Lorre (Ugarté), S. Z. Sakall (Carl), Madeleine le Beau (Yvonne), Dooley Wilson (Sam), John Qualen (Berger), Leonid Kinsky (Sascha), Joy Page (Anna Brandel), Marcel Dalio (Croupier).

Planned as a vehicle for the successful *Kings Row* (Sam Wood, 1942) team of Ronald Reagan and Ann Sheridan, with Dennis Morgan in the Henried role, *Casablanca* went through countless changes of cast and crew during 1942 as war work claimed vital personnel. As last, in a desperate attempt to get the film on the floor, Warners assigned it to Curtiz, and gave him the pick of Hollywood's non-draftables, mostly foreign *émigrés* or, in Bogart's case, men who were physically unfit. Undeterred by such problems, or by the script revision that went on until the last days of shooting, Curtiz created a film that in its effortless style and evocative mood is a masterpiece of the Forties.

Casablanca's impeccable technical credits need no endorsement: Edeson's sinuously craning camera, the mock-Arabic sets then a Warner speciality, and the superb "cutting on action" by Owen Marks, one of Hollywood's supreme editors, continuing a durable legacy from German cinema. Less often commented upon is the script, to which Howard Koch, called in at the last minute, contrived to add a new dimension by making Bogart, in his words, "an arch liberal,"

Casablanca. Humphrey Bogart, Peter Lorre.
"You despise me, don't you Rick?"
"I probably would if I gave any thought to it."

and peopling Casablanca with ingeniously drawn national stereotypes who reflect America's view of the world situation: Rains' French policeman, witty, charming, devious ("I'm just a poor corrupt official"), who—in a superb moment—after having closed Rick's club for illegal gambling, calmly accepts from a suave Marcel Dalio his night's winnings; Conrad Veidt, the stock Nazi beast; Sidney Greenstreet's Ferrari, an Italianate voluptuary, greedy and sly; the Central-European Laszlo, politically idealistic, socially naïve; and at the centre, Bogart's Rick, the tough, independent American, honest broker to all until influenced by higher motives to intervene on the side of the just. The image of a whirling world that opens the film is more significant in retrospect than one imagines.

As the beautiful Ilsa, returning from Rick's past to vex him with reminders of an idyllic Parisian affair on the brink of invasion, Ingrid Bergman, adapting to a project less ambitious than those while under personal contract to David O. Selznick, convinces totally in love scenes where an attachment must be

implied but never stated. Her coaxing of Dooley Wilson to play "As Time Goes By" and the late-night arrival at the bar as Rick urges him to "Play it, Sam. If she can stand it, so can I" outline the personality of a unique woman, vulnerable but finally stronger than those who surround her. Film, director and screenplay all received Academy Awards, and Bogart was nominated. In a remarkable stroke of luck, American forces captured Casablanca just as the film opened, and while it was on general release Roosevelt and Churchill chose the city for a summit meeting, the resultant publicity guaranteeing commercial success to this classic film.

KEEPER OF THE FLAME. M-G-M. Produced by Victor Saville. Associate producer: Leon Gordon. Directed by George Cukor. Script by Donald Ogden Stewart from the novel by I. A. R. Wylie. Photographed by William Daniels. Art direction by Cedric Gibbons and Lyle Wheeler. Edited by James E. Newcom. Costumes by (Gilbert) Adrian. Music by Bronislau Kaper. Players: Spencer Tracy (Steven O'Malley), Katharine Hepburn (Christine Forrest), Richard Whorf (Clive Kerndon), Margaret Wycherley (Mrs. Forrest), Donald Meek (Mr. Arbuthnot), Horace McNally (Freddie Ridges), Audrey Christie (Jane Harding), Frank Craven (Dr. Fielding), Forrest Tucker (Geoffrey Midford), Percy Kilbride (Orion Peabody), Howard da Silva (Jason Richards), Darryl Hickman (Jeb Richards), William Newell (Piggot), Blanche Yurka (Anna), Craufurd Kent (Ambassador).

Although the Hollywood film industry of the Forties had no collective political view except to reflect the ideals of its audience, its liberal film-makers occasionally managed to sneak an ideological statement through the studio machine. To M-G-M and even producer Victor Saville, *Keeper of the Flame* was merely a Hepburn/Tracy romantic melodrama intended to exploit the success of *Woman of the Year* (George Stevens, 1942) but screenwriter Donald Ogden Stewart saw I. A. R. Wylie's "idea for an unwritten novel" (bought by RKO in the late Thirties and only later by M-G-M) as a unique vehicle to attack the tenets of Fascism as many Americans tacitly accepted them in the early days of the war.

Tracy plays a reporter recently back from Europe with a clear understanding of the political scene there, and Katharine Hepburn the widow of Robert V. Forrest, a General MacArthur-like military leader who has died violently in a car crash near his country retreat on the eve of taking up an important government post. Cynically disregarding the lines of reverent mourners queueing in the rain to pay their last respects, and likewise the fashionable boredom of pressmen kicking their heels in the crowded small-town hotel, he penetrates the hilltop mansion and the confidence of its mistress, an emotionless figure in icy white moving calmly among the sheafs of flowers that mark her husband's death, reminiscing about his *corps* of boy-scout followers and the tribute of flowers they brought her. Sensing a secret, O'Malley uncovers the truth about Forrest: he was a crypto-Fascist who intended to exploit his popularity and take over the government. Rather than have this revealed, his household hid from O'Malley the fact of a bridge collapse that led to his death, and only his secretary, played with sinister intensity by Richard Whorf, remains to carry out the plans of his master, a plot prevented when the house, with its plans and papers, is burned down.

Citizen Kane influences are evident in the deep-focus compositions and gloomy interior settings, Cukor's slick style disguising the precise script beneath. Stewart, a playwright, novelist and wit known mainly for his Oscar-winning work on *The Philadelphia Story* (George Cukor, 1940), seemed an odd candidate for Hollywood's liberal conscience, since his background was East Coast high society and the Whitney/Rockefeller circle, but a belated discovery of socialism in the late Thirties (he recalls asking the doorman at London's exclusive Claridges Hotel to recommend a good book on Communism, only to get a baffled stare in reply) was accompanied by a decision to let his political beliefs show in the films he wrote: "This was the picture I was proudest of doing," he said. "By that time, we writers wanted to say something in pictures. It was, I think, partly guilt, but we had a feeling that it wasn't just entertainment that we had an obligation to provide. The story goes that Louis B. Mayer hadn't seen *Keeper of the Flame* until he went to a screening at the Radio City Music Hall and he got up and walked out. I hope it's true." (Donald Ogden Stewart to author, London, 1970) Although Stewart, with the collusion of Cukor and Katharine Hepburn, who possessed more political acumen than either Tracy or Saville, managed to transfer the idea intact to the screen, this act, as well as his involvement in Hollywood anti-Fascist movements, contributed to his blacklisting at the 1951 HUAC hearings, where he was named, inaccurately, by writer Martin Berkeley as an active Communist, and his career virtually terminated as a result.

SULLIVAN'S TRAVELS. Director: Preston Sturges. Sturges so appreciated his own jokes, colleagues confess, that during shooting he would sit with a handkerchief stuffed in his mouth to muffle his own laughter. One sees a key to Sturges' charm in his total absorption in his own world; often frail in their plots and falling back on slapstick or false moralising when comic invention flagged, his films retain their charm because of a whole-hearted conviction, a sense that Sturges, for all his lapses, has something to say. Because of its overt message, *Sullivan's Travels* has more *longueurs* than most. Joel McCrea is Hollywood director Sullivan who, tired of *Hey Hey in the Hayloft* and *Ants in Your Pants of 1941*, insists on the right to make *Brother Where Art Thou*, a plea for internationality amity, full of Significance. Setting out to gather material, he sees only the low life his studio prepares for him, and is ready to return with this *ersatz* vision when chance throws him on a train to the South and into a Georgia chain-gang. Dazed, unrecognised, his circumstances unknown to his friends, he learns through the medium of a cartoon show at a Negro church that his simple comedies have more social value than any drama, and eventually returns willingly to the slapstick factory. But despite the abrupt changes of key, Sturges and McCrea, aided by Sturges's discovery Veronica Lake as the cynical voice of logic who accompanies Sullivan on his first research trip, create a telling parody of Hollywood pretension, a work which, like the Swift satire that suggested it, remains funny when it is at its most acid.

1943

By 1943, 29% of the Hollywood community had joined the services, many of them spurred by the 1942 decision that the cinema could not be claimed as a restricted profession for draft purposes. Most entered the entertainment *corps,* but many technicians and directors were employed on the production of propaganda or training films. The Disney organisation received a Navy commission to produce animated films on air gunnery, later turning to elaborate tracts like *Victory through Air Power* (1943), and *Der Fuhrer's Face* (1942), a broad caricature of the Nazi hierarchy as a comic brass band which encouraged full and prompt payment of taxes. Hal Roach's studios became "Fort Roach," headquarters for stunt flier Paul Mantz and his combat camera teams. Propaganda co-ordination was poor. Each department and service had its film unit. Frank Capra, who enlisted five days after Pearl Harbour, controlled that of the Army, leading a distinguished team including John Huston, Anatole Litvak, William Hornbeck and Anthony Veiller. Their "Why We Fight" series of feature documentaries, mostly directed by Litvak—*Prelude to War, The Nazis Strike* (1942); *Divide and Conquer, The Battle of Britain, The Battle of Russia* (1943); and *The Battle of China* (1944)—as well as series like "Know Your Enemy" and the special *The Negro Soldier,* acquainted fighting men and allies with the strategy and progress of the war, adopting the techniques developed by the de Rochemonts on "Time/Life"'s *March of Time* documentaries, in which newsreel and dramatised incidents were combined with stylish animation and graphics—maps, cartoons, newspaper headlines—to create a visual news style. At the Office of War Information, the non-service propaganda arm of the State Department whose overseas director was playwright Robert E. Sherwood, scenarist Philip Dunne controlled "The American Scene" and other series. Josef von Sternberg's *The Town* (1944) decorously evoked the integrity of American small-town life. John Ford, long a Navy reservist, headed the Office of Strategic Services' Photographic Branch: many old collaborators, including Robert Parrish, Gregg Toland, Joseph August, Robert Montgomery and Jack Pennick, joined the team to make, among other films, *The Battle of Midway* (1942), the war's first documentary of US forces in action, and an Oscar-winner.

Few propagandists attempted an independent view. Some films, like *The Town* and William Wyler's *Memphis Belle* (1943), about bombing raids over Europe, emphasised human dignity and courage, but ignored the morality of war and its cost in human suffering. (Attempts by John Huston after his successful *Report From the Aleutians* (1942) to consider this in *The Battle of San Pietro* (1944) and *Let There Be Light* (1945) were frustrated by the Army.) Since patriotic and thus politically conservative film-makers enlisted first, they soon became controllers of the propaganda output, which reflected their views. Perhaps wrongly, socialist/pacifist directors and writers like John Howard Lawson, Dalton Trumbo and Edward Dmytryk felt more could be done with the fiction film to influence public opinion, but the mildly anti-war and pro-Socialist sentiments of *Tender Comrade* (Dmytryk, 1943) written by Trumbo, and *Action in the North Atlantic* (Lloyd Bacon, 1943) written by Lawson, merely provided ammunition for the HUAC, soon to terrorise Hollywood.

ABOVE SUSPICION. M-G-M. Produced by Victor Saville. Associate producer: Leon Gordon. Directed by Richard Thorpe. Script by Keith Winter, Melville Baker and Patricia Coleman, from the novel by Helen MacInnes. Art direction by Cedric Gibbons. Photographed by Robert Planck. Edited by George Hively. Music by Bronislau Kaper. Players: Joan Crawford (Frances Myles), Fred MacMurray (Richard Myles),

Conrad Veidt (Hassert Seidel), Basil Rathbone (Sig von Aschenhausen), Reginald Owen (Dr. Mespelbrunn), Richard Ainley (Peter Galt), Cecil Cunningham (Countess), Ann Shoemaker (Aunt Ellen), Sara Haden (Aunt Hattie), Felix Bressart (Mr. A. Werner), Bruce Lester (Thornley), Johanna Hofer (Frau Kleist), Lotta Palti (Ottilie).

Tired of seeking a new image for Joan Crawford to replace that of the man-eater (shortly afterwards, she left for a new career at Warner Brothers as a haughty high-society matron), M-G-M cast her in a throwaway spy romance set in pre-war Germany, serving propaganda aims by ridiculing the Reich. An unlikely Oxford lecturer, MacMurray's Richard Myles and his wife Frances fool the Germans with relative ease, even misleading Nazi boss von Aschenhausen, an Oxford-educated intellectual, and regain safety with the magnetic mine formula they were sent to obtain. A wisecracking script finds comedy even in the mechanics of torture; on a tour of the dungeons, neither guide Seidel nor visitors leave behind their sense of humour. "On your left," Seidel says—Veidt's laconic style is perfect for the role—"you see the Iron Maiden of Nuremberg, sometimes known as the German statue of liberty," while Frances characterises the extraction of fingernails as "a totalitarian manicure." During the reunion with von Aschenhausen, a slip that threatens to reveal all is casually covered by Frances at the piano

Above Suspicion. Joan Crawford.

when she strikes a chord, says "Remember this?" and all three join in a spirited rendition of the "Eton Boating Song" ("Jolly boating weather. . . ."). Crawford gives a good account of the silly plot, losing no laughs but adding personality to a role that could have been a mere *cliché*. Her finest moment occurs as Myles is being asked to incorporate espionage into his German study trip. Both are initially uninterested, but as the case is put with greater emphasis and the ramifications made clear, Frances falls into a daze. No longer listening to either her husband or the government man, she stares into the distance and whispers in ecstasy "Spies!".

THE SEVENTH VICTIM. RKO-Radio. Produced by Val Lewton. Directed by Mark Robson. Photographed by Nicholas Musuraca. Script by Charles O'Neil and DeWitt Bodeen. Music by Roy Webb. Art direction by Al D'Agostino and Walter E. Keller. Edited by John Lockert. Players: Tom Conway (Dr. Louis Judd), Kim Hunter (Mary Gibson), Jean Brooks (Jacqueline), Hugh Beaumont (Gregory Stone), Erford Gage (Jason Hoag), Isabel Jewell (Frances), Chef Milani (Mr. Romari), Marguerita Sylva (Mrs. Romari), Evelyn Brent (Natalie Cortez), Mary Newton (Mrs. Redi), Wally Brown (Durk), Ben Bard (Mr. Brun), Feodor Chaliapin (Leo).

An eccentric even by the standards of Hollywood producers, Val Lewton dominated horror and fantasy film during the early Forties. Little in his early career suggested a talent for film-making; the nephew of actress Alla Nazimova, he entered Hollywood with her assistance after a profitable period of writing pornographic novels, one of which, "Yasmin," is now a collector's item. He supervised the Bastille-storming sequence of M-G-M's *A Tale of Two Cities* (Jack Conway, 1935) with Jacques Tourneur directing, and was briefly a Selznick associate, advising David O. against buying "Gone with the Wind" and suggesting, as an alternative epic subject, "War and Peace," which the Mitchell book resembled in plot. Lewton came into his own as head of a unit at the impoverished RKO, where his economical and imaginative horror films reworked the fantasy tradition. *The Seventh Victim,* less famous than *Cat People* (Jacques Tourneur, 1942) or *The Curse of the Cat People* (Gunther Fritsch, Robert Wise, 1944), best exemplifies his genius for mood. The first directing job for former editor Robson and Kim Hunter's screen *début,* its story of a young girl seeking her sister amongst diabolists in an eerie, crepuscular New York combines Lewton's black view of the world and his European sophistication of metaphor. A John Donne sonnet superimposed on a stained glass window ushers in the revelation by the principal of Mary Gibson's school that money for her tuition, usually paid by her older sister Jacqueline, has not arrived, and that she must leave. Seeking Jacqueline in New York, Mary finds her employer and friends evasive, and visiting her apartment discovers only one room, empty but for a chair and a noose above. When Mary has solved the mystery and found her sister to be a devil worshipper cursed by her involvement with the cult, Jacqueline goes to the room. The door closes, and the last sound in the film is that of a chair being kicked over.

The Seventh Victim is ingrained with despondency and pessimism. In Jacqueline's apartment building, a consumptive girl coughs out her lungs, resolving to "go out and live," if only for a few hours, even though she knows it will kill her. She sets out, desperately gay, a symbol of hope terminated by the city's impersonality. Visiting an empty office where she hopes to find Jacqueline, Mary sends a private detective along the dark corridor to investigate. He returns a few moments later, walking slowly from the darkness, blind with terror, in a moment of Lewton's most potent demonstration of horror. Fleeing from her fate, Jacqueline, pursued by footsteps, plunges into an alley. Spread against the wall, she feels in the darkness—and touches the hand of a smiling killer. But suddenly, in an effect Lewton cherished, a door erupts noise, light and actors dressed for a harlequinade. Lewton was not a fantasist in the style of Carné and Clair, devoted to the airy romances beloved of the French, but a Gothic talent, revelling in blood, rape and violence, which he allied with cynical imagination to Beardsley, Wilde and Blackwood to create an arresting synthesis of film and art no later producer equalled.

1944

In two historic decisions, American courts broke the power of the "exclusive personal services" contract. The Supreme Court allowed a claim against Universal by Robert Cummings for $10,700: Cummings, then in the Army, had refused to appear in the film *Fired Wife* on the grounds that it was below his usual standard, and when the company offered no alternative project, announced that he no longer considered himself under contract and sued for back salary. In an even more important decision Judge Charles S. Burrell of the Superior Court, hearing a case brought by Olivia de Havilland against Warner Brothers, overruled a 1917 decision under which a studio could suspend a star for refusing to obey orders, and add the period of suspension to the end of the contract period. Miss de Havilland had been loaned to Columbia, and when she protested at Warners' refusal to put off the transfer (Columbia having failed to produce an acceptable script on time), they suspended her. Pointing out that such a contract constituted "peonage," the Court freed her and established a new autonomy for stars.

The success of *Random Harvest* (Mervyn LeRoy, 1942), *How Green Was My Valley* (John Ford, 1941) and other films of new novels, set Hollywood bidding for the latest best-sellers. In 1936, David O. Selznick had paid $50,000 for the rights to *Gone with the Wind*. In 1944, Edna Ferber sold the film rights to *Saratoga Trunk* for $175,000, and Ambassador Joseph E. Davies and A. J. Cronin those to *Mission to Moscow* and *The Keys of the Kingdom* for $100,000 each. Fox bought *The Song of Bernadette* for $75,000 and RKO *The Robe* for $80,000. Impatient with the novel's slow gestation, M-G-M commissioned proven best-selling authors to write novels specifically for film use. Booth Tarkington, James Hilton, Carl Sandburg and Rose Franken all signed Metro contracts for books to which the company would have sole advance film rights, though their writers could then sell the books in the usual way. Sandburg announced that his "An American Cavalcade" would cover the panorama of US society, and predictably both the Hilton and Tarkington novels, the latter tentatively called "The Man Who Lived," would deal with the problems of the returned soldier. There is no record that this curious project ever produced a filmable property.

At a time when the Cummings and de Havilland court decisions spelt the end of studio star "stables," M-G-M held a lunch to celebrate its twenty-fifth anniversary and solemnly elevated ten of its "featured players" to official "star" status. The most meticulously professional of studios, Metro had made the word "star" official, its emblem the placement of one's name above the film's title in credits and advertising.

SINCE YOU WENT AWAY. Selznick International/ United Artists. Produced and written by David O. Selznick, suggested by the book by Margaret Buell Wilder. Directed by John Cromwell. Photographed by Stanley Cortez and Lee Garmes. Production designed by William L. Pereira. Settings by Mark Lee Kirk. Edited by Hal C. Kern. Music by Max Steiner.* Players: Claudette Colbert (Anne Hilton), Jennifer Jones (Jane Hilton), Joseph Cotten (Tony Willett), Shirley Temple (Brig Hilton), Monty Woolley (Colonel Smollett), Lionel Barrymore (Clergyman), Robert Walker (William Smollett), Hattie McDaniel (Fidelia), Agnes Moorehead (Emily Hawkins), Nazimova (Zofia Koslowska), Albert Basserman (Dr. Sigmund Golden), Gordon Oliver (Marine Officer), Guy Madison (Harold Smith), Lloyd Corrigan (Mr. Mahoney), Craig Stevens (Danny Williams), Jane

---

* Because of possible anti-German sentiment, Steiner's name was shown in the publicity as "Main Steyner."

Devlin (Gladys Brown), Keenan Wynn (Lt. Solomon), Jackie Moran (Johnny Mahoney), Ann Gillis, Irving Bacon, Andrew McLaglen, Barbara Pepper, Byron Foulger, Florence Bates, Dorothy Dandridge, Ruth Roman.

Indefatigable in his search for a successor to *Gone with the Wind,* and inclined to inflate each new production, no matter how inappropriate, to that film's epic status, David O. Selznick approached Margaret Buell Wilder's story of American war-time home life with propagandist fervour and unjustified big-budget expenditure. Seeking to glorify, as the dedication puts it, "An unconquerable fortress, the American home," Selznick rashly wrote his own script. "David Selznick's greatest weakness was the organisation of his professional life," John Cromwell says, "and since he had determined to write the screenplay of the picture—rightfully, I believe—it was not surprising to find we were to begin shooting with twenty pages of script. He hoped, of course, to keep ahead of me. But he had the conviction that the muse would visit him only in the dark hours so his stint was to dictate to two stenographers all night and meet me at the gate of the studio at nine in the morning with the day's labours to be quickly scanned before the cameras started rolling. . . ." (Letter to author, 1971). Nor was this the only technical difficulty. Told that the film should be shot in as near an approximation as possible of the heroine's suburban home, art director William Pereira built sets so substantial that cameramen could not work within them. George Barnes began shooting the film, which, to aid the actors, was made chronologically, but after a few scenes entered the army, handing the project to Stanley Cortez, who after disputes with Cromwell also left for armed service. It was completed by Lee Garmes, only Garmes and Cortez taking credit for a film that, apart from the opening sequence, they shot equally.

For a film made under such difficulties, *Since You Went Away* has surprisingly few signs of strain. One

Since You Went Away. "The unconquerable fortress."

easily forgets the familiarity of all concerned: Claudette Colbert's navy wife Anne Hilton (a $150,000 fee encouraged her to take her first matronly role); Jennifer Jones and Shirley Temple as the daughters; Monty Woolley's crusty lodger; Joseph Cotten's old flame, casually on the make; and Agnes Moorehead, in a role Ruth Gordon refused despite Selznick's importunities and offers of generous salary, as the bitchy, self-interested matron thriving on war-time *ennui* and licence. All play with such ensemble perfection under Cromwell's control that one is immersed in the *ambiance of a country at war*, facing not the threats of enemy action but the faults in human personality that boredom, anxiety and tension can emphasise. Jennifer Jones' husband, Robert Walker, borrowed expensively from M-G-M, provides an emotional balance to the central love affair (Miss Jones' role was expanded in the course of writing by Selznick, whom she later married) and their meetings, particularly a love scene in a barn during a rainstorm and a tearful farewell at the station, her shadow lengthening on the platform as his train disappears taking him away forever, are invested with a touching intensity, reflecting the actress' own tension at the time. After each take, she broke down, and when the film was completed announced she was suing Walker for divorce.

Cromwell captures the feel of war-time with striking accuracy from the very first scene: a pan around an empty room with glimpses of wedding photographs, one of a man in uniform, another of a family group; allied to this, Max Steiner's Oscar-winning score emphasises the point with quotes from "Always," the Wedding March, "You're in the Army Now" and the film's theme. Anne finding a note from her departed husband under the pillow and her tearful retreat into his empty bed are effects delightfully chosen both to tell the story and influence our emotions, as is the friction between Colonel Smollett and his grandson, which leads to his romance with Jane Hilton. Significantly, though the affair progresses through spring rainstorms, it is winter and the kids are collecting scrap in a desolate landscape when the cable arrives telling of his death. A dance for servicemen in a hangar, couples jitterbugging under a vast silhouetted eagle (a subtle use of split-screen to suggest height) while long shadows sprawl on the floor, is one of Stanley Cortez's most audacious shots; and crowded bars where women compete for handsome young officers and deprecate their absent husbands, even a moonlight ride for Anne and Tony Willett where incipient romance is headed off by the conversation of a lonely cycle cop—such scenes convey the sense of a society whose barriers, though strained, remain triumphantly intact and, as Selznick puts it, "unconquerable." Colbert, Woolley, Jones and the picture all received Academy Award nominations (Jones received a 1944 Oscar, but for Henry King's *The Song of Bernadette*) and though critically unsuccessful the film realised $7.1 million on its $2.9 million investment.

FAREWELL MY LOVELY (also known as MURDER MY SWEET). RKO-Radio. Produced by Adrian Scott. Directed by Edward Dmytryk. Script by John Paxton from the novel by Raymond Chandler. Photographed by Harry J. Wild. Edited by Joseph Noriega. Art direction by Albert S. D'Agostino and Carroll Clark. Music by Roy Webb. Players: Dick Powell (Philip Marlowe), Claire Trevor (Mrs. Grayle), Anne Shirley (Ann Grayle), Otto Kruger (Jules Amthor), Mike Mazurki (Moose Malloy), Douglas Walton (Marriott), Miles Mander (Mr. Grayle), Don Douglas (Lt. Randall), Ralf Harolde (Dr. Sonderborg), Esther Howard (Mrs. Florian).

Slickest and most atmospheric of Hollywood's Forties gangster melodramas, Edward Dmytryk's version of Chandler's "Farewell My Lovely" conveys intact to modern audiences the authentic mood of organised crime as it appeared to a country preoccupied by war—an arcane world where no evil was too great not to aspire to tragedy, and where cultivated gang-leaders in penthouse apartments ruled over a world of dark wet streets and desperate men. John Paxton's script uses much of Chandler's dialogue, Dick Powell working comfortably with its wisecracks and Philip Marlowe's sardonic view of the corrupt world in which he lives. The plot (Marlowe made a fall guy in a big-time blackmail racket run by fake psychoanalyst Jules Amthor, and the theft of a jade necklace belonging to the sultry Mrs. Grayle) disguises an exploration of moral decay, a pointed attack on the corruption of the rich, cleverly emphasised by Marlowe perched on a table and staring around with amused contempt at the Grayle mansion's echoing hall, and an edgy sexual conflict between flip detective and acquisitive socialite. Dmytryk's skill in choosing the appropriate face results in an excellent supporting cast, Miles Mander pathetically believable as a cuckolded husband, and Mike Mazurki huge and amiable as the bruiser Moose Malloy.

Dick Powell is effective in his first dramatic role, though the choice was not Dmytryk's, the singer having signed an RKO contract only on the understanding that some of his roles would be dramatic. So successful was his partnership with Dmytryk on this film and *Cornered* (1945) that Powell's subsequent career was made in its mould, with radio series and even the films Powell produced or directed following the hard-bitten private eye pattern. Powell's appearance in the film also dictated a title change in some countries. When "*Farewell My Lovely* with Dick Powell" was previewed, audiences assumed a musical and stayed away; hence the sanguinary renaming.* Dmytryk's technical imagination, the result of his early training as a physicist and later apprenticeship in B-movies like *Tele-*

---

* Similar confusion followed the release of *The Lost Weekend* with Ray Milland (see 1945), audiences expecting a typical Paramount comedy/musical.

vision Spy (1939) where only by technique could one draw studio attention to one's ability, gave *Farewell My Lovely* its share of intriguing devices. Sets in false perspective distort Mazurki's bulk in relation to that of other actors, and window glass was relocated to show the reflection of his head materialise enormously behind Powell's on his first appearance in the office. Dmytryk also used frozen-frames of cigarette smoke to duplicate the muzzy effect of a drug overdose on Marlowe, and an optical illusion at the climax to convince the audience that the star, actually ten feet from Mr. Grayle's gun, had his eyes seared by the blast. For sheer expertise in the deployment of limited cinematic resources, *Farewell My Lovely* has few equals.

1945

Returning to Hollywood after four years of propaganda film-making largely free of box-office considerations and the studios' ingrained conservatism, a number of creative directors and actors determined to enjoy a similar freedom in their civilian careers. Frank Capra, George Stevens, William Wyler and writer/producer Sam Briskin formed Liberty Films, largest of the post-war independents; and Leo McCarey (Rainbow Films), Mervyn LeRoy (Arrowhead), David Selznick (Vanguard), as well as Frank Borzage, Douglas Fairbanks, Jr., James Cagney and an alliance of Alfred Hitchcock and Cary Grant, led a flood of similar production companies.

They immediately encountered strong industrial resistance on all levels. The government, declining to treat such companies on a different basis to major studios, enforced the harsh tax laws, forcing them to deposit large portions of their meagre capital against future tax bills and otherwise impeding their efforts. Paramount's new studio boss Barney Balaban, whose reputation as a financial wizard was then high, promulgated the theory that, with foreign markets shrinking in post-war austerity—Britain had passed a law demanding that 75% of any profits from foreign films be left in Britain, a lead countries like Australia soon followed—no feature could hope to make more than $3 million. It therefore followed that, for safety, the cost of even the largest film could not exceed $1½ million. This upper limit was promptly placed on all studio production, and low-budget production limited in proportion, thus damaging the independents' prospects of success. The issue was further complicated by a strike of the International Alliance of Theatrical and Stage Employees, which controlled most Hollywood technicians. For thirty-four weeks, studio employees demonstrated their resentment of the lay-offs and restricted salaries the studio limit enforced. In the face of such problems, all but a handful of the new independents closed as soon as they opened.

THE LOST WEEKEND. Paramount. Produced by Charles Brackett. Directed by Billy Wilder. Script by Brackett and Wilder from the novel by Charles R. Jackson. Photographed by John F. Seitz. Edited by Doane Harrison. Art direction by Hans Dreier and Earl Hedrick. Music by Miklos Rozsa. Players: Ray Milland (Don Birnam), Phillip Terry (Wick Birnam), Jane Wyman (Helen St. James), Howard Da Silva (Nat), Doris Dowling (Gloria), Frank Faylen (Bim, the Male Nurse), Anita Sharpe Bolster (Mrs. Foley), Mary Young (Mrs. Deveridge), Helen Dickson (Mrs. Frink), Eddie Laughton (Mr. Brophy), David Clyde (Dave), Louis L. Russell (Charles St. James), Lillian Fontaine (Mrs. St. James).

In common with most of the Viennese film-makers who came to Hollywood in the Thirties, capitalising on the work of Lubitsch and his colleagues who had recreated in California the witty, sly and elegant Weimar cinema, Billy Wilder never entirely adjusted to Hollywood's strict categorisation. To him, as to von Sternberg, every comedy had an element of drama, and no tragedy was so profound as not to encourage a satirical approach, a fact dramatised in this memorable version of Charles Jackson's novel about the horrors of alcoholism, which won for Ray Milland a well-deserved Oscar. As the likeable failed writer Don Birnam descends into hell during a lonely weekend of binges, delirium and desperate searches for liquor, Wilder's mocking humour, captured with instinctive skill by Milland, jars our acceptance of a situation that could have been *cliché*. The protective Wick invents an imaginary business trip to explain his brother's non-appearance at a lunch with his *fiancée*'s parents, but the bottle in which Don has drowned his nervousness obstinately rolls from under the couch. Trying on a Jewish holiday to pawn his typewriter for a bottle, Don finds the town's pawnshops closed, the result, a helpful proprietor explains, of an agreement between the Jewish and Irish "uncles": "They stay closed on Yom Kippur; we don't open on Saint Patrick's." And when he tries to steal a woman's handbag, the club pianist, as Birnam is ejected, leads the patrons in "Somebody Stole a Purse." Appropriate, then, that in his suicide note he should urge for his funeral "No flowers and some good jokes."

Though he wanted José Ferrer for the part, Wilder guides Milland into a portrayal of alcoholism more subtle and complex than any seen on the screen, using Birnam's natural dignity and sensitivity as a measure of his decline (an effect heightened in the original novel by the man's homosexuality). Drink, which, as he demonstrates in an outburst of self-approbrium to bartender Nat, makes him a self-parody of a writer, exaggerates his virtues into mockeries of themselves: confidence becomes arrogance, charm self-pity. Stealing the purse, he replaces its contents with a carnation, "for a lovely lady" as he explains to a puzzled rest-room attendant, and when caught he owns up to the charge with a contemptuous "of course," promising even while being manhandled into the street to return and pay his bill. When a drunken fall puts him into the alcoholic ward of a public hospital, the sadism of the male nurse ("Like the doctor was just telling me, delirium is a disease of the night. Good night.") and the horrific delusions of other patients, one of whom wakes the ward with his screams as hordes of imaginary beetles attack him, cannot destroy his self-respect; but the scenes that follow his hospital escape —including the theft of whisky from a liquor store and a terrifying bout of DTs where, alone in the darkened apartment, he sees a bat attack and kill a mouse that struggles through a crack, blood dribbling down the plaster as he dissolves into shrieks of terror—reduce him to total helplessness. Wilder uncharacteristically ends the film with a last-minute reprieve from suicide by the faith of his girl, Birnam dropping a contemptuous cigarette into a glass of whisky and resolving to write a novel about his own experience, but a flashback to the film's first scenes, purportedly showing how Birnam begins his book, stings with the suggestion that the same events may well recur—an endless, vicious circle.

As harshly cynical about human frailty as in *Sunset Boulevard* (1950), Wilder in *The Lost Weekend* abandons even the musty evocation of glamour that distinguishes the later film. Birnam's New York, sweating in early-morning smog or choked on a warm Saturday afternoon with the acid stink of hot asphalt and exhaust fumes, lacks even a vestigial charm. Only liquor and its associations have the air of desirability: the marks left on the bar seem rings of black glass, magically bright; even the bottle hidden in a light fitting by Wick throws a bar of shimmering light on the ceiling. With the appearance of liquor, Birnam's fragile personality, his dignity and perception, are replaced by a mindless spiralling into oblivion. The sight of a bottle at the instant he is inventing the first lines of his novel replaces his determination with a furious search during which he wrecks the apartment. From the opening shot of a bottle hung out of sight below his window, one watches with growing disquiet for its reappearance, the signal for a man's destruction of personality.

THEY WERE EXPENDABLE. Director: John Ford. One of Hollywood's finest films about men at war, Ford's quietly passionate tribute to the Navy with which he fought and was wounded takes its tone from a remark by Ward Bond's Petty Officer Mulcahy in an early scene. Asked to make a speech on the retirement of colleague Jack Pennick, he rejects the suggestion. "I'm not going to make a speech," he says. "I've just got something to say." Ford's "something to say" is the story of a torpedo squadron's gradual destruction at the hands of the Japanese during the Philippines and Pacific campaign of the Second World War, a testing time during which, though the squadron's boats are destroyed and the lives of its men lost, its devotion to Navy discipline and the rituals of respect both to the service and to God affirm the worth of such an existence, devoted to selfless effort and honour. Robert Montgomery plays a character based on John D. Bulkeley, commander of Torpedo Boat Squadron 3 and the officer who smuggled MacArthur off Corregidor, John Wayne his executive officer, and a selection of Ford shipmates and collaborators the rest of the squadron. Although Ford claims to dislike the film, one senses that, for this proselytising director, a work in which emotions are nakedly on show is not one to which attention should be drawn. One means no disrespect in endorsing *They Were Expendable* as a masterpiece.

MILDRED PIERCE. Director: Michael Curtiz. Curtiz never lost the obsession with low life and atmospheric drama developed over years of direction in Vienna, and Warner Brothers, with its predominant interest in *le film noir* (a phrase later coined by French critics to describe the dark, low-key thrillers of the Forties), allowed this talent its complete extension. Remaking her image, Joan Crawford starred as a middle-aged matron who, obsessed with the welfare of her selfish daughter (Ann Blyth) discards husband and likeable but unglamorous younger daughter for success and disillusion as the owner of a chain of restaurants. Curtiz sets the story by the Los Angeles ocean front, alternating between the elaborate brightness of *chic* restaurants to the beach house in which the film's climactic murder takes place. Wet streets, the distant roaring surf, shadows flaring from an overturned lamp, and Crawford's own mask-like face, all combine to create a despairing, heartless world in which Curtiz's imagination thrives.

1946

With studios reporting all-time high profits, and weekly admissions hanging at the highly satisfactory level of eighty million, Hollywood was set to take advantage of post-war optimism, but the revival of federal government suits against the combines, suspended during the war, was a spectre at the feast. Exhibitors increasingly preferred to ignore the big chains, whose restrictive policies now extended to dictating admission prices and the period a film should run. In a 1946 court ruling, the fixing of prices was made illegal, foreshadowing the decision of 1948 which destroyed the monopolies. Yet another IATSE strike crippled Hollywood, dramatising that war-time appeals to solidarity could no longer save studios from implementing the new national salary and fringe benefits structure.

Unconventional Howard Hughes adopted a novel means to oppose the MPAA's withdrawal of a Code seal from *The Outlaw* (Howard Hughes, 1943) because of lurid advertising. (To exploit a relatively tame Western with his newest star Jane Russell, Hughes had developed an advertising campaign based mainly on the prominence of Miss Russell's breasts.) When the authority withdrew its Seal, Hughes sued on the grounds that this was a restraint of trade, but the courts rejected this plea. In a more important move, the Code slightly liberalised its attitude to drug addiction, permitting limited references, though it was not until *The Man with the Golden Arm* in 1955 that the issue received any detailed film examination by Hollywood.

GILDA. Columbia. Produced by Virginia Van Upp. Directed by Charles Vidor. Script by Marion Parsonnett, from a story by E. A. Ellington adapted by Jo Eisinger. Photographed by Rudolph Maté. Edited by Charles Nelson. Art direction by Stephen Goosson and Van Nest Polglase. Music by M. W. Stoloff and Marlin Skiles. Songs by Allan Roberts and Doris Fisher. Players: Rita Hayworth (Gilda), Glenn Ford (Johnny Farrell), George Macready (Ballan Mundson), Joseph Calleia (Obregon), Steven Geray (Uncle Pio), Joe Sawyer (Casey), Lionel Royce (First German), Ludwig Donath (Second German), Robert Scott (Gabe Evans), Gerald Mohr (Delgado), Saul Martell (Little Man).

"There Never Was a Woman Like Gilda" the posters proclaimed, heralding Columbia's confidence that in the young, red-headed Rita Hayworth they had a star whose sex-appeal would establish for her the sort of reputation only Garbo and Dietrich in their heyday had achieved. The twenty-seven year old Hayworth, a promoted night-club dancer previously confined to frothy musicals and B-comedies, responded to Harry Cohn's confidence by producing, under Charles Vidor's suave management, a quintessentially Forties performance. Set in the never-never land of post-war Argentina, a stuffy sub-tropical *milieu* created by Stephen Goosson and RKO's master designer Van Nest Polglase, *Gilda* renounces reality for oblique and intriguingly distorted emotionalism. Cultivated gambling club-owner Mundson rescues crooked crapshooter Johnny Farrell from the thieves of downtown Buenos Aires, adopts him into his business and home to create a relationship more than subtly tinged with latent homosexuality, only to destroy it by marrying Gilda, a leonine playgirl who, unknown to Mundson, is Johnny's discarded lover. Mundson's involvement in an international tungsten cartel complicates an essentially sexual conflict, but his apparent death in a plane crash, Johnny's subsequent marriage to Gilda, his revenge—locking her in her apartment, terrorising her potential lovers, luring her back by trickery when she flees to another country—and Mundson's fortuitous return just as they have reached a new *entente* give the

A moving allegory of the problems facing returning airmen. Dana Andrews in the graveyard of *The Best Years of Our Lives*.

Clarence Brown directing *The Yearling*. Stars Gregory Peck and Claude Jarman Jr., and cinematographer Charles Rosher far right.

The Yearling. Lighting by Charles Rosher.

film a healthy under-current of melodrama.

Since the issues throughout are sexual—sensitive, attractive gambler against cynical voluptuary ("Hate *warms* me. It is the only emotion I enjoy") with Gilda, sensuous, emotional, alone, as the prize—all Vidor's skill is lavished on Hayworth's role, so essential is it to create a character for whom two men might well choose to destroy themselves. Using Sternberg techniques, he dresses her in sequined gowns which Rudolph Maté's camera transforms into fields of darting light, places her in the soft glow of the moon with leaves and vines outlined like metal shapes on the walls around her, and uses her hair as the focus of her personality, so that every scene (from her first appearance in Mundson's bedroom to her sultry strip-tease with "Put the Blame on Mame" in which she personifies Johnny's view of her as a heartless tramp and thus crystallises his real love) has her tossing this delicious mane in our faces. The skill of Hollywood's Forties film-makers to render the best of the past with contemporary skill shows notably in *Gilda*: Sternbergian photographic style, improved by new lacquers for prints and higher-contrast stock, is blended with Vidor's harsher dramatic skill; and the plot of *Casablanca* is rendered by veteran scenarist Virginia Van Upp, here producer, with more cynicism and precision. It is interesting to compare *Casablanca's* sympathetic "chorus" Dooley Wilson with the harsher cracks of Steven Geray's Uncle Pio in *Gilda*: confident in his estimate of Johnny as "a peasant" and Gilda as a whore, Pio betrays emotion only when the "Little Man" commits suicide in his washroom, and even then the reaction is only a bemused purse of the lips and distracted dab with his brush at the arm of a bystander. Most of all, Hayworth's Gilda is neither the *femme fatale* Dietrich personified nor the beautiful clothes-horse Fifties films were to make fashionable, but a living personality, provocative, intelligent, unforgettable.

THE BEST YEARS OF OUR LIVES. Director: William Wyler. One of his last jobs for Goldwyn before an unsuccessful attempt to enter independent production, *The Best Years of Our Lives* is Wyler's finest film. Based on McKinlay Kantor's "Victory For Me," it charts the repatriation of three fighting men into a society for which they find their skills have no value. The mutilated veteran reduced to dependence on his family, the bank manager who finds comradeship incompatible with business methods, the skilled pilot now fit for nothing but labouring—their problems were typical of a social adjustment in which many suffered. Cameraman Gregg Toland creates a stirring visual poem, notably in a sequence in which the pilot, Dana Andrews, visits the grave-yard of the planes he flew, relives briefly the moments of power and fear he experienced in them, and then, cleansed of bitterness, takes a job in the crews that prepare these wrecks for scrap.

THE YEARLING. Director: Clarence Brown. Though Brown's business interests made further work in the cinema a financial irrelevance, he continued exploring the world of an earlier America to which his interest had increasingly shifted after the Garbo fashion declined. In *Of Human Hearts* (1938) and *Ah Wilderness!* (1935) his vision of American culture was revealed as one of the strongest and most coherent in the cinema, but his version of Marjorie Kinnan Rawlings' story of a boy's life and growth to maturity in the bayous of the South proved its finest statement. Gregory Peck played the phlegmatic father, Jane Wyman the mother and Claude Jarman Jnr. the son whose affection for a yearling deer brought him into a confrontation with the reality of life. Although Brown recreates the swamps and thick forests of the setting on a sound stage, an atmosphere is evoked more redolent of heat and humidity than any location work could achieve, and Charles Rosher's colour photography, livid with reds and greens, sustains the vision unfalteringly.

1947

Following Roosevelt's death and resulting US reaction against Socialism as Soviet power increased, conservatives pressed for the purging of "Communist" elements in industry and the arts. Eric Johnston, President of the Motion Picture Producers' Association, urged Hollywood to avoid Congressional investigation by "cleaning its own house," dismissng self-confessed Communists and sympathisers. Most studio heads, notably Schary of RKO, Zanuck of Fox, Mannix of M-G-M and the independent Sam Goldwyn, condemned the idea of a blacklist, but in July 1947 the House Un-American Activities Committee served notice of its intention to investigate Communism in the cinema by placing under subpoena a number of Hollywood personalities, ranging politically from Gary Cooper and Adolphe Menjou on the far right through liberals like Dore Schary to nineteen leftists—directors Lewis Milestone, Irving Pichel and Edward Dmytryk, producer Adrian Scott, and many writers active in the Screen Writers' Guild, including president John Howard Lawson.

Some witnesses welcomed the investigation, but the "unfriendly" nineteen retained legal counsel to attack the investigation's legality via the then-untested First Amendment of the Constitution, guaranteeing freedom of speech. As Charles Katz, one of the five-man legal team, put it, "A strategy was evolved for the men to protest audibly that they were not declining to answer but they would answer in their own way, never quite answering the question, berating those who asked the question and explaining why it wasn't being answered, all the while relying on the First Amendment as a barrier to answering the question." (Charles Katz to author, London, 1971) Hearings began on October 20, and the "friendly" witnesses' parade of unsupported accusations, bigotry and absurd speculation quickly earned national contempt for the Committee and its chairman J. Parnell Thomas. In the second week, the nineteen, led by Lawson and reassured by a statement made to the committee by Johnston of the MPPA in which he rejected totally the idea of blacklisting and implied support for those refusing to expose their beliefs to scrutiny, opened their assault on the Committee, only to be totally routed. Legalities were ignored, witnesses given no opportunity either to state their case or cross-examine accusers; prepared statements, allowed in the case of "friendly" witnesses, were ruled inadmissible. Hearings were abruptly suspended during the second week after only ten leftists had testified: the eleventh, Robert Rossen, and eight colleagues, were never called. Quizzed in New York by pressmen, all nineteen refused to answer in public the questions put to them by the Committee, and public opinion turned against them.

After the American Legion threatened a boycott of films on which these men worked, Hollywood's Wall Street backers became nervous. On November 25, after a meeting at the Waldorf Astoria Hotel in New York, the MPPA repudiated Johnston's promise of support, and undertook not to employ any witness who refused to assist the HUAC. Even anti-blacklisters like Schary were forced to comply with this order. All the ten witnesses called so far were dismissed by their studios, and J. Parnell Thomas (later himself jailed for nepotism) cited them for Contempt of Congress. Each was fined $1,000 and sentenced to a year in jail (Edward Dmytryk, whose involvement with Communism had ended long before the investigation, offered after two months to testify and was released) : those who served their sentences were Adrian Scott, Ring Lardner Jr., Alvah Bessie, John Howard Lawson, Sam Ornitz, Lester Cole, Albert Maltz, Dalton Trumbo and Herbert Biberman. Civil suits were later brought by Scott, Lardner and Cole against the studios for breach of contract, won in the lower courts but reversed on appeal. They were then re-won and re-reversed until set-

Captain from Castile. Jean Peters.

tled with unsatisfactory sums out of court. The careers of all nineteen "unfriendly" witnesses as well as more than three hundred actors, directors and writers were ruined by a blacklist that persisted until the early Sixties, and is only now fading out.

CAPTAIN FROM CASTILE. Director: Henry King. This lively account of Samuel Shellabarger's novel of Spain under the Inquisition and the Mexican campaign of Hernan Cortez gave good roles to Tyrone Power as a fugitive *hidalgo* and Jean Peters as his servant girlfriend, with John Sutton combining religious fervour and self-interested sadism in the role of villain. Rich colour location work by Charles Lang Jr. and an interesting script by Lamar Trotti, who also produced, make this one of the best of 20th. Century-Fox's historical romances.

CROSSFIRE. Director: Edward Dmytryk. When scenarist Richard Brooks wrote his novel "The Brick Foxhole," it was as an attack on the mindless bigotry that could lead a man, unsure of his own sexuality, to murder a homosexual, but in his adaptation Dmytryk, recognising that Brooks aimed his polemic at bigotry and not the problems of homosexuals, altered the victim to a Jew (Sam Levene) and the killer (Robert Ryan) to an anti-Semite. *Crossfire*'s harsh criticism of anti-Semitism contrasts favourably with that in Elia Kazan's *Gentleman's Agreement,* made the same year, in which Gregory Peck's journalist professes Jewish parentage in order to investigate the problem, aware, as is the audience, of WASP birth as a haven in the background.

CRY WOLF. Director: Peter Godfrey. In a comparatively rare directorial assignment, actor Godfrey remade "Jane Eyre" as a thinly-disguised contemporary thriller, with resilient and inquisitive heiress Barbara Stanwyck visiting the estate of her mysteriously deceased husband to find a mansion presided over by a saturnine brother (Errol Flynn, badly miscast), noises in the night and a close-lipped staff hiding a family skeleton, predictably the very-much-alive husband (Burgess Meredith) whose insanity they wish to hide. Godfrey, an expert in gloomy thrillers, creates a chilling sense of mystery, effectively using the mansion, with Stanwyck clambering over roofs and into dumbwaiters with the same earnestness with which she rides on horseback through the woods and skirmishes with the reluctant Flynn.

1948

A black year for Hollywood. On March 24, 1944, the "New York Times" had reported: "'Any fears Hollywood may hold that TV will injure motion pictures are ungrounded,' says Niles Trammell, President of the National Broadcasting Company. He asserts that 'nothing will hurt a good picture' and that TV will increase the box-office value of film performers." But when the 1947 Presidential election campaign was nationally telecast in the US—historians claim this as the beginning of TV's dominance as a medium—the cinema began a fatal decline. Cinema admissions sagged to sixty-two million a week at one point in 1948, but the average figure hovered around ninety million. After a long struggle, the first companies began observing government "consent decrees" to divest themselves of their theatre chains, the means by which they had kept a check on public taste and both catered to and formed it. TV, with its ratings analysis system, was to exploit the feedback of public opinion in a similar way while Hollywood lost touch with its audience.

The government action was fatal to at least one major company. After two disastrous years, Floyd Odlum sold RKO-Radio to Howard Hughes. There is apparently no truth in the famous story that the new owner visited the lot only once, and after a quick tour ordered only "Paint it"; he may never have visited the studio at all, since his work was carried out in an office hired on the Goldwyn lot. Directors occasionally heard of rushes being spirited away at night to be seen by Hughes, and on one occasion a set that required his approval was built at RKO, then dismantled and re-built at Goldwyn before being returned to RKO for shooting.

The few independent companies that survived the Hollywood recession were hard-hit by a financial crisis at United Artists, their main distribution outlet. John

The RKO studio.

Ford's Argosy Films, shaky Frank Capra Films, all that remained of Liberty, and the George Stevens, William Wyler and James Cagney companies all left UA, protestations on the studio's part as to its solvency being met by recriminations and lawsuits. Most of UA's independents were politically of the right, and the decline of Capra, Wyler and Ford was mainly a result of the uncommercial films they had produced for a market increasingly oriented towards realism. The trend alarmed conservative Hollywood, especially when staid organisations like the Bank of America financed new independents who produced the popular leftist crime dramas. This alarm was probably the motive for a statement from the MPPA's Eric Johnston that "no picture shall be approved dealing with the life of a notorious criminal of current or recent times which uses the name, nickname or alias of such a notorious criminal in the film, nor shall a picture be approved if based upon the life of such a notorious

154

Fort Apache. Henry Fonda, Shirley Temple.

criminal unless the character shown in the film be punished for crimes shown in the film as committed by him." Productions like *Dillinger* (Max Nosseck, 1945), *This Gun for Hire* (Frank Tuttle, 1942) and *The Killers* (Robert Siodmak, 1946) were accordingly withdrawn.

Almost unnoticed, D. W. Griffith, whose long obscurity had been interrupted only briefly by the Academy's award of a commemorative Oscar in 1936 (mainly a stunt to re-establish confidence in the Academy after various blunders) and a belated admission to the Directors' Guild, died on July 23, but the Hollywood he knew had died long before him.

FORT APACHE. Argosy/RKO-Radio. Directed by John Ford. Script by Frank S. Nugent from "Massacre" by James Warner Bellah. Photographed by Archie Stout. Art direction by James Basevi. Music by Richard Hageman. Second-unit director: Cliff Lyons. Players: Henry Fonda (Col. Owen Thursday), John Wayne (Capt. Kirby York), Shirley Temple (Philadelphia Thursday), John Agar (Lt. O'Rourke), Ward Bond (Sgt. Major O'Rourke), Pedro Armendariz (Sgt. Beaufort), George O'Brien (Capt. Collingwood), Victor McLaglen (Sgt. Mulcahy), Dick Foran (Sgt. Quincannon), Anna Lee (Mrs. Collingwood), Irene Rich (Mrs. O'Rourke), Miguel Inclan (Cochise), Grant Withers, Guy Kibbee, Mae Marsh.

By the time *Fort Apache* was made, John Ford's critical reputation, high at the time of *Stagecoach* (1939) and *The Grapes of Wrath* (1940), had sagged so low that even his champions, the editors of the English magazine "Sequence" led by Lindsay Anderson, considered it a failure. Yet viewing the film today, one is refreshed by its sophisticated imagery, and the realism Ford and Frank Nugent* give to Fonda's Owen Thursday, the Custer-like cavalry commander, ambitious but short-sighted, who leads his men into an unnecessary massacre for the sake of a prestigious victory.

Usually considered as the inferior of a trilogy including *She Wore a Yellow Ribbon* (1949) and *Rio Grande* (1950), since all three feature John Wayne as a cavalry officer (he plays the same man, Kirby York, in both *Fort Apache* and *Rio Grande*), *Fort Apache* and *She Wore a Yellow Ribbon* should be more correctly grouped with *Stagecoach* (1939), since in these three films Ford explores the encroachment of urban values, which he despises, on the rugged morality of the frontier, with its society based on a balance of power among equals. *Fort Apache's* cavalrymen are

young and ambitious, the comedy is robust, the songs lusty, the action exciting and heroic to a degree rare in Ford's films, but with the end of Thursday's command in a massacre recalling Custer's, this energy, reminiscent of Northern confidence following the Civil War, evaporates. *She Wore a Yellow Ribbon* opens with an evocation of the Little Big Horn—"Custer is dead, and around the bloody guidons of the 7th Cavalry lie the 212 officers and men he led . . ."—from which the film takes its tone. Wayne is now an ageing captain on his last raid against the Indians before retirement. Politicians and capitalists, personified by the crooked store-keepers who cheat cavalry and Indians in both films, are destroying the frontier myth. Pointedly, Ford asked cameraman Winton Hoch to evoke the twilight mood of frontier painter Frederic Remington, efforts for which Hoch received an Oscar. *Stagecoach*, though made earlier, completes the process by showing a town forcing its moral views on the frontier, ejecting a prostitute, gambler and drunken doctor who exhibit, during a dangerous coach ride across Indian territory, greater integrity and honour than their "decent" associates. But the town still wins: history is on its side.

The conflict between Northern pragmatist Thursday and Southern gentleman York motivates *Fort Apache*, the men taking opposite sides even in their sense of duty. Thursday demonstrates his contempt for ancient rituals by failing to disguise his distaste for the non-commissioned officers' ball, at which tradition demands he officiate—dances to Ford are a powerful affirmation of community spirit to which his heroes always subscribe—and in adopting an insulting brevity for his parley with the Indian chiefs, men whose courtliness and honour find an instant response in York and his sergeants. Setting their confrontation before one of Monument Valley's pinnacles, Ford suggests that Thursday, in accusing the Indians of being "without honour," opposes a moral precept as indestructible as the peak, and significantly it is in a valley at the base of this rock that his men are ambushed, Thursday's riderless horse, aptly symbolising his abrogation of duty, leading them into the trap.

Fort Apache ends on a typically symbolic note, often passed over by critics. With Thursday dead and York in command, he is questioned by newsmen, afire with legends of "Thursday's Charge," who suggest it was a privilege to know the dead Colonel. York acknowledges ambiguously "No man died more bravely, nor brought more honour to his regiment," implying that Thursday's importance, like that of all Ford heroes, is in the lessons other people draw from his life rather than in any abstract virtue. We are all servants of our society, Ford says, to be used as the forces of history see fit. Disliking individuality, he emphasises in all his films a belief based on his own Catholicism and devotion to the Navy's harsh discipline, in a divine scheme mere men cannot comprehend but which all must obey without question.

---

* Nugent had been a "New York Times" film critic with literary ambitions. After some damning reviews of Fox films, Zanuck offered him a scripting contract, mainly to keep him quiet; none of his scripts were ever used. Zanuck had also hooked free-lance Fonda to an eight-film contract in 1939 by threatening to cast Don Ameche or Tyrone Power in the role of Tom Joad in *The Grapes of Wrath,* a part Fonda coveted.

The Lady from Shanghai. Orson Welles and Everett Sloane.

THE LADY FROM SHANGHAI. Director: Orson Welles. Welles earned the enmity of Harry Cohn by casting his own wife Rita Hayworth in this cynical thriller of a destructive woman devouring both husband and lover before meeting her end in a bullet-shattered hall of mirrors, a role that, Cohn alleges, impaired her image as a sex symbol. Exploring his tropical *milieu*, Welles creates a haunting parable of deception and desire, himself playing the Irish sailor intrigued by Hayworth into conniving at the murder of her crippled attorney husband. Palms and jungle vines, an oily tropical sea, heat and the omnipresent samba create an equatorial accidie that engenders desire.

1949

As TV established itself, admissions dropped to an average of seventy million a week but, on the crest of a realist wave, the leftist independents enjoyed unaccustomed prosperity. Some introduced socialist principles into their working methods as well as their films. David Loew's Enterprise Studios offered top salaries and free life-insurance to its technicians, relative autonomy and a share of the profits to directors and stars, and free coffee and doughnuts at all hours for everybody. Enterprise had such artists on its staff as John Garfield, Abraham Polonsky, Robert Rossen, Robert Aldrich, Robert Parrish and Don Weis, and while films like *Body and Soul* (Rossen, 1947) and *Force of Evil* (Polonsky, 1948) represented the best of socialist cinema, its reckless working methods and the growing blacklist brought bankruptcy. Stanley Kramer who, with director Mark Robson and writer Carl Foreman (later replaced by publicist George Glass), led one of the most forceful new companies, criticised some independents who entered the field at this time, derogating get-rich-quick operators who extorted advances from banks on illusory films or exploited blacklisted directors and writers unable to work at regular studios. This irresponsibility contributed to the reaction against independents in the Fifties and a decline of vitality in the field.

Enterprise, Kramer and others survived while some major studios suffered in the adjustment to a smaller market and the lack of guaranteed outlets for their films. Warner Brothers was hit hard. Bette Davis left the Warner lot after eighteen years, and fading stars found their contracts not renewed. David O. Selznick, whose Vanguard Films was floundering, exploited the general lack of capital for new screen properties by selling off story rights he owned, including some to Warners. Producer Henry Blanke, whom Warners had signed to a twenty-five year contract at $5,000 a week, refused to agree to a termination, and was so harassed by Warners' management that he only entered the studio when surrounded by a group of his lawyers. The most pathetic sign of change was B. P. Schulberg's paid advertisement in "Variety" appealing for work in an industry he had helped to found.

An Oscar awarded to Eastman-Kodak in 1949 for the development of safety-base film also heralded technical changes. Films had been shot on nitro-cellulose "nitrate" stock, the same material as the explosive gun-cotton, rendered transparent by fusel oil, camphor, alcohol or amyl acetate (banana oil). The resulting material was inflammable, brittle, deteriorated chemically after some years in storage and burned fiercely when decomposed. After the Eastman advance, "nitrate" was gradually replaced by safety stock which, though lacking the faint attractive sepia tone of the earlier material, was safe and stable. To studios' already large overheads was added the cost of adapting to the new film. Also recognised in the 1949 technical Oscars were André Coutant and Jacques Mathot for their development of Eclair's "Camerette," precursor of the hand-held cameras that revitalized cinematography in the next decade.

ACT OF VIOLENCE. M-G-M. Produced by William H. Wright. Directed by Fred Zinnemann. Script by Robert L. Richards from a story by Collier Young. Music by Bronislau Kaper. Photographed by Robert Surtees. Art direction by Cedric Gibbons and Hans Peters. Edited by Conrad A. Nervig. Players: Van Heflin (Frank R. Enley), Robert Ryan (Joe Parkson), Janet Leigh (Edith Enley), Mary Astor (Pat), Phyllis Thaxter (Ann), Berry Kroeger (Johnny), Taylor Holmes (Gavery), Harry Antrim (Fred), Connie Gilchrist (Martha), Will Wright (Pop).

The death of Mark Hellinger in 1947 ended one of Hollywood's most notable careers. A newsman and columnist turned screenwriter, Hellinger had already provided the original story for *The Roaring Twenties* (Raoul Walsh, 1939), one of the most politically precise gangster films of the pre-war period, and produced, among other films, *High Sierra* (Raoul Walsh, 1941), *The Killers* (Robert Siodmak, 1946) and Jules Dassin's harsh *exposés* of urban corruption, *The Naked City* (Hellinger's last, released in 1948), and his prison film *Brute Force* (1947). Hellinger reflected the best of Hollywood's political conscience, and his premature death, combined with the HUAC witch-hunt, did much to arrest the growth of "idea" films after the war-time slump.

Among the projects left uncompleted at his death was *Act of Violence*, a crime film that focused on the social dilemma of the Second World War veteran as *The Roaring Twenties* had on those of the First, facing the contradictions of a society that condemned men in peace-time for acts of violence which were condoned, even praised, during war, and of a code of honour under which a man who sacrifices a group of fanatic prison-camp escapees to protect the safety of a larger number can be regarded as more of a murderer than one who encouraged their suicidal course. Frank Enley, successful and ambitious small-town building contractor widely praised for his work on houses for veterans, crumbles into a desperate, confused fugitive when the limping Joe Parkson arrives in town and calmly goes about finding a convenient place to murder him. The question of force as an answer in human affairs is opened up in the intricate script, which has Enley, hiding out with an embittered prostitute, accept the offer of a crooked lawyer and professional killer to have his pursuer shot. Only at the last moment does he realise that this merely endorses the illogic Parkson represents and, in trying to save his hunter's life, loses his own.

Zinneman prefers to tell his stories less through a central hero than those who surround him, and this technique gives *Act of Violence* much of its strength. Mary Astor's prostitute, cynical and down-at-heel, her oblique conversation conveying a world of disillusion behind the hard face; the falsely jovial, rumpled lawyer Gavery manipulating the desperate Enley into parting with his money in return for a murder; Parkson's nervous *fiancée* whose obvious love makes one see him as more than a menace—a man deformed by the same forces that twisted Enley into betraying his men. Like many films of the time, Zinnemann's avoids

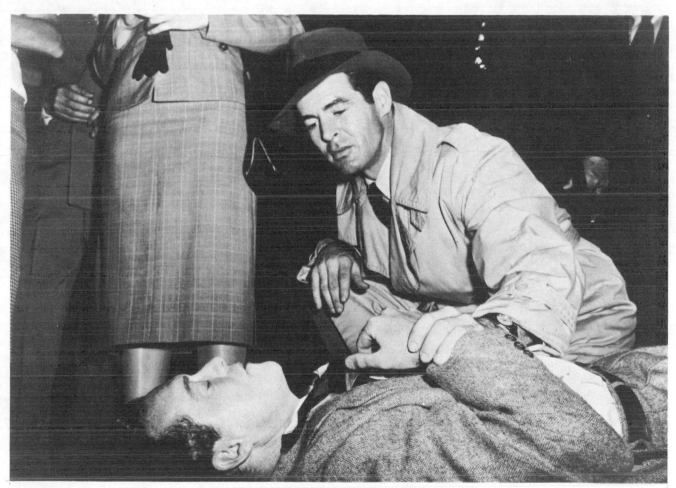

Act of Violence. Van Heflin, Robert Ryan.

The Fountainhead. a) Patricia Neal, Gary Cooper;
b) King Vidor directs.

a

b

the obvious in its style. The terrified Enleys sit in the dark behind closed blinds while Parkson's car hunches across the street, a silent threat. The first attempt on Enley's life comes on the sunny surface of a lake, Zinnemann shooting the scene from a hunter's point of view, long lens foreshortening perspective as we appear to track the unsuspecting victim through a hunting rifle's scope. Sequences like the chase in a roaring subway tunnel and the final death on a deserted railway platform show Zinnemann investing the urban world with its own sinister life, and revealing the city not as a refuge but a trap in which the innocent are soonest caught.

THE FOUNTAINHEAD. Warner Brothers. Produced by Henry Blanke. Directed by King Vidor. Script by Ayn Rand from her novel. Music by Max Steiner. Photographed by Robert Burks. Art direction by Edward Carrere. Set decorations by William Kuehl. Players: Gary Cooper (Howard Roark), Patricia Neal (Dominique Wynand), Raymond Massey (Gail Wynand), Kent Smith (Peter Keating), Robert Douglas (Ellsworth Toohey), Henry Hull (Henry Cameron), Ray Collins (Enright), Jerome Cowan (Alvah Scar-rett), Paul Harvey, Moroni Olsen, Harry Woods, Paul Stanton.

It is a typical Hollywood inconsistency that, at a time when America's socialist minority was most strongly under fire, a film should be produced in which the artist's right to his own ideas is expressed with the greatest passion, and that the vehicle for this statement should have been a book whose author, a fierce conservative, gave "friendly" testimony in the HUAC hearings. Though dissatisfied with *The Fountainhead* because of a restricted budget, and marred as the film is by Gary Cooper's unconvincing portrayal of architect Howard Roark (Cooper was another "friendly" witness), King Vidor made it one of his most powerful works, turning restricted funds to his advantage by reducing sets to the simplest forms and gradations of light, exploiting a powerful supporting cast to sustain the frail central performance.

Ayn Rand saw her uncompromising architect as a super Frank Lloyd Wright, the ultimate *Übermensch* fated to control the world by his force and courage, but to Vidor, always more interested in personal striving than in ideology—as his view of socialism in *The Crowd* (1928) and *Our Daily Bread* (1934)

161

shows—Roark is first a man, only later a symbol. His appeal to the frustrated intellectual Dominique is essentially sexual, dramatised in scenes of his pneumatic drill biting into rock as she watches hungrily from the cliff above,* and by the final shot of him astride the world's largest phallic symbol, a skyscraper; for all his profession of principles it is the assistance of newspaper tycoon Gail Wynand and his wife, both emotionally involved with him, and the jealous opposition of architecture critic Toohey ("'I play the stockmarket of the spirit and I sell short"), that control his fate. The film's sparse style is an original answer to the problems of an impossible narrative. Decoration literally does not exist. Slabs of light on plain walls represent an office, newspapers fanned behind Wynand's head his publishing empire. A futuristic lampshade filled with goldfish suggests Dominique's incarceration in her husband's Roark-designed mansion, though the most ingenious emphasis of her individuality and freedom from reliance on others is an appearance at a party dressed in full evening dress but without a handbag. The effect is of a woman almost armed by her refusal to rely on the conventional feminine props, a device that economically and precisely encapsulates *The Fountainhead's* unique style.

ON THE TOWN. Directors: Stanley Donen, Gene Kelly. M-G-M wisely accepted the recommendation of scout Lillie Messinger to buy into the Leonard Bernstein/Betty Comden/Adolph Green musical of which the enterprising backers had given her a pre-Broadway preview. For $165,000, they received a share both of its stage and film success. In a leaping style set halfway between musical and ballet, *On the Town* revitalised the musical form and established Kelly (an ex-chorus boy) over Fred Astaire as the cinema's major dancer. The athletic energy of "We're Going on the Town,"

On the Town. Gene Kelly, Frank Sinatra, Jules Munshin.

growing from a stevedore's dawn lament "I feel like I ain't outta bed yet" to the returning sailors' romp through Manhattan, emblematised a generation.

---

* Miss Neal dislikes the role, her first major film part, and remembers it as "a constant battle," but she and Cooper became romantically involved as a result of the film.

1950

President Truman recognised the stars' growing power by criticising those who formed temporary companies to escape crushing tax bills, but since the ruse was a legal one most of Hollywood's leading earners soon had their own permanent companies or made arrangements to spend part of their year abroad. A growing interest in foreign films and the start of an "art house" circuit emphasised the new activity of the European cinema, Hollywood's traditional rival which European wars had in the past kept in check. Now, with the American industry suffering a setback with the outbreak of the Korean conflict, Truman throttling back on private spending and restricting vital materials, foreign film-makers used their advantage. Almost, one senses, in revenge, the MPAA issued a waspish manifesto on the exploitation of stars' indiscretions in film advertising, aimed at a campaign for Roberto Rossellini's *Stromboli* which dwelt on the current notoriety of Ingrid Bergman, the film's star and Rossellini's mistress. *Stromboli* nevertheless did good business.

Under one of the ubiquitous "consent decrees," the Technicolor Corporation was forced to relax its grip on colour film. By government order, ninety-two of its basic patents were released to all producers on a no-royalty basis, and twelve others for a "reasonable royalty." The system under which studios had been forced to contract with Technicolor for the supply of stock, processing and cinematographic staff was also outlawed.

As admissions dropped to a weekly sixty million, a gloomy survey showed that 17.9% of American homes had TV, a number growing daily. By now, the TV networks' reassurances had lost credibility, and Hollywood faced a fight for survival. Various methods were tried to absorb the new medium. Cinemas equipped with large TV screens presented sports events live to audiences, an idea experimented with again in the early Seventies with even less success than in 1950. Pay TV was tentatively tried by the Zenith Company as "Phonevision." Three features not seen before on TV—*Homecoming* (Mervyn LeRoy, 1948), *Welcome Stranger* (Elliott Nugent, 1947) and *April Showers* (James V. Kern, 1948)—were offered to a sample audience of three hundred Chicago subscribers who could watch any of the films by feeding coins into their sets, the signal being relayed to them via landline. Zenith's experiment was inconclusive, but others persisted in the project that was to occupy much time and publicity in subsequent years without any real signs of success.

STARS IN MY CROWN. M-G-M. Produced by William H. Wright. Directed by Jacques Tourneur. Script by Margaret Pitts based on the novel and adaptation by Joe David Brown. Photographed by Charles Schoenbaum. Art direction by Cedric Gibbons. Editor: Gene Ruggiero. Players: Joel McCrea (Josiah Doziah Gray), Ellen Drew (Harriet Gray), Dean Stockwell (John Kenyon), Alan Hale (Jed Isbell), Lewis Stone (Dr. Harris Snr.), James Mitchell (Dr. Harris Jnr.), Amanda Blake (Faith Samuels), Juano Hernandez (Uncle Famous Prill), Charles Kemper (Prof. Sam Houston Jones), Connie Gilchrist (Sarah Isbell), Ed Begley (Lon Backett), Jack Lambert (Perry Lokey), Arthur Hunnicutt (Chloroform Wiggins). Narrated by Marshall Thompson.

Son of Maurice Tourneur and heir to the subtle decorative tradition of European art, Jacques Tourneur has always been a film-maker of immense visual flair. From Val Lewton fantasies like *Cat People* (1942) and *I Walked with a Zombie* (1943) through the cold elegance of *Out of the Past/Build My Gallows High* (1947), his most accomplished crime drama, to the sardonic humour of Westerns like his Wyatt Earp story *Wichita* (1955), he exemplifies craftsmanship and restraint. Superficially, *Stars in My Crown* (one of a series of well-planned B-features instigated by Dore Schary on taking over as M-G-M studio head) is his least forceful work, but it is precisely the rural setting and domestic charm, redolent of Griffith, its episodic story and calculatedly downbeat playing by Joel McCrea as the ex-gunfighter parson, that provide the film's charm. Tourneur follows his quietly spoken hero —a low voice is, he has said, to him the perfect representation of sincerity—through the problems of a summer: a plague which the townspeople fear the minister may be carrying (it actually comes from an infected well near the school), the difficulties of a young doctor taking over the practice of his dying father, and the attempt of a greedy landowner to drive a freed slave from his tiny property. Tourneur's flair for subtle and sinister effects gives the climax notable atmosphere allied to the charm that characterises the film. As the rich man's hirelings in Ku Klux Klan robes gather to scare the old man, McCrea intervenes and, identifying each of the men under his robes, reads an imagin-ary will in which the victim purportedly leaves his pathetic belongings to them, with a shrewdly accusing comment to accompany each bequest. One by one, the would-be lynchers melt away, ashamed.

ALL ABOUT EVE. 20th Century-Fox. Produced by Darryl F. Zanuck. Written for the screen and directed by Joseph L. Mankiewicz. Photographed by Milton Krasner. Music by Alfred Newman. Art direction by Lyle Wheeler and George W. Davis. Players: Bette Davis (Margo Channing), Anne Baxter (Eve Harrington), George Sanders (Addison De Witt), Celeste Holm (Karen Richards), Gary Merrill (Bill Sampson), Hugh Marlowe (Lloyd Richards), Thelma Ritter (Birdie), Gregory Ratoff (Max Fabian), Marilyn Monroe (Miss Carswell), Barbara Bates (Phoebe), Walter Hampden (Aged Actor), Randy Stuart (Girl), Eddie Fisher (Stage Manager).

A screenwriter turned director/writer, Joseph Mankiewicz predictably delights in words and those whose business they are. Entertainment media, he suggests

Stars in My Crown. Joel McCrea, Dean Stockwell.

164

All about Eve. Anne Baxter, Bette Davis, Marilyn
Monroe, George Sanders.

in *A Letter to Three Wives* (1949) and *The Barefoot Contessa* (1954), place special stresses on the relationships of those involved and demand a morality and private assurance denied most—a philosophy which finds its highest expression in *All about Eve.* Through his mouthpiece, the cultivated, waspish critic Addison De Witt (based on Alexander Woollcott, many of whose phrases George Sanders employs in his Oscar-winning performance), Mankiewicz expresses his delight in the power of the stage and the charisma of its people, while Bette Davis as the ageing Margo Channing, in her nervous, spiteful and finally ferocious response to a newcomer's challenge, draws the human parallel to De Witt's intellectual explanation of the theatre's attraction. Both in the end understand and respect the other because they are united in addiction to their craft. One wonders if Mankiewicz's original choice for Margo, Marlene Dietrich, would have carried off the subtleties of the part, but she declined when he refused to insert a song for her into the central party scene, with its discussion between De Witt,

director Bill Sampson, playwright Lloyd Richards and newcomer Eve Harrington, in which the last of these expresses nakedly her own drive to achieve the magic of stardom ("If there's nothing else, there's applause . . . like waves of love coming up at you over the footlights"). The role of Margo then went to Claudette Colbert, who withdrew because of a back injury, leaving Bette Davis, as with *Of Human Bondage,* the only suitable actress available. (Ironic, since Claudette Colbert's 1934 Oscar for *It Happened One Night* deprived Miss Davis of recognition for the Cromwell film made in the same year.)

Ostensibly "all about Eve," the film is more correctly all about Margo, since it is she whom the ambitious and decisive Eve supplants and her circle she manipulates to aid her career. Merely by exploiting human qualities she does not share—Karen's compassion to obtain an audience with the star; Bill's ambition to undermine Margo's self-possession; Lloyd's artistic temperament to steal the play she knows will make her famous—Eve achieves her ends, but ironically

165

there is no savour in the success, owed as it is to her mentor De Witt and coarsened by a Hollywood contract which, Mankiewicz implies, will make her just another movie star, distrusted and patronised by the "real" theatre people. Confronted in the final scene with her own image, the ambitious Phoebe, she can only sink deeper into disinterest and despair. Anne Baxter's performance shows a skill that makes her misuse in the Fifties, when a lowering of Hollywood sights made her brand of unglamorous authority unfashionable, all the more tragic.

A sense of performance permeates Mankiewicz's script. Eve is always on stage, and others instinctively adopt the position and interest of audiences, even the cynical Birdie who, entering in the middle of Eve's spurious biography, instinctively takes up her position behind the enraptured listeners and offends them at the conclusion with a critic's admiring reaction—"What a story! Everything but the bloodhounds snapping at her rear end." Typical, then, that Eve's downfall should come through her failure to realise that, as she can dominate people with her skill, she also must have her master, and she automatically acknowledges the authority of the callous De Witt. Cleverly, Mankiewicz shows only the aftermath of any stage performance, but his stars' domestic scenes are no less delicately directed. Piqued by Eve's growing interest in Bill, Margo delivers her famous "Fasten your seatbelts. It's going to be a bumpy night," with theatrical precision, alerting her audience to a show more dramatic than any play. Mankiewicz's tart dialogue, New York oriented and informed with the astringency of a dry martini, belongs like the action of *All about Eve* to the Thirties; his style declined during the Sixties, when an emphasis on visuals diverted attention from content, but even in *Cleopatra,* a film he refuses to discuss, one senses the irony of a man who in his time defined conclusively the limits of intelligence in the American cinema.

1951

A changing pattern of film exhibition in the US, the growth of European cinema that had thrived in the post-war freeze of US funds, encouraging Hollywood to instigate production in other countries and to leave behind a nucleus of trained technicians who put their skill to use in films with native directors, and an expansion of general corporations into the capital-hungry film industry, all forced drastic changes on Hollywood internal structure. At loggerheads with M-G-M over its expansionist policy, Louis B. Mayer resigned abruptly at the climax of a series of disputes with studio head Dore Schary, a liberal and progressive film-maker whose backing for William Wellman's war film *Battleground* (1949) had particularly incensed Mayer. Cashing in his story and other interests for $2.7 million, Mayer entered speculative independent production, financing the TV series *Dragnet* and the Cinerama process. (Lillian Ross described some of the Schary/Mayer conflict's more abrasive moments in her book "Picture.") The Decca Record Company bought Universal, first of many studios to be absorbed by a non-film conglomerate. With 23,100 cinemas in the US, and 2,100 drive-ins (most of them built since the war) pointing to a new trend, Hollywood increasingly slanted its material towards a tempting but fickle section of its audience—the mobile and wealthy eighteen-to-twenty-fives.

A contracting industry began to shed its stars and resisted growing demands from major names for rewards equal to their contribution to a film's profit. Spyros Skouras, new President of 20th Century-Fox, enforced cuts of between 25% and 50% in executives' salaries, and both Tyrone Power and Betty Grable were suspended when they baulked at unsatisfactory roles. Universal suspended Shelley Winters for refusing to visit Hollywood for costume fittings she considered superfluous, and Kirk Douglas bought his Warner Brothers contract for $100,000 to become one of the first independent actor/producers. Less highly publicised was the studios' campaign against blacklisted artists, a practice now attracting extortioners who published lists of *personae non gratae* and accepted money to "forget" individuals. Columbia cancelled a projected Larry Parks film after his successful *Jolson Sings Again* (Henry Levin, 1950) when his political views became known, and Howard Da Silva was only one of many talented actors whose name was removed from the credits of a film already shot to forestall picketing. Joseph Losey, Cy Endfield, Carl Foreman, Donald Ogden Stewart, Jules Dassin and other artists known for their socialist sympathies came to Europe, where for the most part their work exceeded in artistic and commercial success anything they had done in Hollywood. Among those who stayed, Stanley Kramer, once an independent liberal producer, toed the Hollywood line, and signed a $25 million contract with Columbia for thirty films over five years.

THE ENFORCER (also known as MURDER INC.). Warner Brothers. Produced by Milton Sperling. Directed by Bretaigne Windust. Original screenplay by Martin Rackin. Photographed by Robert Burks. Art direction by Charles H. Clarke. Music by David Buttolph. Edited by Fred Allen. Players: Humphrey Bogart (Martin Ferguson), Zero Mostel (Big Babe Lazich), Ted de Corsia (Joseph Rico), Everett Sloane (Albert Mendoza), Ray Roberts (Capt. Frank Nelson), King Donovan (Sgt. Whitlow), Bob Steele (Herman), Adelaide Klein (Olga Kirshen), Don Beddoe (Thomas O'Hara), Tito Vuolo (Tony Vitto), John Kellogg (Vince), Jack Lambert (Philadelphia Tom Zaca).

Hollywood has traditionally drawn the themes and characters of its crime films from real life, a practice pioneered by newsmen like Ben Hecht who used their reporting experience in creating screenplays like *Underworld* (Josef von Sternberg, 1927) and *Street of Chance* (John Cromwell, 1930), and confirmed by Darryl Zanuck's "spot news" policy at Warner Brothers in the Thirties. Production Code restrictions on the glamourising of underworld figures impeded the studios only slightly, nobody doubting that it was John Dillinger on whom W. R. Burnett based the story of *High Sierra* (Raoul Walsh, 1941) or special investigator Thomas Dewey's 1936 arrest of Mafia boss "Lucky" Luciano on compulsory prostitution charges that motivated *Marked Woman* (Lloyd Bacon, 1937). Mafia activity also suggested *The Enforcer*,* a recognisable re-enactment of Dewey's enquiry into New York racketeering that uncovered a murder service run by the Mafia, in which anonymous hired killers carried out murders on behalf of inter-state criminals on a fee basis. (Although the film is signed by Bretaigne Windust, a minor stage director whose other work shows minimal imagination, writer Martin Rackin has revealed that Raoul Walsh directed most of it. The Walsh style is apparent throughout.)

Bogart, who played a character based on Dewey in *Marked Woman,* gives a hard-bitten performance, betraying little emotion even when his investigations reveal a mass grave containing dozens of pairs of shoes. The first breakthrough in Dewey's inquiry, the admission by Abe "Kid Twist" Reles that he had been a Mafia killer for the service journalist Harry Finey dubbed "Murder Inc.", is paralleled in the film by the inquisition of sweating informer Zezo Mostel in a sequence replete with Germanic shadows, though it is the organiser Rico who falls to his death shortly afterwards, as Reles mysteriously did from a Coney Island hotel. Mostel's role accurately depicts the Mafia recruitment methods, and Ted de Corsia is an effective cell leader. "Burn that tent you're wearing," he snarls at Mostel, "and get yourself a suit." The taut ending, with both sides racing to reach a vital witness, shows Hollywood improving on reality, but since the killers used rural New York and New Jersey to execute and hide their victims (of whom fifty-six were found), the sense of death striking without warning in the sunny streets of a country town is a legitimate invention. (The same material provided the plot of *Murder Inc.* (Stuart Rosenberg, Burt Balaban, 1961), a more violent and accurate retelling of the episode).

A PLACE IN THE SUN. Director: George Stevens. Theodore Dreiser's rambling, passionate Twenties novel "An American Tragedy" struck at the social basis of crime, showing how a working-class boy,

George Stevens experiments with a Polaroid camera to check exposure, watched by Montgomery Clift on *A Place in the Sun.*

through early involvement with his parents' street-corner preaching, a succession of jobs designed to break down any remaining moral fibre, and eventual seedy liaison with a young factory worker whom he makes pregnant, is led to murder her, the only way he knows to keep his new, rich girl friend and the comfortable future she represents. Originally to have been one of Sergei Eisenstein's projects during his ill-fated visit to the US in 1929, and later filmed with limited success by Josef von Sternberg in 1931, the story received its best film treatment in George Stevens' adaptation, with Montgomery Clift as Clyde and a young Elizabeth Taylor as the aristocratic Sondra Finchley. Stevens, no socialist, understandably muted the story's message, but invested its dramatic possibilities with much suspense. Clyde becomes a young hustler punished more for excessive ambition than in a miscarriage of social justice, and Sondra a thrill-seeking *débutante* dazzled by the sexuality of her new plaything, an attraction ingeniously suggested in Clyde's lone snooker game during a formal Finchley party, a symbolic display of masculinity with which she is immediately won.

---

* The title is inexplicable and inappropriate. Anthony "The Enforcer" Accardo was a post-war leader of Chicago gangsterism.

1952

William Fox died, and after disputes over administration in which Darryl Zanuck was outvoted, exhibitor Spyros Skouras and his group became controllers of 20th Century-Fox, Zanuck remaining Vice-President in Charge of Productions. The studio's product sagged alarmingly in the disputes that followed. Zanuck, whose production system involved elaborate previews of new films, after which a feature might be re-edited or re-recorded entirely (as happened with *Three Coins in the Fountain,* Jean Negulesco, 1954), was forced to release films "cold," without preview and to recall films for revision even after they had already begun their cinema release. Towards the end of the year, Zanuck instigated development work on the anamorphic projection system of Henri Chrétien, later to be known as Cinemascope.

Among the technical Oscars distributed in 1952 were awards to both Eastman-Kodak and Ansco for the development of colour negative film. Although the two processes differed fundamentally, each produced a sensitive colour film requiring none of Technicolor's elaborate printing nor its beam-splitting technique. M-G-M backed Ansco but switched to Eastmancolor when it proved the Hollywood trend.

Reporting on its Hollywood investigations, the House Un-American Activities Committee charged that studios had been half-hearted and un-cooperative in their anti-Communist activities, an accusation that brought protests from the MPAA and all the studios. Senator Richard Nixon and other HUAC members held up as an ideal the response of Howard Hughes, who at one point in his personal anti-Red purge closed down the RKO studios altogether to "clean house." In 1954, Hughes, a fanatical anti-Communist, was to offer detailed suggestions to the Committee on ways to prevent the processing, distribution and exhibition of *Salt of the Earth,* the feature on labour exploitation of Mexican-Americans made by blacklisted writer/director Herbert Biberman and a similarly unemployable crew.

THE BAD AND THE BEAUTIFUL. M-G-M. Produced by John Houseman. Directed by Vincente Minnelli. Script by Charles Schnee based on a story by George Bradshaw. Photographed by Robert Surtees. Art direction by Cedric Gibbons and Edward Carfagno. Edited by Conrad A. Nervig. Music by David Raksin. Players: Kirk Douglas (Jonathan Shields), Lana Turner (Georgia Lorrison), Walter Pidgeon (Harry Pebbel), Dick Powell (James Lee Bartlow), Barry Sullivan (Fred Amiel), Gilbert Roland (Victor "Gaucho" Ribera), Leo G. Carroll (Henry Whitfield), Vanessa Brown (Kay Amiel), Paul Stewart (Syd Murphy), Sammy White (Gus), Elaine Stewart (Lila), Ivan Triesault (von Ellstein).

Films on Hollywood, falling into two main categories, the jokily affectionate tribute or hard-bitten *exposé,* seldom achieve any sense of a place where people live and work in a profession they admire, nor of the film industry philosophy that forgives much in a man if he has talent and the ability to use it. All these, however, are captured precisely in Vincente Minnelli's drama, perhaps his finest film and the best ever made about Hollywood. Intricately scripted by the brilliant Charles Schnee (who received the year's Best Screenplay Oscar and died in 1963 aged forty-six), the story of ruthless producer Jonathan Shields runs parallel with the careers of many Hollywood personalities without quite corresponding to any, though Minnelli acknowledges resemblances to David O. Selznick in his handling of Kirk Douglas' performance. Shields' Poverty Row beginnings recall those of a hundred men, and though his decision to make a horror film about "cat people" using light effects to replace tatty monster costumes recalls Val Lewton's similar decision for *Cat People* (Jacques Tourneur, 1942), his subsequent rise to be one of Hollywood's most prestigious film-makers, always at the expense of his associates, is too common to be easily attributable. Shields' speech to the drunken Georgia, sunk in a maudlin obsession with her dead father, evokes the Barrymore legend, even though the voice that croaks a "Macbeth" soliloquy from the phonograph is Louis Calhern's. He smashes the record, raging, "Because he drank, you're a lush. Because he loved women, you're a tramp." He scrawls a moustache on the portrait reverently preserved in an improvised shrine. "You will be until you can do this, and laugh as he would have done"— a classic encapsulation of the Barrymore *élan*.

Minnelli's instinctive love for the glamour of film-making permeates the film: Amiel's appearance in the seat of a camera crane and the yelled "Number one" carrying him away from Harry Pebbel's news that Shields, now on hard times, needs help to start a new film; the same crane shot that begins with a close-up of Georgia playing a love scene, then pulls back to show director, crew, executives and finally a lonely electrician high in the gantry absorbed in her performance; even the appalled and silent attention Shields and Amiel give to a prop man's description of how the ridiculous cat-man costumes can be renovated to look effective evokes its own idiocy and charm, the fascinating gadgetry, the sense of a dream made real. As an extension of this, Minnelli even parodies its traditions, inflating a *clichéd* situation, then pricking it with a barbed joke. After the formal funeral of Shields' hated father (almost certainly based on Lewis J. Selznick, father of David O.), black-coated mourners line up to shake the hand of the bereaved son and, after being revealed as extras, receive

The magic of the movies: Lana Turner and Gilbert Roland play a scene watched by Kirk Douglas, Leo G. Carroll in the film within a film from *The Bad and the Beautiful*.

their payment for attending. Carrying a drunken Georgia through the grounds of his mansion in approved Douglas Sirk fashion, Shields pauses, head raised in apparent ecstasy, then drops her into a suddenly-revealed swimming pool. Even the illusion of Shields the monster wears thin, and one regrets that the ambiguous original title, *Tribute to a Badman*, was discarded (later to be used for Robert Wise's 1956 Western). In the last scene, as each of Shields's collaborators—writer Bartlow, director Amiel, star Lorrison—rejects the suggestion that they should collaborate with their mentor on a new film, Pebbel takes the call from Rome in which he will break the news. In an outer office, all three hear the phone ring, pause curiously, nervously; then Amiel picks up an extension and listens, the others gather close, absorbed, attentive —Shields' creatures, unable and unwilling to escape.

HIGH NOON. Director: Fred Zinnemann. This pioneer adult Western, with its insistent Oscar-winning theme tune sung by Tex Ritter (to editor Elmo Williams goes the credit for suggesting it should be featured throughout as a musical *motif*, an idea pioneered by Lewis Milestone in *A Walk in the Sun*, 1945), broke the ground that Delmer Daves, John Sturges and Budd Boetticher later farmed. Seen by many as a comment from scenarist Carl Foreman on American abrogation of principles in the face of the HUAC witch-hunt (which had terminated Foreman's Hollywood career), the film is muddled in its morality. Sheriff Gary Cooper, standing by his principles in refusing to run when an old enemy returns to kill him, survives only because his pacifist wife compromises her belief to help in his defence; after endangering his life and hers for the common good, despite non-support from those he protects, Cooper invalidates the gesture by, in true heroic fashion, walking callously away from his contemptuously-discarded badge. One misses the moral rigour of John Ford in the idea's development. Cooper, his career in decline, shrewdly accepted a share of the profits rather than a salary for *High Noon*, a film costing only $750,000 but making millions, and he found himself again in demand to play the indomitable lawman which was his speciality: refusing to wear a hair-piece, he went on to star in *Vera Cruz* (Robert Aldrich, 1954), *Garden of Evil* (Henry Hathaway, 1954) and *Man of the West* (Anthony Mann, 1958) without, even when asleep, removing his hat.

1953

The wide-screen/three-dimensional film revolution, like that of sound, has a longer history than most people realise. Wide-screen, 3-D and 70mm films existed in the 1910s, and Chrétien's "anamorphic" lens was developed as long ago as 1937 (see that section). 3 D cinema employing polarised light was known in the Twenties and used in features, *Danger Lights* (George Seitz, 1930) among others, though technical problems and cost hampered wider exploitation. In 3-D film, lenses spaced roughly the distance between the human eyes record a scene on separate negatives; the completed films are then projected simultaneously on the same screen through lenses of different polarisation, and audiences view the image with spectacles in which each lens is polarised to receive one projected image only. Each eye sees, in fact, a different film, resulting in a partially three-dimensional image, creating the impression of depth but not roundness. The same effect, though only in black-and-white, can be achieved by double-printing films in cyan and magenta, producing an image which, if viewed through cyan/magenta spectacles, appears in 3-D.

Cinerama marginally led the wide-screen trend, the documentary *This Is Cinerama* (first shown on September 30, 1952) briefly preceding Arch Oboler's *Bwana Devil,* the first 3-D feature in "Natural Vision," released on November 27. It was not until September 17, 1953 that 20th. Century-Fox, hastily accelerating its development of the Chrétien process, unveiled *The Robe* (Henry Koster) in Cinemascope, trumpeted as "the wide-screen miracle you see without glasses." Cinerama never solved the problem of synchronising its three images nor of removing the wavering joins between them, and it abandoned the system in 1963 for Super-Panavision, a 70mm widescreen process. The difficulties of 3-D, which demanded precise synchronisation—the loss of even one frame from a print ruined the effect—led to its early demise, and many

3-D films were released in a "flat" form. Less novel than either, and plagued by problems of focus and composition—the early Bausch and Lomb lenses fattened faces in close-up and accentuated the characteristic distortion of the wide-angle lens—Cinemascope alone survived, and introduction of the spherical Panavision lens in the early Sixties finally solved its optical difficulties. Today, only the conventional wide-screen ratio of 1.85:1 remains from the boom, and many films shown in wide-screen are in fact shot on 35mm without an anamorphic lens.

70mm, brought in to outdo Cinemascope in size, was already well-known in Hollywood, M-G-M having fitted a number of its cinemas in the Thirties with 70mm projection equipment for its "Grandeur" system, in which productions like *Billy the Kid* (King Vidor, 1930) and *The Big Trail* (Raoul Walsh, 1930) had been shot. (In a variation, films like *Portrait of Jennie*—William Dieterle, 1947, for Selznick—had their final reel boosted to wide-screen size to emphasise the impact, in above case of a storm sequence.) The process flowered briefly, but high costs led to corner-cutting. Paramount introduced VistaVision which used 35mm film running horizontally to create a double-frame 70mm, and Todd-AO, promoted by producer Mike Todd, exploited 5mm of the 70mm film with high-quality magnetic soundtracks and an effective stereophonic sound "programme" (magnetic sound recording, like colour, boomed on patents captured from Germany after the war). Technirama cut the 35mm frame in half horizontally to create half-frame images of great sharpness which were then projected on to 70mm-sized screens. There were many other inventive variations, but few were successful.

High costs of exhibition spelt the decline of these processes, which, unlike sound, did not bring in sufficient extra audiences to justify the adaptation of a theatre. Even when Cinerama was at the height of its

Adolph Zukor is a willing subject for a 3D camera crew (double 3D camera at right) for the shooting of a promotional short.

popularity, only one hundred cinemas in the world had Cinerama equipment, from which it was necessary to recoup the cost of a $14 million film like *How the West Was Won*. Few cinemas outside the US and Britain bothered to re-equip for a complex process like Vista-Vision or Todd-AO, and when films in either system were shown there, 35mm reduction prints were used, though the original advertising was almost always retained, as were promotional shorts describing the process in which audiences imagined they were seeing the film. 70mm's high costs and improvements in film resolution led to the paradox of films being shot in 35mm, then blown up to 70mm for the production of release prints only; but the sharpness and accuracy of the best 70mm films, like *Lawrence of Arabia* (David Lean, 1963, photographed by Freddie Young), created critical standards for cinematography seldom reached later.

IT CAME FROM OUTER SPACE. Universal-International. Produced by William Alland. Directed by Jack Arnold. Script by Harry Essex from a story by Ray Bradbury. Photographed in 3-D by Clifford Stine. Art direction by Bernard Herzbrun and Robert Boyle. Edited by Paul Weatherwax. Players: Richard Carlson (John Putnam), Barbara Rush (Ellen Fields), Charles Drake (Sheriff Matt Warren), Russell Johnson (George), Kathleen Hughes (Jane), Joe Sawyer (Frank Daylon), Alan Dexter (Dave Loring), Dave Willock (Pete Davis), George Eldridge (Dr. Snell).

An obscure and interesting figure whose science fiction and horror films during the Fifties boom far outclassed those of his contemporaries, Jack Arnold marked his work with an extraordinary mood and visual signature. Even though hampered by 3-D, with its obligatory demands for visual shocks, this film and the memorable *Creature from the Black Lagoon* (1954) have a detached subtlety and Cocteauesque fantasy rare in Hollywood. With the desert setting creating a quintessential symbol of the threatening American landscape, Leslie Fiedler's "unhumanised vastness," and a reflective story of mankind struggling to encompass visiting aliens whose actions appear evil, *It Came from Outer Space* demands attention and respect. Based on a Bradbury story outline of which Arnold and his scenarist used only the plot and a few sentences, the film develops Arnold's characteristic interest in the essence of xenophobia and the presence of a metaphoric alien in our own personalities and environment, presaging a Sixties interest among sf addicts in the concept of "inner space," the enigma of human emotion and mentality. Except for an unfortunate shot of the egg-shaped creature trundling from a mine entrance, the visitors are never seen except as men taken over and changed in order to serve their controllers. Arnold, by careful setting, contrives to render even familiar actors in the tones of another existence. Barbara Rush stands untroubled by an icy desert wind while Richard Carlson cowers from its bite; Russell Johnson stares without flinching into the sun; the actions of all the captives are deliberate, and

quietly horrific. With the desert as an evocative background, intruding into normal life, Arnold reveals our world as a battleground where even the strongest must fight to assert their individuality or go under.

PICKUP ON SOUTH STREET. Fox. Produced by Jules Schermer. Directed by Samuel Fuller. Script by Fuller from Dwight Taylor's story. Photographed by Joe MacDonald. Art direction by Lyle Wheeler and George Patrick. Set decoration by Al Orenbach. Edited by Nick de Maggio. Music by Leigh Harline. Players: Richard Widmark (Skip McCoy), Jean Peters (Candy), Thelma Ritter (Moe), Mervyn Vye (Capt. Dan Tiger), Richard Kiley (Joey), Willis Bouchey (Zora), Milburn Stone (Winocki), Henry Slate (Macgregor), Jerry O'Sullivan (Enyart), Harry Carter (Dietrich), George E. Stone (Police Station Clerk), George Eldridge (Fenton), Stuart Randall (Police Commissioner), Victor Perry (Lightning Louie).

Advertising for 3D films often misled audiences about the nature of the spectacle to which they were to be exposed.

Like many other newsmen turned scenarists, notably Ben Hecht and Charles MacArthur, Samuel Fuller brought to Hollywood a sharp political sense, demonstrated in a heightened consciousness of the degree to which those in power manipulate the weak, whether in government, business or personal relationships. In *Pickup on South Street,* one of Fuller's most assured works and the film which drew European attention to him as a master, a superficial story of international politics—a Soviet spy-ring's messenger has a microfilm stolen from her by a pickpocket, who is then sought by carrier, spies and the police—disguises a deeper examination of sexual politics, and finally of moral politics in which the apparently amoral thief, played with clarity and restraint by Richard Widmark, proves a man of unshakeable integrity. Through the character of Candy, the cynical tart from whom the plans are stolen, Fuller explores the exploitation of women with an insight into sexual manipulation that Jean-Luc Godard was later to demonstrate in *Two or Three Things I Know about Her (Deux ou Trois Choses que Je Sais d' Elle)*. She carries the microfilm as a gesture of fidelity to the lover who has abandoned her, not in the hope of reviving their affection but as a recognition that, like all human beings, he needs help, a weakness he exploits by forcing her into the spy game. McCoy, though moral, uses her with equal brutality as a weapon for his advancement, driven by a capitalism so blatant that it often borders on obsession. Sex to him is interchangeable with business—"Look for oil" he remarks as they kiss passionately "and you hit a gusher"—and largely a means of furthering his ends. The fevered embrace ends abruptly when she has revealed the facts he needed, yet its passion is unmistakable. Like all Fuller's heroines a casual possession, insulted, beaten and mistreated by her owners, Candy wins with a total passivity, a negation of emotion—availability that McCoy is prepared to interpret as love. He kisses the bruised face—a familiar Fuller *motif*—in acceptance, and returns to his anti-social trade with her as willing accomplice.

Pickup on South Street lacks the force of his later *Underworld USA* (1960), where Cliff Robertson reproduces Widmark's role as an apparently nihilistic avenger undeviatingly true to his personal code, or the sexual subtlety of *The Naked Kiss* (1964) with its memorable scene of prostitute Constance Towers stuffing money into the mouth of madame Virginia Grey, a Fuller symbol of the curious politics of exploitation, but the synthesis of these elements, combined with harshly atmospheric lighting and delightful playing from Thelma Ritter as the ageing tie-selling informer Moe and Richard Kiley as a nervous Communist spy, makes it a remarkable work. Fuller's delineation of Candy's trampish face, cigarette wedged into the corner of her mouth, legs provocatively visible through a thin skirt, hair foaming over the forehead like the crest of a wave, is as perfect as his picture of New York; its crowded subways with masses rocking in unison, remote from one another except for the alert pickpocket, who unites them as a collective victim; the clattering anonymity of an office building's marble foyer; McCoy's shack perched at the end of a pier, disdainfully remote from the city. Fuller's looming close-ups, presaging TV style of the late Fifties, the tracking camera, his habit of flinging victims into heaps of breakable objects to accentuate the violence of their fall are intriguing superficialities of technique that do not divert attention from the fact that his films are among the most thoughtful and provocative of their time.

FROM HERE TO ETERNITY. Columbia. Produced by Buddy Adler. Directed by Fred Zinnemann. Script by Daniel Taradash from the novel by James Jones. Photographed by Burnett Guffey. Edited by William Lyon. Art direction by Cary Odell. Set decorations by Frank Tuttle. Music by George Duning. Song: "Re-enlistment Blues" by James Jones, Fred Karger, Robert Wells. Players: Burt Lancaster (Sgt. Milton Warden), Montgomery Clift (Robert E. Lee Prewitt), Deborah Kerr (Karen Holmes), Frank Sinatra (Angelo Maggio), Donna Reed (Lorene), Philip Ober (Capt. Dana Holmes), Mickey Shaughnessy (Sgt. Leva), Harry Bellaver (Mazzioli), Jack Warden (Corp. Buckley), George Reeves (Sgt. Maylon Stark).

Fred Zinnemann's version of James Jones' sprawling realistic war novel has little of the almost stifling depiction of military life in Hawaii in the first days of the war, nor the cynicism that curdles its sexual encounters. Donna Reed is a prissy dance-hall girl rather than Jones' original lacquered snobbish whore, Montgomery Clift lacks the intellectual self-esteem that makes Prewitt not so much an indomitable individualist as a stubborn drop-out, and Deborah Kerr (in a role originally intended for Joan Crawford), though effective as the bored, amoral captain's wife having an affair with a virile sergeant, seldom rises above miscasting. "That was the toughest role I ever played," she recently said, "since I had to make myself into the absolute reverse of everything I am. . . . She was a nut. A rather pathetic nymphomaniac who was always seeking after something from a man, sexually, which she never found satisfying. . . ."

Unfilmable under Hollywood Code rules of the time (which still forbade the showing of navels) and opposed by the Army because of its brutality theme, *From Here to Eternity* presented scriptwriting problems Zinnemann and writer Daniel Taradash could not hope to solve. Twenty-four scripts were produced before finding one acceptable to all concerned, and the result understandably is only a shadow of the original. Prewitt has become a bugler who earns the dislike of his effete commanding officer by refusing to box in the company championships, and the raids of December 7 arrive just as interest is beginning to lapse. Burt Lancaster gives a positive and well-constructed performance as Warden, the sergeant who will "draw a line he thinks fair and not step over it," complementing Deborah Kerr, though their much-publicised beach embrace seems feeble by Seventies standards and, as the only scene with music, bears the mark of studio interference. Zinnemann's delicate sense of mood, so apparent in his best work, is exercised in purely visual sequences, notably Prewitt's blowing of "Taps" for his friend Maggio (Frank Sinatra, in the Oscar-winning supporting role that revived his failing popularity) * who has been killed in prison. From a stripped bed and rolled mattress, Zinnemann cuts to the distant Prewitt at the far side of the parade ground. Men listen spell-bound; Warden turns out the light in his office and stands in appreciative silence as the clear notes drift on the evening air. In the hush that follows, the regular bugler takes his instrument and looks at it with disbelief. Such romanticism, alien to Jones, briefly evokes the dead and forgotten war years.

---

* Oscars also went to Zinnemann, Burnett Guffey and Donna Reed. Miss Kerr was nominated as Best Actress.

1954

In the confusion following 20th. Century-Fox's wide-screen breakaway, other studios struggled to re-adjust. Banking on 3-D as an adequate answer to Cinemascope, M-G-M found audiences reluctant to endure its paraphernalia even for major features, and many films were issued in 3-D and "flat" versions. After an unsuccessful week in Los Angeles as a 3-D film, *Kiss Me Kate* (George Sidney) was offered in 2-D and billed "See it without special glasses." Although exhibitors of 20th. Century-Fox features complained about limited product, high rentals and unsatisfactory material chosen for many Cinemascope films cheap epics with minor stars and trivial adventure stories constituted the company's main output—Spyros Skouras claimed that theatre-owners had spent $50 million on converting to Cinemascope in 1953-4, and predicted a further $25 million investment in 1955. To assist struggling exhibitors, the company, after a brief public argument, tacitly accepted the discontinuing of stereo sound for Cinemascope in all but the large city cinemas, and films were thereafter issued with a single sound track suitable for conventional theatre sound systems. The concession made easier the metamorphosis of Cinemascope into "wide-screen"; though only a percentage of films were produced in the anamorphic process, theatres retained a modified Cinemascope screen size, lopping films at the top and botton even when shot in conventional 35mm.

Television was the fastest growing and most dangerous force in the entertainment industry, and one already creating its own style and work force. NBC announced a 1953 turnover of $100 million, 18% more than in 1952. Such networks had unprecedented power, and many stations charged that block-booking had become a regular TV practice, regional stations being forced to accept poor programmes in order to obtain the high-rating specials. It is appropriate that such a charge should have been made in the year when the last big theatre/studio film combine, M-G-M/Loew's Inc., obeyed the government "consent decree" and divorced its production and exhibition operations.

SEVEN BRIDES FOR SEVEN BROTHERS. M-G-M. Produced by Jack Cummings. Directed by Stanley Donen. Script by Albert Hackett, Frances Goodrich and Dorothy Kingsley based on "The Sobbin' Women" by Stephen Vincent Benet. Photographed by George Folsey. Music by Gene de Paul, lyrics by Johnny Mercer. Dances and musical numbers staged by Michael Kidd. Art direction by Cedric Gibbons and Urie McClearly. Edited by Ralph E. Winters. Costumes by Walter Plunkett. Players: Howard Keel (Adam), Jeff Richards (Benjamin), Russ Tamblyn (Gideon), Tommy Rall (Frank), Marc Platt (Daniel), Matt Mattox (Caleb), Jacques d'Amboise (Ephraim), Jane Powell (Milly), Julie Newmayer (Dorcas), Nancy Kilgas (Alice), Betty Carr (Sarah), Virginia Gibson (Liza), Ruta Kilmonis (Ruth), Norma Doggett (Martha), Ian Wolfe (Rev. Elcott), Howard Petrie (Pete), Earl Barton (Harry), Dante Di Paolo (Matt), Kelly Brown (Carl), Matt Moore (Ruth's uncle), Dick Rich (Dorcas's father), Marjorie Wood (Mrs. Bixby), Russell Simpson (Mr. Bixby).

One is grateful that Stanley Donen's maturity as a director of musicals came before the late-Fifties shrinkage of interest and a switch in Hollywood orientation from original musicals of moderate budget to massive recreations of Broadway shows, twin influences that snuffed out the form, as well as the careers of stars like Howard Keel who, though incomparable in such films, were ill-suited to drama. *Seven Brides* showcased M-G-M's new mastery of Cinemascope, the optical problems of which directors and cameramen had now overcome, and its Ansco colour process, shortly to be

Seven Brides for Seven Brothers. Jane Powell and the brothers watch Russ Tamblyn.

discarded for the more popular Eastmancolor. The slightly muted Anscocolor, with its clear rendition of softer tones, and of low-lit browns and reds, was ideal for this backwoods musical loosely based on the Roman legend of the Rape of the Sabine Women, with frontier orphans as the Romans and town girls as the kidnapped women who learn to love them. One wonders if even Keel's flowing red beard may not have been chosen with Ansco's good points in mind.

Gene de Paul's *forte* is the melancholy ballad ("You Don't Know What Love Is," "I'll Remember April," "Star Eyes") and his score is not among the most distinguished with which Donen worked. When de Paul is obviously on his home ground, as in the mournful "Lonesome Polecat," Donen and Kidd ingeniously find visual equivalents to the song's mood, in this case creating a slow-motion ballet for the brothers as they chop wood in a landscape as frozen as their emotions. "Point" songs like "Sobbin' Women" in which Adam

Pontipee relates the Sabine story to his brothers, and "Bless Your Beautiful Hide," stating his marital ambitions and outlining the kind of woman for whom he is searching, create their own logic. The greatest imagination is reserved for the action numbers, notably "Goin' Courtin'," Jane Powell's crash-course in etiquette for the Pontipees, and the barn-raising sequence, where an amicable community event deteriorates into mayhem as the brothers tangle with their town opposition, finally reducing the building to ruins. A deserved classic, this number has the romping violence typical of the American musical at its best.

THE WILD ONE. Director: Laslo Benedek. Produced by Stanley Kramer, this low-budget drama belongs to the school of quasi-*exposés* he manufactured with increasing assurance during the Fifties, with Edward Dmytryk's *The Sniper* (1952) his best. Purporting to examine the breakdown in law and order when a

The Wild One. Marlon Brando.

Stanley Kramer and Marlon Brando on the set of *The Wild One*.

motor-cycle group, initially tolerated by an ineffectual sheriff and self-interested tradespeople, takes over a country town, Kramer and director Benedek actually exploit the motor-cycle cult's glamour and violence, with Marlon Brando as its potent symbol, a vessel of undirected power and sex appeal. Noting the "Black Rebels MCC" on his jacket, a girl asks, "What are you rebelling against, Johnny?" The pout increases slightly. "What have ya got?" he growls. Brando and small-town girl Mary Murphy make memorable lovers, their affair portrayed in a tradition of chivalry remote from the film's alleged concern with contemporary social issues. Capturing her from menacing followers, Brando throws her on his cycle and they whirl away along a moon-dappled road, she clutching his leather-jacketed body as a muttering muted trumpet echoes the bike's exhaust. (Jazz virtuoso Milton "Shorty" Rogers composed the score and led the group performing it, though only after a lawsuit did Leith Stevens relinquish credit.) A *cause célèbre* in many countries, including England, where for some years it was denied a release, *The Wild One* nevertheless remains a powerful evocation of sexual and social violence, in which even the punishments meted out to Johnny and his boys are shown by Brando's masochism to be aspects of pleasure.

1955

In a contracting industry, weaker companies suffered first. Technicolor Corporation, its income cut drastically by the 1950 consent decree, laid off four hundred employees and reluctantly turned to the more prosaic job of processing, setting new standards of excellence in both black-and-white and colour printing. Having tried since 1948 to keep RKO in business, Howard Hughes finally opened negotiations for its sale, eventually disposing of the company to General Tire and Rubber Company's media subsidiary General Teleradio. Though Thomas Francis O'Neil of General promised to keep the studio running, this takeover virtually ended RKO; the following year, Hughes bought back two features, Josef von Sternberg's *Jet Pilot* and Dick Powell's *The Conqueror*, both starring John Wayne, and, after substantial reshooting on the first, which had been in production since 1949, released them independently.

The RKO sale's most important aspect was Hughes' concurrent disposal to C&C Super Corp. for $15.2 million of the TV rights to RKO's 740 features and 1,100 shorts. Hollywood had thus far resisted mass sales of films to TV, but Hughes' deal instigated a flood of them, studios squandering a vital reservoir of future income in return for quick profit. One Jeremiah with a head for figures estimated that, of 5,500 features made in Hollywood since sound, 2,900 were available to TV.

1955's most discussed film was Delbert Mann's *Marty*, a low-budget drama adapted from Paddy Chayefsky's TV play, with Ernest Borgnine as a lumpy New York bachelor, that earned him an unexpected Oscar. Its success was hailed as a breakthrough for low-cost realistic films comparable to that of 1947, but as other rueful independents pointed out, *Marty* made a profit because producer Harold Hecht made its costs appear low by "cross-collateralizing," the book-keeping practice whereby a weak film is made technically prof-

Jet Pilot. John Wayne.

itable by sharing its costs among more commercial productions, and keeping rentals artificially low. These practices and the much-maligned block-booking system had given most of Hollywood's serious dramas their only chance of a showing. Independent producers still found it impossible to succeed with solo efforts, and as

181

late as 1963, Frank Perry's fêted *David and Lisa* encountered indifference from exhibitors when it was offered at a fair rental. "Give exhibitors ten *David and Lisa*s," Robert Aldrich remarked, "and no one would finance you an eleventh."

A STAR IS BORN. Warner Brothers. Produced by Sidney Luft. Directed by George Cukor. Script by Moss Hart, based on the Dorothy Parker, Alan Campbell, Robert Carson screenplay from a story by William A. Wellman and Robert Carson. Photographed by Sam Leavitt. Art direction by Malcolm Bert. Edited by Folmar Blangsted. Set decorations by George James Hopkins. Art direction and costumes by Irene Sharaff. Production design by Gene Allen. Music by Harold Arlen. Lyrics by Ira Gershwin. ("Born in a Trunk": Music and Lyrics by Leonard Gershe.) Players: Judy Garland (Vicki Lester), James Mason (Norman Maine), Jack Carson (Matt Libby), Charles Bickford (Oliver Niles), Tom Noonan (Danny McGuire), Lucy Marlow (Lola Lavery), Amanda Blake (Susan), Irving Bacon (Graves), Hazel Shermet (Miss Wheeler), James Brown (Glenn Williams), Lotus Robb (Miss Markham).

This most memorable of Hollywood fantasies had a confused history. Originally produced in 1937 by David O. Selznick, with William Wellman directing, it used a script by Wellman and Robert Carson based on the former's Hollywood experiences and the death of John Bowers, an actor ruined by sound who sailed out to sea in his boat in 1936 and drowned. Feeling the script could be improved, Selznick hired Dorothy Parker and her husband Alan Campbell (who received screen credit with Carson and Wellman), Adela Rogers St.John, Gene Fowler, Budd Schulberg and Ring Lardner Jr. (who did not), and Rowland Brown, who was fired for suggesting to Selznick that the script needed no revision.* The success of this version with Fredric March as the failing leading man and Janet Gaynor as his *protégée* and wife who supplants him encouraged Warners twenty years later to revive it as a "comeback" vehicle for Judy Garland who had declined since leaving M-G-M after being fired from *Annie Get Your Gun* and replaced by Betty Hutton. George Cukor achieved some of his most striking work in it, creating a film that, as well as exploiting Hollywood glamour, exposes also its emotional aridity.

Working for the first time in colour and Cinemascope, Cukor courageously refused to adopt the bland, highly-lit technique more pedestrian directors used with the difficult new medium, and opted for atmospheric low-key lighting effects, often almost Expressionist (as in "The Man That Got Away," sung by Vicki at an after-hours jam session while she is still band vocalist Esther Blodgett), and for documentary

accuracy, as in the murky, chancily side-lit appearance of the drunken Norman Maine on stage at a benefit, first disrupting, then being absorbed into a dance number with Esther and two chorus boys. The film's opening, with crackling arc lights and flash-bulbs recording the arrival of the stars at a *première* (Cukor used newsreel footage of the opening of *The Robe* in Hollywood), instantly captures the tawdry thrill of film-making that is the strongest *motif*. One admires the development of a romance between star and unknown, but the real attraction of *A Star Is Born* lies in its depiction and parody of Hollywood: Maine casually involving producer Niles in conversation, then "allowing" him to hear Esther's voice, piped on the loudspeakers (Cary Grant was to have played James Mason's Maine, but baulked at its drama); the runaway marriage in a desert town, recalling that of Pickford and Fairbanks, with the stars giving their true, prosaic names, the locals gawking, and the studio PR man berating them with superficially amiable acidity for failing to observe Hollywood ritual; Esther's solo playing out of "Somewhere There's a Someone," her production number for some grotesque musical. The film's structure is often that of a dramatic musical, with the musical's quality of parody, as in Esther's metamorphosis at the hands of the studio make-up and costume departments, which Cukor handles with the fanciful unreality of a production number that mocks its absurdity.

Few people associated with the film were satisfied with its fate. Considerable re-editing to tighten the structure was done by Cukor and Hart at the studio's insistence, and many scenes, in James Mason's view some of Judy Garland's most effective, were deleted. The studio later removed Esther's pause on her way to the *première* to be sick behind an oil pump, a visit by Maine to her sleazy apartment, and his proposal delivered on a movie sound-stage, and added "Born in a Trunk," a two-reel musical number in the most vapid Hollywood style where Miss Garland performs a medley of popular songs and allegedly reviews her theatrical career. Though the excerpt is represented as being from one of her films, its use, unlike that of "Somewhere There's a Someone," lacks any satiric edge, and its inclusion mars a notable work of art.

NIGHT OF THE HUNTER. United Artists. Produced by Paul Gregory. Directed by Charles Laughton (additional scenes by Terry Sanders). Script by James Agee from the novel by Davis Grubb. Photographed by Stanley Cortez. Music by Walter Schumann. Edited by Robert Golden. Special effects by Jack Robin and Louis de Witt. Players: Robert Mitchum (Rev. Harry Powell), Shelley Winters (Willa Harper), Billy Chapin (John Harper), Sally Jane Bruce (Pearl Harper), Peter Graves (Ben Harper), James Gleason (Uncle Birdie Steptoe), Don Beddoe (Walt Spoon), Evelyn Varden (Ise Spoon), Lillian Gish (Rachel Cooper), Gloria Castillo (Ruby).

---

* It has been suggested that it was on this occasion that Brown "socked a supervisor," i.e., Selznick, rather than while making *The Devil is a Sissy* (see 1933).

A Star Is Born. Judy Garland in "Born in a Trunk."

Directing *Night of the Hunter*. Robert Mitchum at
left, Charles Laughton and Lillian Gish right.

Recalling Val Lewton in its frugal style and pre-occupation with ancient magic, Charles Laughton's sinister fairy-tale springs from the most durable tradition of American art. With a spirit inspired by Griffith, whose films Laughton ran before shooting, and whose star Lillian Gish he cast in a central role, Laughton tells a story more related to Japanese myth: pursued by a religious psychopath, two children whose mother he has murdered turn their backs on the unfeeling adult world and trust in Nature; guarded by insects and night creatures, borne on the river, they drift to a haven where a fundamentalist grandmother protects them with Biblical fervour from The Hunter. Meticulous as an actor to the point of mania, Laughton the director shows a rare ability to integrate the contributions of others, exploiting the project's low budget by stripping scenes to the bone. Shadows blanket all but the vital playing areas of the Harper house, oppressing the cellar in which the children hide or creating a Gothic solemnity for Powell's ritual murder of Willa, lit only by the icy moonlight of madness. For the fleeing children, peace becomes the shadow of a birdcage seen through an open window,

horror the distant silhouette of Powell riding by on his horse (for sets built in false perspective, a midget on a pony replaced Mitchum). Schumann's music, and special effects of remarkable graphic power similarly transmute the prosaic. Powell's delight in the hymn "Leaning on the Everlasting Arms," and Schumann's tinkling minor orchestration of Pearl's song ("Once there was a pretty fly/ And he had a pretty wife/But one day she flew away . . .") as the river takes them into its care and forest creatures watch, are uses of music to sustain the threatening but fanciful mood. Where money is spent, the result more than justifies it. A few helicopter shots precisely evoke the Ohio countryside against which the myth is set, tiny summer towns clinging to river and forest, to them the only reality. Even the elaborate tableau of the murdered Willa, blonde hair waving among the river grasses as she sits, a tranquil passenger, in the drowned car, repays with a stinging sense of horror the expense of sinking wind machines into the tank at Republic Studios and creating a convincing wax dummy of Shelley Winters. Such expertise hints at Laughton as a great talent, sadly discovered too late.

184

1956

Warner Brothers sold control of the company to Boston bankers Serge Semenko and Charles Allen Jnr. Dore Schary terminated his position as M-G-M studio head when Joe Schenck was elevated to "'honorary chairman" of the company and Arthur Loew took over Loew's Inc. Darryl Zanuck also resigned as Vice-President in Charge of Production at 20th Century-Fox after disagreements with Spyros Skouras over the sacking of staff writers, directors and stars, becoming an independent producer making five features a year, Fox paying half the negative cost in return for release. He also drew $150,000 "consultant's fee" from the company and retained his stock holdings. From his headquarters in the Paris office of 20th Century-Fox he watched the decline of the company he created, until later events (see 1962) put him back in charge.

In the fragmentation of Hollywood, some cherished institutions disappeared. Since nobody could argue that the industry was even close to capacity production, unions for the first time forced a forty-four hour five-day week. Belatedly bowing to new audience sophistication, the Production Code liberalised its provisions to cover Otto Preminger's *The Man with the Golden Arm,* dealing with the forbidden subject of drug addiction. Preminger had earlier illustrated his and the industry's contempt for the Code by issuing his comedy *The Moon Is Blue* (1954) without a Seal when one was refused after star Maggie Mac-Namara had described herself in the film as a virgin. Canvassing independent exhibitors, now in the majority since the studios had been divorced from their cinema chains. Preminger found them indifferent to the Code ruling, and obtained good releases for his film. The 1956 concession marked the end of Hollywood's rigorous self-censorship, though it had really ceased when the MPAA lost the power to enforce its rulings.

ATTACK! The Associates and Aldrich/United Artists. Produced and directed by Robert Aldrich. Script by James Poe from the play "The Fragile Fox" by Norman Brooks. Photographed by Joseph Biroc. Art direction by William Glasgow. Edited by Michael Luciano. Music by Frank DeVol. Players: Jack Palance (Lt. Joe Costa), Eddie Albert (Capt. Erskine Cooney), Lee Marvin (Col. Clyde Bartlett), Robert Strauss (Pfc. Bernstein), Richard Jaeckel (Pfc. Snowdon), Buddy Ebsen (Sgt. Tolliver), William Smithers (Lt. Harry Woodruff), Peter Van Eyck (Nazi Captain), Jon Shepodd (Cpl. Jackson).

Hollywood's pacifist conscience that declined in the post-Korea boom was revived by Aldrich's brutal, precise attack on the corruption too often forgiven in men under pressure. Moving from the fashionable "war is hell" line employed in film like John Ford's 1952 remake of *What Price Glory?* to excuse false heroics and cosy combat humour, Aldrich emphasised the distortion of morality that, at one extreme, can bring about the horrors of a Belsen, but at the other can cause essentially honest men to abrogate their responsibilities at a time when they are most needed. Faced with the fact that a company commander, the Southern aristocratic weakling Cooney, is an alcoholic and paranoid cripple unfit to lead his men, those around him react differently. Lee Marvin's Colonel, once a clerk in the office of Cooney's powerful father, protects him as a lever to later political power. Woodruff, the cautious high-principled executive officer, accepts the situation in the name of peace, sustained by the Colonel's assurance that their unit will almost certainly not go into battle again. On the other hand, Costa, working-class, professionally skilled at making war, and fanatically devoted to the safety of his men, sees the situation in terms of almost Biblical retribution: Cooney's negligence has led to the deaths of eleven men, who must be avenged, and he is determined to execute the man responsible with his own hands. A sudden eruption of enemy action—the Battle

Attack. Jack Palance.

of the Bulge—into their casually held town headquarters catalyses the conflicts. Through cowardice and ineptitude, Cooney again lets the company down, stranding Costa and four men in enemy territory as part of an abortive raid. Costa gets some of his men out, struggles back into town where a pitched battle is now being fought, is horribly wounded when a German tank crushes his arm, but presses on, only to die before he can fulfil his promise to kill Cooney. Triumphant, preparing to surrender, Cooney is shot by the liberal Woodruff, after which each member of the platoon fires his rifle into the corpse, disguising his act. Even though the Colonel too is happy to let Cooney's death seem heroic ("The judge wanted a son. Seems I can only give him one dead."), Woodruff reports the facts to High Command, responding not to the distorted values of personal gain but the higher ethics of human society. Looking down at the corpse of Costa, he says, "You would have done the same, Joe."

Expanding the focus of the play on which *Attack!*

is based, Aldrich externalises the moral conflict. The hard winter landscape becomes a sterilised slide where life is reduced to essentials, and despite intrusions by Frank DeVol's appalling score, the overall effect is of silence, broken only by the slithering whistle of the wind and distant crump of artillery. In their cosy billet, Bartlett, Cooney and their unwilling subordinates play poker and appreciatively sip the bonded bourbon supplied by the doting judge, as his son speculates with adolescent eagerness on how to draw attention to the medal he confidently expects from Bartlett. A pathetic figure, Cooney, as played by Eddie Albert, becomes the film's most rounded character, contemptible but human, a weak boy crushed by the burden of an ideal, reduced at last to a snivelling wreck clutching a fur-lined slipper in memory of a lost childhood. Palance, with a furious attack on the role of Costa, makes him an embodied Fury, an expression of pure moral force. Horror film has nothing more terrible than his sudden appearance at the top of the stairs, one arm mangled and dripping blood, the other clutching a .45, and his sliding, gasping descent to end powerless at the feet of the triumphant Cooney, a curse of fearful nihilism on his dying lips. If Aldrich meant to destroy totally the concept of heroism, he could have chosen no better vehicle.

FORBIDDEN PLANET. Director: Fred Wilcox. Improving special effects and the perfection of Cinemoscope put new facilities into the hands of science fiction film-makers, and as a showcase for such expertise M-G-M created *Forbidden Planet*, the most lavish of modern sf films. Fred McLeod Wilcox, a minor director whose best film to date had been the saccharine *Lassie Come Home* (1943), did little more than supervise the special effects team gleaned from Disney and other studios, to whom credit for the creation of the planet Altair IV alone belongs. The plot, a retelling of Shakespeare's "'The Tempest," sets up a planet inhabited by sardonic scientist Morbius, played by Walter Pidgeon, a Prospero whose Miranda is Anne Francis. Ariel is a Robot named Robby, omniscient, omnipresent but alarmingly humourless in his response to his mistress' needs and those of the spacemen, led by Leslie Nielsen, who visit Altair IV to investigate the death of Morbius' colleagues and the destruction of their ship. Their investigations reveal the island's Caliban, an invisible monster who eventually destroys the entire world. Simple-minded in its plot and dialogue, *Forbidden Planet* is light enough in its approach and of sufficiently high technical quality to invalidate critical objections. Few films can be watched with quite such pleasurable suspension of disbelief as this technological fantasy.

Advertisement for *Forbidden Planet*.

1957

United Artists' management, who bought out the last of UA's original partners, Mary Pickford, in 1956, went public and diversified into TV, records and music publishing, the end of a concept of independent cinema impractical in the Fifties. To boost sagging box-office figures, the MPAA brainstormed a plan for reviving national interest in the cinema. Under the slogan "Get More out of Life—Go to a Movie," it recommended sweepstakes on the Academy Awards results, an Audience Awards Poll in which picture-goers would have the opportunity to vote for their favourite films and stars, and extensive radio, TV and cinema publicity to be financed by a studio consortium. None of these ideas, and particularly not those threatening to involve the studios in any expense, were adopted, although some radio and TV publicity did emerge, to little effect.

The more realistic Academy of Motion Picture Arts and Sciences offered suggestions of more gravity: a Hollywood cinema museum, the sponsorship of a Film Festival, travelling shows to stir interest in crafts like costuming and camerawork, a magazine, assistance to educational foundations and film schools. More realistic than anything discussed by the MPAA, these projects nevertheless collapsed through industry conservatism and selfishness, though producer Sol Lesser and others devoted years to the museum project. Unions and guilds were particularly averse to any suggestion that their ranks, protected by rules demanding the payment of huge bonds for admission and making dismissal or redundancy almost impossible, should be open to young newcomers. An industry where even focus-pullers were in their fifties, and where studio drivers were kept employed by a rule calling for stars to report first at the main studio before being driven to a location, even if that location were nearer to their home than the head office, had no room for those with only talent and the willing-ness to make films. Nevertheless, film schools proliferated, and TV was happy to absorb their graduates.

WRITTEN ON THE WIND. Universal-International. Directed by Douglas Sirk. Script by George Zuckerman, from the novel by Robert Wilder. Photographed by Russell Metty. Art direction by Alexander Golitzen and Robert Clatworthy. Edited by Russell F. Schoengarth. Music by Frank Skinner. Title song by Victor Young and Sammy Cahn. Players: Rock Hudson (Mitch Wayne), Lauren Bacall (Lucy Hadley), Robert Stack (Kyle Hadley), Dorothy Malone (Marylee Hadley), Robert Keith (Jasper Hadley), Grant Williams (Biff Miley), Harry Shannon (Hoak Wayne).

One of the most arresting rediscoveries by the French "Cahiers du Cinéma" critics was Danish director Detlef Sierck who, after a Thirties career in Germany and France, moved to Hollywood in 1943 and, as Douglas Sirk, became the master of romantic melodrama. Where directors like Peter Godfrey (*The Woman in White*, 1948) and Mitchell Leisen (*Frenchman's Creek*, 1944; *Bride of Vengeance*, 1949) employed costume and historical backgrounds to tell stories of furious emotionalism, Sirk did so in the more complex field of contemporary melodrama. Only Alfred Lewin in *The Picture of Dorian Gray* (1944) and Gordon Wiles, Lewin's set-designer turned director, in *The Gangster* (1947) showed even comparable flair. But in *Lured* (1947), where London becomes a sinister backdrop to a girl's search for her friend, and *Thunder on the Hill* (1951), a convent murder mystery exploited for its Gothic horror and stylish visual opportunities, Sirk outclassed both.

Sirk's great days were the post-Cinemascope years at Universal, whose limited star roster and garish visual style he exploited superbly in a series of modern romances superior to those of 20th Century-Fox,

188

a specialist in this field. In *Imitation of Life* (1959), his last Hollywood film, and *Magnificent Obsession* (1954), both remakes of John Stahl Thirties successes, and in a sparse, almost Pabstian adaptation of William Faulkner's "Pylon," *Tarnished Angels* (1958), he showed contemporary existence in terms of the costume picture, grand gestures in modern dress hinting at the capacity for personality which even the least prepossessing exterior masks.

Written on the Wind, his most complex and extravagant work, exercised the Universal star stable in a story of superficial insipidity. Oil millionaire Kyle Hadley, apparently sterile, suspects boyhood friend Mitch Wayne of responsibility for the pregnancy of his wife Lucy, while bad sister Marylee tries to intrigue Mitch away from a chaste devotion to his friend's wife by encouraging the rumour. But played against a panorama of tireless oil wells, in a world of elegant, empty mansions or in the darkness among the derricks where car headlights glare into a meaningless sky, the story achieves the dignity of high drama. Leaves blow through a mansion's open door and skitter crisply across the tiled floor, a semi-nude Marylee dances narcissistically in a private act of drunken self-indulgence (Dorothy Malone earned an Oscar for her performance), idylls by the river make even so simple a ritual as the picnic into a sexual confrontation that leads to violent death. Sirk reworks the melodramatic tradition into something approaching the work of Sternberg and Murnau who pioneered this complex form.

COWBOY. Phoenix/Columbia. Produced by Julian Blaustein. Directed by Delmer Daves. Script by Edmund H. North based on Frank Harris' "My Life and Loves." Photographed by Charles Lawton Jr. Edited by William A. Lyon. Music by George Duning. Players: Glenn Ford (Tom Reece), Jack Lemmon (Frank Harris), Anna Kashfi (Maria Vidal), Brian Donlevy (Doc Bender), Dick York (Charlie), Victor Manuel Mendoza (Mendoza), Richard Jaeckel (Paul Curtis), King Donovan (Joe Capper), Vaughn Taylor (Mr. Fowler), Donald Randolph (Señor Vidal), James Westerfield (Mick Adams), Eugene Iglesias (Manuel Arriega).

Frank Harris' reminiscences of his experience as a cowboy in the early 1910s occupy only a few chapters of the huge and seldom extramural "My Life and Loves," but Delmer Daves, a master of frontier narrative (*Broken Arrow*, 1950; *The Last Wagon*, 1956; *3.10 to Yuma*, 1957), saw that they contained the elements of a satisfying if unconventional Western. (As early as 1949, John Huston had proposed to shoot the Harris story with Montgomery Clift and Walter Huston.) *Cowboy* is Daves' most assured film, mixing Edwardian elegance with Western adventure, superbly exploiting the American landscape. In roles offering few opportunities for their usual specialties, comedy and romance respectively, Jack Lemmon and Glenn Ford are convincing as Harris and Reece, callow

Glenn Ford takes a horse fall during the filming of *Cowboy.*

hotel clerk and reluctant trail-boss employer, who form a relationship that grows through the film to a mutual respect. Harris the womaniser, intellectual and social reformer has little place in Lemmon's conception of the man, whom he presents as a clever but starry-eyed youngster eager to please, prepared to help the hell-raising cattleman who runs short of money during an all-night poker game at the Chicago hotel where he is night clerk, but correspondingly stubborn at holding Reece to his agreement, made in the heat of fatigue and eagerness, to sell him a share in the herd and take him on the drive. Their argument in the stockyard at sunrise among lines of haystacks—Lawton's camerawork is memorably sharp—is the epitome of concise, exciting dialogue, Reece outlining the hard work he has put into his business and asking "Do you think you can just buy a part of that?", Harris countering hotly "I'm buying what you're prepared to sell," and the laconic Mendoza commenting "He is right. If he were not, you would have killed him by now." Such precision is typical of Edmund North's aphoristic and terse script: an employee characterises Reece as the kind of man who "if you asked him in the middle of a river for your money, he'd pay you off and he'd pay you in dry bills"; and when Harris, embittered over Reece's physical superiority and the hopelessness of his love for the Mexican girl, devotes himself to becoming more hard-bitten than the trail hands, Reece sums up the distinction between them as "You ain't got tough—you've just got miserable." *Cowboy* lacks stereotypes. Even the trail hands have idiosyncrasies that mark them as individuals, with Brian Donlevy's retired gunman the most real. In a few scenes the character is so indelibly impressed on the audience that his death in a meaningless argument at the hands of a former friend, even though it occurs off-screen, has remarkable poignancy. Such attention to detail marks *Cowboy* as one of Hollywood's most professionally made Western adventures.

1958

The lowest ebb in Hollywood history, when weekly admissions dropped to 39.6 million, the worst since records began in 1922. In September, traditionally the month in which new features went on the floor, only fifteen films were in production, less than half the number of 1957. Republic went out of business, Universal lost $861,247 in the thirty-nine weeks to August 2, and was bailed out of bankruptcy by the agenting and entrepreneurial Management Corporation of America—MCA—grown fat on production deals for independent producers and stars. MCA bought Universal from Decca and leased its studios back to it; in 1962, it acquired Decca as well. Harry Cohn's death during the production of *Bell, Book and Candle* contributed to the Columbia deficit, though its fortunes were partially revived by investment in the British-made *The Bridge on the River Kwai* (David Lean). Paramount, almost the sole company to show a profit, did so only because of a $10 million payment made by MCA on a $50 million purchase of seven hundred pre-1948 Paramount features for TV. MCA's rise typified the new trend in Hollywood, with power passing to artists from the hands of studio bosses. Almost unnoticed, producers Samuel Z. Arkoff and James H. Nicholson founded American-International, a small company whose economical methods of exploitation of the teenage audience with horror films and pop musicals were to make it one of the most successful of the Sixties.

BELL, BOOK AND CANDLE. Columbia. Produced by Julian Blaustein. Directed by Richard Quine. Script by Daniel Taradash from John Van Druten's play. Photographed by James Wong Howe. Edited by Charles Nelson. Art direction by Cary Odell. Music by George Duning. Players: James Stewart (Shepherd Henderson), Kim Novak (Gillian Holroyd), Jack Lemmon (Nicky Holroyd), Ernie Kovacs (Sidney Redlitch), Hermoine Gingold (Mrs. DePass), Elsa Lanchester (Queenie), Janice Rule (Merle Kitteridge), Philippe Clay (French Singer).

Talkative, and far from ideal as film subjects, John Van Druten's plays have seldom transferred well to the screen, an exception being Irving Rapper's 1947 version of *Voice of the Turtle* with a charming Eleanor Parker. Journeyman comedy director Quine does better, however, than one expects with this airy and amusing film, aided by James Wong Howe whose photography of New York locked in the blue gloom of winter and the idol-crammed interior of Gillian Holroyd's apartment makes *Bell, Book and Candle* a continuing delight to watch. Miss Novak is a modern witch, Jack Lemmon her impish brother, and Elsa Lanchester and Hermoine Gingold delightfully eccentric colleagues. When publisher Shepherd Henderson catches the eye of Gillian, he becomes enmeshed in their peculiar world, one in which writer Sidney Redlitch, then in Mexico, can be cajoled by magic into flying all night to turn up, hung-over and unshaven, in his office the next day with a bemused "'Mr. Henderson, I *think* I want to see you," or hexes can be set of his *fiancée* and phone, forcing him into countermagic and the choking down of a foul porridge-like concoction of Mrs. DePass to lift the spell.

Quine, a director whose early use of Miss Novak in *Pushover* (1954), when she was merely Harry Cohn's latest *protégée*, showed an understanding of her feline charm and cold sex appeal, employs her with care and skill as an unblinking iceberg able to chill the most insistent charmer but thawing with alarming swiftness under the touch of a man she loves. Driving Shep's *fiancée* into a hysterical state by playing on her fear of thunder storms—Quine uses trumpet duo Pete and Conte Candoli in the nightclub scene to create a shrieking version of "Stormy Weather"—or playing with her Siamese cat Piwacket as she conjures

The Bridge on the River Kwai. Sessue Hayakawa, Alec Guinness.

Bell, Book and Candle. Kim Novak.

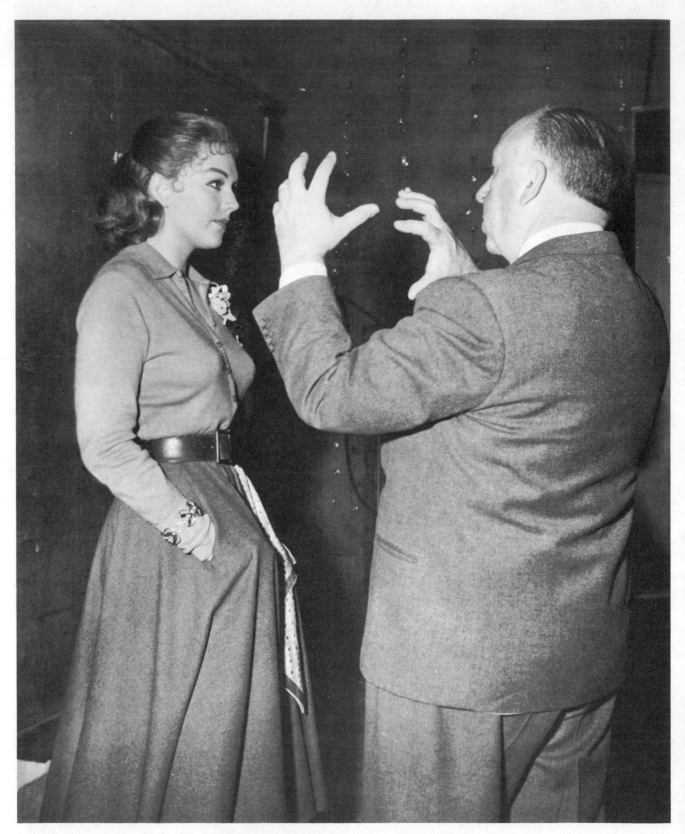

Directing *Vertigo*. Kim Novak and Alfred Hitchcock.

up a spell against her chosen victim, Kim Novak personifies something more than simply the character in Van Druten's intellectual spellbinder—a sex symbol whose sinuousness and almost masculine assertiveness made her more legitimate a figure of the spirit world than any ghost.

VERTIGO. Director: Alfred Hitchcock. Also released in 1958 was another film teaming James Stewart and Kim Novak, but one so different in its form and content as to provide a revealing contrast. The most silkily insistent of Alfred Hitchcock's modern thrillers, appearing to defy the rules of drama in its convoluted plot but actually manipulating the audience with insolent ease, *Vertigo* owes much of its personality to its detachment from Hollywood style and form. Based on a novel by Boileau and Narcejac, authors of *Les Diaboliques (The Fiends)*, Henri-Georges Clouzot's 1954 classic, and taking San Francisco, a city of recusant, almost European character as its setting, the film achieves a delicate, corrupt charm, accentuated by Kim Novak's precise performance in the difficult central role, where communication depends on her subtle evolution of personality. As the cop driven to nervous collapse by a fear of heights, and later haunted by a girl who changes his life, dies and appears again, James Stewart replaces his usual amiability with obsessional ruthlessness, pursuing the girl greedily through what appears a reliving of a dead past, and after her apparent death setting out to transform the new girl in whom he sees the image of a lost love. Hitchcock here examines the roots of his own personality, his fascination with cool, enigmatic blondes common to many of his films (*Marnie, The Birds, To Catch a Thief*), and his own religio-necrophilic interest in death and resurrection.

A precise contrast of tingling triangles and strings in Bernard Herrmann's score underlines a nervous visual style, where pastel exteriors softened by gauze into the texture of a dream alternate with the calmly factual: a forest of sequoias whose passive survival evokes the eternity of existence on which Stewart and Novak seem merely passing shadows; the luminous space of an art gallery where Novak sits contemplating an ancient portrait, seemingly of herself; harshly threatening scenes beneath the Golden Gate bridge where she attempts suicide. Hitchcock consistently disguises the underlying tensions of his work with a delight in the exercise of technique, simultaneously tracking away and zooming in to create a dizzying sense of falling, or manipulating his plot to reveal its twist in the middle yet still keep his audience's attention. It is the unique insight into personality, however, that draws us back again and again to this cryptic work.

1959

The problem of "runaways" dominated studio discussion and was to do so for five years. In silent days, film-making had been a mobile activity. Most Hollywood companies owned studios on both the East and West coasts, and regularly sent units to other countries for big-budget films. Many had financial interests in German, Italian, French or British film concerns. But the coming of sound impeded, then halted this process almost entirely, as producers found that only an established home studio with a nucleus of contract technicians and stars guaranteed the continuity of style and high technical quality audiences demanded. As late as 1927, King Vidor shot *The New Klondike* in Miami, working from a hired bungalow and recording the details of a land boom as it occurred around him, but shortly after, the famous Laemmle dictum "A rock is a rock; a tree is a tree—shoot it in Griffith Park"* became Hollywood policy. Improvements in set design, back projection and process work, allowing the smooth integration of stock footage into studio films, and the invention of effective fog machines and studio tanks made it unnecessary for a crew to leave Hollywood even for the most lavish adventure story.

This situation persisted into the Fifties, and even in 1955 overseas location work could be sufficiently rare for M-G-M to advertise *Bedevilled* (Mitchell Leisen) as "the first film ever made on location in Paris." But studios with "blocked funds" in Britain and British Commonwealth countries, accumulated under laws demanding that a proportion of revenue earned from film distribution must be spent in the country in which it was made, had already instigated production in Britain, and in 1951 20th Century-Fox sent Lewis Milestone to Australia to make *Kangaroo*

---

* An area of natural terrain outside Los Angeles commonly used by low-budget producers to stand in for most landscapes.

(1952). Independents Stanley Kramer (*On the Beach*, 1959) and Fred Zinnemann (*The Sundowners*, 1960) followed. With unreal U.S. tax laws, high salaries and the unions' restrictive practices making Hollywood increasingly unattractive as a film-making centre, more studios sent units overseas, particularly for epics demanding unusual backgrounds. Samuel Bronston, a minor Hollywood producer of the Forties, built a huge studio near Madrid and offered Hollywood producers cheap labour, ample working space and reliable weather in return for shares in the films made there. Dino De Laurentiis in Rome's Cinecittà studios and many of Yugoslavia's autonomous regional film industries followed suit. When *Ben Hur* (William Wyler), an epic made on location in Rome by M-G-M, took eleven Oscars in 1960 and returned its costs in one year, the studios felt they had discovered the elusive grail of profit snatched from them by the 1948 consent decrees. Of the one hundred and twelve foreign-made features released in the US in 1961, fifty eight were Hollywood-financed, and by 1962, 30% of Hollywood film production was going on in other countries.

NORTH BY NORTHWEST. M-G-M. Produced and directed by Alfred Hitchcock. Script by Ernest Lehman. Photographed by Robert Burks. Art direction by William H. Horning and Merrill Pye. Production designed by Robert Boyle. Music by Bernard Herrmann. Edited by George Tomasini. Titles by Saul Bass. Players: Cary Grant (Roger Thornhill), Eva Marie Saint (Eve Kendall), James Mason (Philip Vandamm), Jessie Royce Landis (Mrs. Thornhill), Leo G. Carroll (Professor), Philip Ober (Townsend), Josephine Hutchinson (Housekeeper), Martin Landau (Leonard), Adam Williams (Valerian), Edward Platt, Robert Ellenstein, Lee Tremayne, Philip Coolidge, Patrick McVey, Edward Binns, Ken Lynch.

Advertisement for *Bedevilled.*

Alfred Hitchcock addicts respect this film as his most skilful, a tribute as much to Ernest Lehman's crisp original screenplay as to Hitch's mastery of suspense. Lehman has incorporated all the characteristic Hitchcock obsessions—the cool blonde heroine of suspect allegiances and frank sexuality, the eccentrically plausible plot that sacrifices logic for surprise, the climax (in this case on Mt. Rushmore Memorial) that combines tension with fantasy—without sacrificing the central narrative core. Hitchcock recalls that the film grew out of his collaboration with Lehman on an abortive version of Hammond Innes' '"The Wreck of the Mary Deare" (eventually filmed in 1959 by Michael Anderson) and took a year to write, after a New York journalist had suggested the basic plot of an innocent businessman being mistaken for a spy, an idea Hitchcock further tested by making the spy an illusory one created by spy-master Leo G. Carroll

William Wyler lines up a shot on the 70mm camera for *Ben Hur.*

to trap James Mason's Vandamm, an art dealer selling secrets to the enemy.

The revelation that Kaplan, the spy for whom advertising executive Roger Thornhill is mistaken, does not exist instigates a series of prestidigitations: the girl who accosts him on the train is not what she seems; the suave Vandamm, who greets Thornhill's protestations of innocence with a weary "Games, Mr. Kaplan? Must we?", is more brutal than anybody is aware; and in Hitchcock's most astonishing *coup de théâtre,* a rendezvous to meet on a flat plain outside Chicago is inverted when a crop-spraying plane turns on him with machine guns. Even in details, the ele-ment of sudden surprise is cunningly exploited by Lehman. Someone notices the monogram "ROT" on Thornhill's match-books. "What does the O stand for?". "Nothing," he says blithely.

Hitchcock's films have a unique durability; even when one has seen them a dozen times, a residual tension and surprise remain in the subliminal relationships between individuals, and between characters and setting. Vandamm's obviously homosexual relationship to his waspish, jealous secretary Leonard, and the mutual need that unites Thornhill and Eve, outlined tersely in a meeting in a forest grove, provide unique sexual electricity. The climax as the fugitives

Ben Hur. Charlton Heston.

Ava Gardner in one of the runaway productions that earned union enmity. *On the Beach*.

clamber over the Rushmore faces is an enduring parody of patriotism, as the early scenes at the United Nations building mock the concept of international amity, and one regrets Hitchcock was not allowed, as he wished, to have Thornhill, hiding in Lincoln's nose, stifle the impulse to sneeze. Never frivolous without meaning, Hitchcock has given *North by Northwest* an intriguing moral undercurrent, unfortunately not sustained by the many films of the Sixties seeking to achieve a similar weighted suspense.

ON THE BEACH. Director: Stanley Kramer. This story of atomic war and its aftermath was one of the most historic runaway productions, made in Australia with an international crew (appropriate since the novel's original author Nevil Shute was Australian) and designed to express a universal moral. Set in 1964, it shows Australia as the last continent uninfected by radioactivity from a war that has destroyed the big powers. Those lucky enough to have fled there, including US submarine commander Gregory Peck and his crew, listen in horror as the radio emissions are snuffed out. The submarine explores the dead cities of America's West Coast in search of a phantom radio transmission, only to discover its source as the random tapping of a morse key by a bottle caught in a window blind. Back in Australia, people prepare for the end. Old friends draw closer together, new ones—sub. commander Towers and his cynical lover Moira Davidson (Ava Gardner)—are haunted by the hopelessness of their lives. As radiation sickness shows that the tide has reached even this last outpost, death pills are handed out at street-corners, and the Americans decide on death in familiar surroundings, taking their craft back to the US. From a headland Moira watches it go, alone on the last beach. Soon all are dead. Papers blow in the empty streets, a brutal statue of "War, the Destroying Warrior" spreads a bronze cloak over the city, and the wind flaps a revivalist's banner with its prophetic legend "There Is Still Time."

1960

The events of 1960 both crystallised the Fifties' changes in Hollywood's structure and keynoted the alterations to come. Continuing the trend towards diversification, M-G-M went into the hotel business and acquired Verve Records, United Artists bought the Ziv company which specialised in distributing features for TV, and most major studios embarked on TV series, often in hired studios, their own having been sold for real estate development or oil drilling. The runaway and foreign film issues remained sources of friction between independent stars and producers and the studios that still adhered to traditional working methods. Facing growing unemployment and refusing to vary their strict rules that demanded large crews even for productons that neither needed nor could afford them, the unions threatened to picket theatres showing runaway productions, beginning with the films of Ava Gardner, whose career had blossomed anew in Italy and Britain. As admissions wavered back to 43½ million, the 1923 figure, Hollywood seemed ill-placed to take any such stand on principle.

The decline in standards was dramatised in two strikes that paralysed the industry in the first half of 1960. In the preceding five years of shrinking returns, Hollywood had solved its problems in the short term by squandering its resources. Feature libraries were sold cheap for ready cash, and costs curtailed by failing to renew the contracts of artists and technicians who constituted the reservoir of talent on which studios depended. In 1945, studios had 490 screenwriters under contract; in 1950, the figure had shrunk to sixty-seven and in 1960 to forty-eight. All studios had also dropped their talent training programmes and restricted new acting contracts to low-cost stars who had made a small reputation in TV, performers to whom they expected to offer less money and fewer benefits than at any other time in the industry's history. To stop the rot, on January 15 the Screen Section of the Writers' Guild of America went on strike for fairer contracts, greater tenure and a share of TV revenue from films written by its members. The strike lasted twenty weeks, and was later joined by most Hollywood unions. On March 7 the Screen Actors' Guild struck for a raise in minimum salary, pension, health and welfare provisions, and a more equitable share of residuals from TV; the IATSE and Directors' Guild soon followed. All those striking gained from the action, most notably the actors who received raises in salary of between 11% and 81%, but the move, by raising already crushing overheads, merely made Hollywood even less viable an industrial complex than before.

1960's most bizarre technical innovation was Smello-vision, developed from the Aromarama technique of Charles Weiss. *Scent of Mystery* (Jack Cardiff) was accompanied by a "programme" of odours fed into the theatre air-conditioning. To nobody's surprise, scents varied in strength and timing from threatre to theatre, or blended with the preceding selection to create some appalling effects. The process, in the words of its backer Mike Todd Jr., was "almost instantaneously rejected by the public," and *Scent of Mystery*, retitled *Holiday in Spain*, went out *sans* smells to unsuccessful general release.

THE RISE AND FALL OF LEGS DIAMOND. Warner-Pathé. Produced by Milton Sperling. Associate Producer: Leon Chooluck. Directed by Budd Boetticher. Script by Joseph Landon. Photographed by Lucien Ballard. Art direction by Jack Poplin. Edited by Folmar Blangsted. Music by Leonard Rosenman. Players: Ray Danton ("Legs" Diamond), Karen Steele (Alice Shiffer), Elaine Stewart (Monica), Jesse White (Leo), Simon Oakland (Lt. Moody), Robert Lowery (Arnold Rothstein), Judson Pratt ("Fats"), Warren Oates (Eddie Diamond), Frank de Kova

(Bodyguard), Gordon Jones (Sgt. Cassidy).

Few directors did more than Budd Boetticher to establish a new dignity for the B-film in a Hollywood determined to exploit the form for its violence and superficial action without taking note of its value as a vehicle for comment on urban life, a role it played with distinction throughout the Forties and Fifties. A former bullfighter whose film career was built on harsh Westerns reminiscent of Ince, notably *Seven Men from Now* (1956), *The Tall T* (1957), *Buchanan Rides Alone* (1958), and *Ride Lonesome* (1959), made for the Ranown company formed by Randolph Scott and producer/writer Harry Joe Brown, Boetticher found work scarce in the Sixties when producers were seldom prepared to instil into gangster, war or Western films the extra dimension he regarded as essential. *Legs Diamond*, his last major work, stands out strikingly among a horde of meagre gangster films for its original view of an unconventional character and Boetticher's imaginative use of the B-film's restrictions—cheap interior sets, often weak supporting cast, the necessity for non-stop action and simple dialogue.

The career of Ray Danton's "Legs" coincides only occasionally with that of the real criminal, but Boetticher uses a few known facts about the man—his background as a dancer; an almost paranoid belief, based on early recoveries from gunshot wounds, that he could not be killed; his one original contribution to criminal activity, the idea of robbing only other criminals who are thus prevented from calling the police—to build the portrait of a wisecracking smart operator whose physical agility is rivalled by a remarkable mobility in rising to the top of the criminal tree. Popping out of dumb-waiters or off fire-escapes, casually dropping hand-grenades at the feet of relaxed bodyguards, bursting from cover with pistols in each fist to expunge a pair of rivals, he is too elusive a ghost even for the suave Arnold Rothstein, on whose staff he makes his greatest advances. In all these exploits, Diamond is sustained by a belief in his own indestructability, but as he sheds encumbrances like a tubercular brother and a Rothstein mistress who has helped him, one sees the price of this confidence, a total emotional self-containment that echoes his economy of physical movement. His embittered wife realises the truth when "Legs," frozen out of the rackets by a new well-organised Mafia machine, tries to dispose of her to be totally independent; his invulnerability lay not in confidence but in the belief of others in his unique personality. "As long as one person in the world loved you, you were safe. That was the magic . . . You can't be killed; you're as good as dead now." Later, over his corpse, she delivers a harsh valedictory. "A lot of people loved my husband but he never loved anybody. That's why he died."

THE MAGNIFICENT SEVEN. Mirisch Brothers/United Artists. Produced and directed by John Sturges. Script by William Roberts based on "Seven

The Rise and Fall of Legs Diamond. Ray Danton.

Samurai," directed by Akira Kurosawa (script by Shinobu Hashimoto, Hideo Oguni and Kurosawa). Photographed by Charles Lang Jr. Art direction by Edward Fitzgerald. Music by Elmer Bernstein. Edited by Ferris Webster. Players: Yul Brynner (Chris), Eli Wallach (Calvera), Steve McQueen (Vin), Horst Buchholz (Chico), Charles Bronson (Bernardo O'Reilly), Robert Vaughn (Lee), Brad Dexter (Harry), James Coburn (Britt), Vladimir Sokoloff (Old Man), Rosenda Monteros (Petra), Jorge Martinez de Hoyos (Hilario), John Alonzo (Miguel), Alex Montoya (Sotero).

Even in the confusion of the early Sixties, it is unlikely that any Hollywood studio would have financed a Western adaptation of Akira Kurosawa's medieval war drama *Seven Samurai (Shichinin no Samurai)* to be made by a relatively routine craftsman with a cast of character actors lacking even a moderately big star, and it was from the independent Mirisch brothers that John Sturges and Yul Brynner finally found support for what became one of the Sixties most important Westerns. A modest $2½ million success in the US, it grossed $9 million world-wide, sparking European interest and a revival of action film-making in many countries on the continent.

In his Hawksian script, William Roberts retains much of the Japanese original, including most of the characters and incidents. The seven become out-of-

The Magnificent Seven.

work gunmen and fugitives in a border town and their task the protection of a Mexican village from a bandit gang led by the gold-toothed Calvera. Their reasons for taking the job are developed with the relaxed detail typical of an American cinema in which the two-hour film had become the norm. Chris, the leader, is moved by the villagers' offer of everything they have—"I've been offered a great deal before, but never everything." Vin restlessly seeks activity and employment; tyro Chico the prestige of riding with professionals; Harry a chance at the riches which, despite Chris' denials, he continues to believe are their motive for taking so arid a commission. Fugitive gunman Lee needs asylum and an escape from his failing ability; and the cool Britt an opportunity to test his skill to its limit. Only Bernardo, half-Indian and a wanderer, sympathises with and understands the people they are to defend. Even Calvera resembles the Seven more than he does the villagers on whom both sides prey. "If God had not wanted them shorn," he reasons to Chris, "he would not have made them

sheep," and when Chris kills him during the final battle he dies without comprehension. "'But why? A man like you . . . why?''

Sturges charts in detail the tentative integration of gunmen and peasants, and the settling down of seven egotistical specialists into a functioning force. The battles, when they come, are as concisely managed as a ballet: peasants springing from the brush to cut down galloping bandits; Lee, after waiting numb with terror, his face pressed against the stone wall, leaping into a room crowded with the enemy and shooting them all in a motion as superbly choreographed as any dance routine. The dialogue has a laconic humour not present in the original. As Britt's long-distance pistol shot brings down a fleeing rider, Chico praises his aim. "'That was the best shot I ever saw!'' The older man sheathes his pistol, disgusted. "It was the *worst* shot. I aimed for the horse." Elsewhere Vin comments, "I've been in towns where the girls weren't very pretty, and I've been in towns where the girls were downright ugly, but I've never been in a town where there were no girls at all." Chico solves the mystery when he finds Petra hiding with other young women in the woods. "Their fathers told them we would rape them," he says angrily as he dumps his sample in the dust. "Well, so we might have," Chris says evenly, "but they could have given us the benefit of the doubt." The blend of glamorously amoral specialists, stylish violence and a Mexican background intrigued the world's film-makers. Sensing a trend already started in Germany, where some Westerns had been made on location in Yugoslavia with expatriate American and British stars, Italian directors Sergio Leone and Duccio Tessari interested waning TV actor Clint Eastwood in a Western based on Kurosawa's *Yojimbo,* to be called *A Fistful of Dollars (Per un Pugno di Dollari,* 1964). The bloody school of "spaghetti Westerns" followed, coming full circle when Ted Post made *Hang 'Em High* (1968) with Eastwood as bounty hunter and Pat Hingle as hanging judge, a Hollywood film that in its violence imitated the Leone/Tessari/Corbucci product of Italy.

1961

Higher costs accelerated rationalisation. With its Screen Gems TV subsidiary booming, Columbia sold its Sunset Boulevard studio and relied on leased space elsewhere. As admissions hovered at 41 million, distributors convinced airlines that films could entertain bored passengers, and in-flight movies began. Still hoping to stem the runaways, the MPAA held a conference at which possible remedies were mooted, ranging from the Screen Actors' Guild's suggestion of all-out war to a counsel of caution from the MPAA, which foresaw the risks of too-strict condemnation. Significantly, the one organisation not present at the conference was the agents' union, the Artists' Managers' Guild, whose members were mainly responsible for the runaway trend. Not surprisingly, the meeting brought no major changes, though tax laws were changed later in the Sixties to close some loopholes.

The MPAA advised restraint on the runaway issue, recognising that to endorse recommendations with no chance of implementation would impair further its credibility as the official voice of Hollywood, already damaged by a decision to accept the cinema's new sexual sophistication. The 1956 Preminger case had proved that a Production Code ban had no real force, and the MPAA now chose to recognise officially the standing of films like Louis Malle's *The Lovers* (*Les Amants*), then the subject of litigation in many states (and immense public interest in the rest) over its alleged obscenity, by interpreting the Code's "Sexual perversion or any inference of it is forbidden" as "a recommendation that producers should use care, discretion and restraint," a ruling that totally compromised the basis of self-censorship and paved the way for its demise in 1968.

LOVER COME BACK. Universal-International. Produced by Stanley Shapiro and Martin Melcher. Directed by Delbert Mann. Script by Stanley Shapiro and Paul Henning. Photographed by Arthur E. Arling. Art direction by Alexander Golitzen and Robert Clatworthy. Edited by Marjorie Fowler. Music by Frank DeVol. With: Rock Hudson (Jerry Webster), Doris Day (Carol Templeton), Tony Randall (Peter Ram-

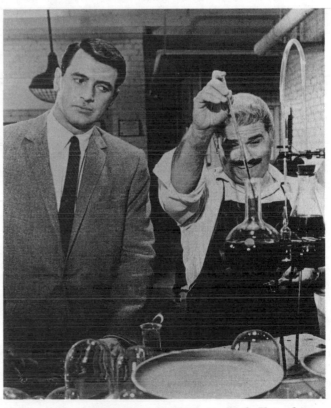

Lover Come Back. Rock Hudson, Jack Kruschen.

sey), Edie Adams (Rebel Davis), Jack Oakie (J. Paxton Miller), Jack Kruschen (Dr. Linus Tyler), Ann B. Davis (Millie), Joe Flynn (Hadley), Karen Norris (Kelly), Jack Albertson (Fred), Charles Watts (Charlie), Donna Douglas (Deborah), Ward Ramsey (Hodges).

Universal-International's production *Wunderkind* Ross Hunter, single-handedly responsible for the company's survival in the Sixties slump, exploited the fact that audiences like what they know by casting ageing Forties stars, notably Lana Turner and Susan Hayward, in remakes of sentimental Thirties classics like *Back Street* (John Stahl, 1932; Robert Stevenson, 1941; David Miller, 1961), *Imitation of Life* (John Stahl, 1934; Douglas Sirk, 1959) and *Madame X* (Lionel Barrymore, 1929; Sam Wood, 1937; David Lowell Rich, 1965), and with a successful comedy cycle starring Rock Hudson and Doris Day. *Pillow Talk* (Michael Gordon, 1958) established the pattern of brisk, assertive career woman Day matching wits with professional competitor Hudson who is also an infamous rake, and besting him before collapsing gratefully into his arms. The success of *Pillow Talk* and its progeny depended on Miss Day's aggressive girlishness, all smart suits and no-nonsense pillbox hats, and Hudson's arrogant *bonhomie* disguising a petulant, almost childish vulnerability; with a comedy stylist like Cary Grant in a Hudson role (e.g. *That Touch of Mink,* Delbert Mann, 1962) the situation became totally implausible.

Lover Come Back—by then Miss Day's husband Marty Melcher had taken over production—has the series' sharpest script and playing. Day and Hudson are rival advertising executives, she resenting the fact that he gets business by holding orgies for visiting clients and bribes accomplices to cover up when his practices are investigated. Hudson's Webster gets caught in his own ingenuity when fake commercials shot to bribe showgirl Rebel Davis are broadcast at the order of his firm's ineffectual owner Peter Ramsey. A national clamour rises for "VIP," the non-existent product advertised, and eccentric chemist Linus Tyler is hired to provide one. He concocts a sweet that turns to pure alcohol in the blood. "Just what this country has always needed," he trumpets as the Advertising Council munches itself insensible, "a good ten-cent drunk." The parody of Madison Avenue idiocy, though amusingly presented in a party scene where executives wield their charm while, in the foreground, large fish gobble smaller ones in an ornamental aquarium, proves less durable than the three-cornered relationship between Hudson, Day and Randall, the last playing the stock figure of Hudson's confidant and stooge which Gig Young executed superbly in most of the series. Randall leads a supporting cast of more than usual strength: Jack Kruschen as the wild-eyed scientist whose laboratory periodically explodes, always with smoke of a different colour which Ramsey, entering the door, receives full in the face; Edie Adams' deep-south dumb showgirl with bra

made from a Confederate flag; and veteran comic Jack Oakie in the minor role of a tycoon victim of the agency's H-bomb hospitality. Carol Templeton finds him alone in his suite at daybreak, draped with ladies' underwear and plucking dreamily at the strings of an abandoned bass fiddle, the case of which contains a semi-naked and unconscious girl. When she proffers her designs, he waves them languidly away. "I've seen *everything*," he says, with the tone of one who has glimpsed paradise.

ONE EYED JACKS. Pennebaker/Paramount. Executive producers: George Glass and Walter Seltzer. Produced by Frank P. Rosenberg. Associate producer: Carlo Fiore. Directed by Marlon Brando. Script by Guy Trosper and Calder Willingham from "The Authentic Death of Hendry Jones" by Charles Neidler. Photographed by Charles Lang Jnr. Art direction by Hal Pereira and J. McMillan Johnson. Edited by Archie Marshek. Costumes by Yvonne Wood. Music by Hugo Friedhofer. Players: Marlon Brando (Rio), Karl Malden (Dad Longworth), Piña Pellicer (Louisa), Katy Jurado (Maria), Ben Johnson (Bob Emery), Slim Pickens (Lon), Larry Duran (Modesto), Sam Gilman (Harvey), Timothy Carey (Howard Tetley), Miriam Colon (Redhead), Elisha Cook (Bank Teller), Rodolfo Acosta (Rurales Leader), Ray Teal (Bartender), John Dierkes (Bearded Townsman), Hank Worden (Doc).

Marlon Brando bought the rights to the novel of *One Eyed Jacks* in 1957 and tried for three years to set up a production. When the package was organised, with Stanley Kubrick as director and Brando deferring his salary in exchange for a substantial slice of the film's profits and rights to the negative after a certain period, friction between director and star caused Kubrick to resign, after which Brando, with no previous directing experience, decided to direct the film himself. Its problems remain a Hollywood legend. Brando kept the crew waiting on Monterey, California, locations for days, at $50,000 a day, through his insistence that waves in a sequence satisfy his requirements; he also encouraged his supporting cast, many of them from John Ford's strictly-disciplined "stock company," to improvise their dialogue and action, and even offered rewards of $200 from his own pocket for the extra who produced the most believable reactions. *One Eyed Jacks* ran disastrously into the red and even though its popularity has grown in the intervening years, put an end to Brando's directorial ambitions.

The film remains one of Hollywood's most memorable Westerns, Brando showing substantial ability as a film-maker in a story more pedestrian directors would have made merely routine. Aided by cameraman Charles Lang Jr., whose use of the VistaVision process allows Brando to create dazzling landscape-poems and light effects never bettered even in the best of Hollywood's outdoor films, the film is a unique visual experience (it was also the last VistaVision film,

One-Eyed Jacks. Marlon Brando (director and star).

Paramount shortly afterwards abandoning the difficult and expensive process). As Rio, abandoned on a hilltop after a bank raid by his friend Dad Longworth, searches America for his mentor and enemy, only to find him settled as sheriff of a sleepy seaside town, Lang and Brando catch the beauty of America's most spectacular scenery. Dust streams from treeless hills while Rio shoots it out with the *rurales;* lines of white foam march towards a rocky shore as he broods in the salt wind, recuperating from the mutilation Dad has inflicted; the light as he seduces Longworth's step-daughter on the beach at dawn is tinged with copper, making their figures as inflexible as hammered metal. Although Brando's obsession with mutilation has ample rein in *One Eyed Jacks,* his exploration of Oedipan conflicts, suppressed homosexuality and the complexities of the familial relationship justify even the brutal flogging sequence. Few Westerns have realised so successfully the potential for psychological and psychosexual comment that exists in this most powerful of American art forms.

1962

Among the studios—20th. Century-Fox, Paramount and M-G-M—that had chosen to concentrate on big-budget production overseas rather than diversify into TV, the balance sheets proved alarming reading. After a long and disastrous location visit to Tahiti during which the original director Carol Reed resigned and costs spiralled to unanticipated heights, M-G-M's ambitious remake of *Mutiny on the Bounty* (Lewis Milestone) with Marlon Brando received lukewarm reviews. The company's earnings dropped to $2½ million, compared with $12½ million in 1961, and during the year it released only twelve features; at one point in 1962, for the first time since its foundation, M-G-M had no feature in production at its studios. Gambling on the epic trend, even then faltering, Paramount signed with Samuel Bronston for the films that were to be released as *Circus World* (also known as *The Magnificent Showman;* Henry Hathaway, 1964) and *The Fall of the Roman Empire* (Anthony Mann, 1964). The first ran into production problems, director Frank Capra being replaced, and neither made much money, the result partly of Bronston's terms, which demanded half the production cost in return for Eastern hemisphere distribution rights only.

Hardest hit in the epics slump was 20th. Century-Fox which, mostly as a result of enormous expenses on *Cleopatra* (see 1963), showed a loss of $16.8 million for the thirty-nine weeks to September, 1962. The previous year it had lost $11 million for the same period. Seeing his heavy investment in the company threatened, Darryl F. Zanuck stepped in and took the presidency from Skouras, who was elevated to Chairman of the Board and then forced to resign. The Skouras-appointed Chairman Judge Samuel Rosenmann, Head of Production Peter Levathes, the head of Fox Movietone, the Chief of Sales and many moribund chiefs of foreign subsidiaries were also ejected, and most remaining executives had their salaries cut

by half. Zanuck closed the studios, but reopened them shortly afterwards with much reduced staff and his son Richard, already a producer of proven skill, in charge. A year later, Fox showed a profit of $14.7 million and was again one of Hollywood's most solvent companies.

HOW THE WEST WAS WON. Cinerama/Metro-Goldwyn-Mayer. Produced by Bernard Smith. Directed by John Ford (*The Civil War*), George Marshall (*The Railroad*), Henry Hathaway (*The Rivers, The Plains, the Outlaws*). Script by James R. Webb, suggested by a series in "Life" magazine. Photographed by William Daniels, Milton Krasner, Charles Lang Jr., Joseph La Shelle. Art direction by George W. Davis, William Farrari and Addison Hehr. Set decorations by Henry Grace and Don Greenwood Jr. Edited by Harold F. Kress. Music by Alfred Newman. Players: Carroll Baker (Eve Prescott), Lee J. Cobb (Marshall), Henry Fonda (Jethro Stuart), Carolyn Jones (Julie Rawlings), Karl Malden (Zebulon Prescott), Gregory Peck (Cleve Van Valen), George Peppard (Zeb Rawlings), Robert Preston (Roger Morgan), Debbie Reynolds (Lilith Prescott), James Stewart (Linus Rawlings), Eli Wallach (Charlie Gant), John Wayne (General Sherman), Richard Widmark (Mike King), Brigid Bazlen (Dora), Walter Brennan (Colonel Hawkins), David Brian (Attorney), Andy Devine (Peterson), Raymond Massey (Abraham Lincoln), Agnes Moorehead (Rebecca Prescott), Harry Morgan (General Grant), Thelma Ritter (Agatha Clegg), Mickey Shaughnessy (Deputy), Russ Tamblyn (Rebel Soldier). Narrated by Spencer Tracy.

The metamorphosis of the Hollywood Western evident in the development from *The Magnificent Seven* to *One Eyed Jacks* to *How the West Was Won* shows in microcosm the inflation and consequent destruction

Rome re-created near Madrid by Veniero Colasanti and John Moore for *The Fall of the Roman Empire* (Anthony Mann, 1964), produced by Samuel Bronston.

Colasanti and Moore: sets for *55 Days at Peking* (rear).

of forms that was typical of Hollywood in the Sixties. Intended as the second and most ambitious use of Cinerama to tell a story—its first story film, *The Wonderful World of the Brothers Grimm* (Henry Levin, George Pal, 1962) was actually released after—*How the West Was Won* offered nothing new either in content or style, using traditional Western talents in an anthology of tried plots. Those involved in the film soon became impatient with the restrictions of Cinerama, with its 146° horizontal plane of action and the complicated three-film process which dictated two shimmering vertical areas where sections joined. Shooting was further impeded by the bulky eight hundred pound camera that allowed as little movement as had the enclosed cameras of the early sound era. Henry Hathaway shot much of his material on an effects stage in Hollywood—none of his principals came anywhere near the rapids in which the river sequences were shot—and even found a way to employ back-projection by shooting backgrounds in 70mm and splitting the negative into three. Such technical short-cuts and the annoyance directors felt at the unwieldy system spelt the end of Cinerama, and its next story effort, Stanley Kramer's *It's a Mad, Mad, Mad, Mad World* (1963) was, like all subsequent Cinerama films, shot in 70mm Cinemascope (Super or Ultra-Panavision), a process that reduced the horizontal plane to 120° but solved many problems.

James R. Webb's script makes a brave attempt to encompass the sweep of Western expansion which the original series of "Life" magazine articles conveyed in well-matched illustrations and text unhampered by the necessity to tell a dramatic story. With only a little distortion, Webb is able to cover the West's history in the life of one woman. Lilith Prescott, first seen as youngest daughter of a family going West, then as a St. Louis dance-hall girl becoming involved in the wagon trains' Westward journeys and the California gold rush, participates in the Civil War by proxy when her nephew and brother-in-law fight at Shiloh, and reappears in the aftermath to counsel her ageing nephew when, as a lawman, he disposes of the last outlaws, clearing the way for peaceful expansion. Despite some attractive landscapes, *How the West Was Won* makes little use of Cinerama to evoke America's vastness, its focus shrinking to the trivialities of personal melodrama and romance. As mountain man Linus Rawlings, James Stewart gives the greatest sense of backwoods relaxation in Hathaway's episode *The Rivers,* paddling phlegmatically along the muddy Ohio, falling for the bland Eve Prescott when he meets the family during its trip West, and saving them from river pirates after he himself has been stabbed and left for dead, the result of having gone with a seductive accomplice to see "the varmint" allegedly penned up in a cave. Stewart's loose walk and homely features fit comfortably into the pattern of a frontier society in a way that the Prescotts never do.

George Marshall's superficial depiction of railroad building, with hard-driving rail boss opposed by ideal-istic cavalry lieutenant, is perfunctory, and the film's best section remains John Ford's *The Civil War.* Beginning with an evocative Fordian tableau of Lincoln with his back to the camera, half-silhouetted in the effect Ford often used to connote approaching death, he shows the Civil War with characteristic humanity. Rawlings enthusiastically leaves the home farm, trusty dog following after him as he disappears down the sun-dappled road, watched by his mother as she leans wearily on the rails of the family graveyard, and is not seen again until, a bloodied smoke-stained survivor, he wanders among the corpses of Shiloh and drinks from a river red with blood. Lines of silent men shovel earth into mass graves, dust rising in another Fordian evocation of the Biblical "dust to dust"; a surgeon operates in a primitive theatre, water sluicing blood from the table before another patient is dumped down; and Sherman and Grant are dragged from the eminence of command to become unshaven and exhausted men. For all his proselytising, Ford has few equals in getting under the skin of history, and it is his contribution that gives *How the West Was Won* more than associational value as the most ambitious exercise of a doomed technical process.

THE MANCHURIAN CANDIDATE. United Artists. Produced by John Frankenheimer and George Axelrod. Associate producer: Joseph Behm. Directed by John Frankenheimer. Script by George Axelrod from Richard Condon's novel. Photographed by Lionel Lindon. Production designed by Richard Sylbert. Music by David Amram. Edited by Ferris Webster. Players: Frank Sinatra (Bennett Marco), Laurence Harvey (Raymond Shaw), Janet Leigh (Rosie), Angela Lansbury (Raymond's Mother), Henry Silva (Chunjin), James Gregory (Senator John Iselin), Leslie Parrish (Jocie Jordan), John McGiver (Senator Thomas Jordan), Khigh Dhiegh (Yen Lo), James Edwards (Cpl. Melvin), Douglas Henderson (Colonel), Albert Paulsen (Zilkov), Barry Kelley (Secretary of Defence), Lloyd Corrigan (Holborn Gaines), Madame Spivy (Berezova—Lady Counterpart):

John Frankenheimer's contribution to the revitalisation of Hollywood cinema in the Sixties can scarcely be underestimated. As the hedge of technical expertise behind which Hollywood had hidden for decades crumbled under the impact of the *nouvelle vague* and shock of new modes and ideas, Frankenheimer, a graduate of live TV, established himself as the most adventurous of the new arrivals, combining New York energy and Hollywood professionalism to create the first viable synthesis of the two. Although his setting is Washington and New York, his collaborators East Coast men—ex-pulp novelist and playwright Axelrod, jazz musician and French horn virtuoso Amram—his stars are Hollywood regulars from whom he extracts telling performances.

Science fiction and documentary blend in Condon's story of a priggish mother-fixated young aristocrat who, kidnapped with his platoon in Korea and brainwashed by a beaming Chinese mind-manipulator, is returned to Washington political circles programmed to assassinate a Presidential candidate, allowing another agent, his brainless stepfather, to gain power. Although, as inquisitor Yen Lo says with satisfaction, the minds of the platoon "have not merely been washed, but dry-cleaned," a recurring dream draws the attention of one member, Bennett Marco, to the truth.

Avoiding the surrealism of the Hitchcock's *Spellbound* to show a mind in distress, Frankenheimer evokes the horror of this situation by dramatising the increasingly restrictive technological jungle in which we live; reducing the platoon to robots is, he suggests, not much worse than the controls to which we daily submit. TV monitors reflect Iselin as a grainy parody when he rises in a Congressional hearing to reveal yet another nest of Communists in the Civil Service, and the final dramatic shooting is seen through the telescopic sights of a rifle as Shaw crouches in a booth hung high over Madison Square Garden's stage. Photo-

graphs flash on a screen as soldiers identify the men who brainwashed them, and a vital meeting, that between Marco and Rosie, the girl whose appearance saves him from suicide, takes place in the vibrating corridor of an express train. Even the comic aspects of Shaw's conditioning—when the key phrase is accidentally spoken in a bar, followed by a suggestion that he "jump in the lake," he obligingly does so—become horrible through the calm logic of their execution, as in the murder of a political commentator in a feathered bedjacket belonging to his wife, and that of Senator Jordan as he pours a midnight glass of milk, the carton punctured by the bullet so that milk streams out blood-like as he collapses. But Frankenheimer's humour is sardonic, and the result a mirthless picture of what technology may do to the man whose spirit cannot withstand its power.

THE HUSTLER. Director: Robert Rossen. Another scenarist of the Forties doomed, one would have thought, like Richard Brooks, to a death by profitabil-

The Manchurian Candidate. Laurence Harvey, Angela Lansbury, James Gregory.

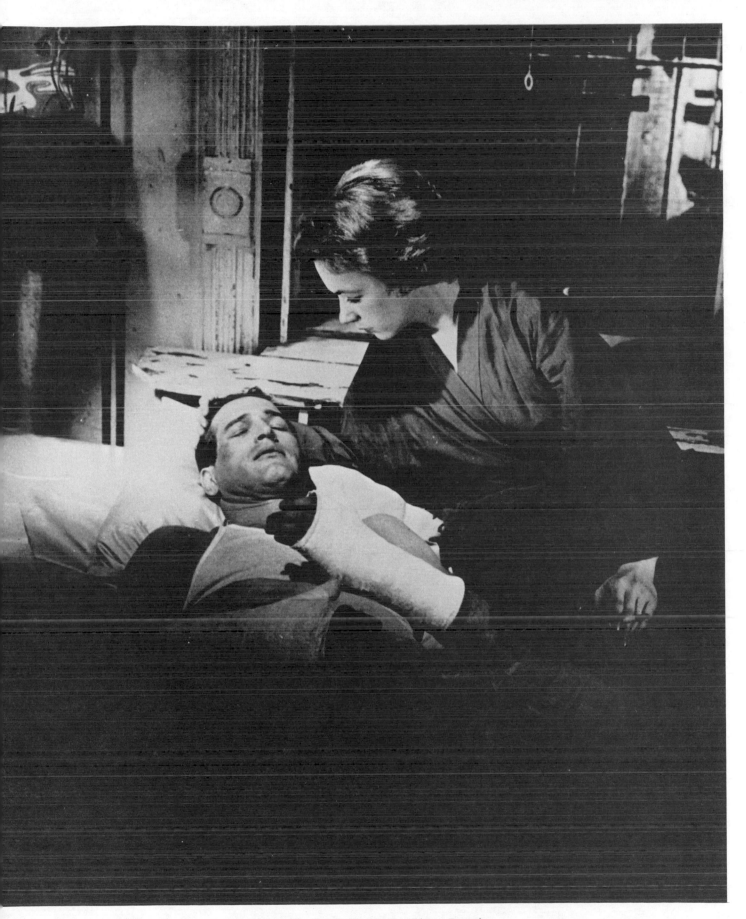

The Hustler. Paul Newman, Piper Laurie.

ity, Rossen rose above disasters like *Mambo* (1955) and their romanticism to create in *The Hustler* an entertaining and energetic work. Not the masterpiece it was hailed to be—Rossen inherited too much of Hollywood to make a film in which the professionally skilled hero is not also an Adonis, the evil mastermind (George C. Scott) does not wear black and talk glibly of morality and "character," and the essential conflict, here the contrast in temperament between top pool players "Fast Eddie" (Paul Newman) and "Minnesota Fats" (Jackie Gleason), is not symbolised by an exciting action sequence, the climactic marathon pool match between these giants—*The Hustler* nevertheless stands out in a period of near-misses for its accurate technique and perception. Rossen's control, if slipping in the use of faded actress Piper Laurie as a maudlin, drunken and crippled girl friend, never falters with either Newman, Murray Hamilton's effete Southern *dilettante* or Gleason's "Fats," a role so precisely appropriate to this actor that one imagines no other in it. His rhetorical "D'ya think this boy's a hustler?" to the assembled onlookers, like the poolroom manager's response when newcomer Eddie asks if the big-time pool hall has a bar ("No bar, no pinball machine; just pool. This here is *Ames*, son."), carries the authentic tone of patient condescension, the feel of professional aristocracy which a few individuals achieve in every human endeavour.

1963

As the 41.9 million people who still went weekly to the movies demonstrated their preference for British films over the bland local product by making David Lean's *Lawrence of Arabia* an all-time hit, the Academy ratified their judgement, awarding it ten

Lawrence of Arabia. Peter O'Toole.

Oscars. Towards the end of the year, Tony Richardson's *Tom Jones* showed signs of enjoying similar success—it won four Oscars in 1964—and many companies ruefully recalled that they had rejected this project, United Artists finally providing the modest $1.4 million that was returned many times over. Richardson promptly received offers to work in the US, where his earlier *Sanctuary* (1961) had been less than popular, and directed *The Loved One* (1964) which, though profitable, achieved none of *Tom Jones*'s mass acceptance. The climate improved for European directors hoping to crash Hollywood, and American companies, encouraged by the Eady Plan under which cash incentives were offered to films wholly produced in Britain, participated increasingly in UK production.

The number of features available to TV from Hollywood rose to 10,427—594 more than the previous year—and the situation, for Hollywood, worsened when Seven Arts bought 215 Universal post-1948 films and NBC a further sixty from M-G-M and Fox. Actors received less than $1 million from residuals during the year, dramatising the loss studios had sustained by selling libraries to TV without adequate provisions for such fees. Any night on network TV, Hollywood could watch itself bleeding to death.

CLEOPATRA. 20th. Century-Fox. Produced by Walter Wanger. Directed by Joseph L. Mankiewicz. Script by Mankiewicz, Ranald MacDougall and Sidney Buchman, based on Plutarch, Suetonius, Appian and Carlo Maria Franzero's "The Life and Times of Cleopatra." Photographed by Leon Shamroy. Second unit directors: Ray Kellogg and Andrew Marton. Second unit photography by Claude Renoir, Pietro Portalupi. Edited by Dorothy Spencer. Production designed by John de Cuir. Art direction by Jack Martin Smith, Hilyard Brown, Herman Blumenthal, Elven Webb, Maurice Pelling and Boris Juraga. Music by Alex

North. Miss Taylor's costumes by Irene Sharaff. Players: Elizabeth Taylor (Cleopatra), Rex Harrison (Julius Caesar), Richard Burton (Mark Antony), Roddy McDowall (Octavian), Cesare Danova (Apollodorus), Hume Cronyn (Sosigenes), Robert Stephens (Germanicus), Kenneth Haigh (Brutus), George Cole (Flavius), Martin Landau (Rufio), Andrew Keir (Agrippa), Pamela Brown (High Priestess), Isabelle Cooley (Charmian), Gwen Watford (Calpurnia), Francesca Annis (Eiras), Gregoire Aslan (Pothinos), John Doucette (Achillas), Richard O'Sullivan (Ptolemy), Martin Benson (Ramos), Herbert Berghof (Theodotus), John Cairney (Phoebus), Jacqui Chan (Lotos), Andrew Faulds (Canidius), Michael Gwynn (Cimber), Michael Hordern (Cicero), John Hoyt (Cassius), Carroll O'Connor (Casca), Douglas Wilmer (Decimus), Marne Maitland (Euphranor), Jean Marsh (Octavia), Marina Berti (Queen at Tarsus), Furio Meniconi (Mithridates), John Karlsen (High Priest.)

20th. Century-Fox's disastrous exercise in big-budget epic production brought palace revolutions in which president Spyros Skouras was purged by Darryl F. Zanuck, who returned to control the company he created (see 1933). Suggested by independent producer Walter Wanger, *Cleopatra* began in 1958 as a modest $1.2 million Joan Collins vehicle to be shot on the Fox backlot. Skouras even suggested a script based on their 1917 Theda Bara success. But Wanger held out for Elizabeth Taylor, ignoring such Fox nominees as Audrey Hepburn, Marilyn Monroe and Shirley MacLaine. Noël Coward was also suggested for Caesar. By 1961, Wanger had persuaded Fox to finance a $5 million English-location production with Stephen Boyd as Antony, Peter Finch as Caesar and Miss Taylor in the star role. Work began at Pinewood under Rouben Mamoulian, but after disputes with the star he left, to be replaced by Mankiewicz. In March 1961, filming stopped while Miss Taylor recovered from a throat infection. Cast and sets were scrapped, and when work recommenced in September Richard Burton and Rex Harrison had replaced Boyd and Finch. Discarding the script expanded by Ludi Clare, Lawrence Durrell, Marc Brandel and Nigel Balchin from an indifferent biography bought for $15,000 by Wanger, Mankiewicz created another in collaboration with Sidney Buchman, Fox's celebrated scenarist of the Thirties and Forties, and Ranald MacDougall, his Warners counterpart.

The writers cribbed liberally from Shaw's "Caesar and Cleopatra," Cleopatra becoming an eager girl who learns from and loves the urbane and weary Caesar, and becomes involved with the weak, hero-worshipping Antony only in an attempt to save her throne from Rome. Poorly cast, Miss Taylor succumbs to a role from which her affair with her co-star during production in Rome often diverted her attention. Acting honours go to Harrison, who revels in the occasional witty lines: meeting the Egyptian court, he extends his compliments to Pothinos, "Chamberlain and Chief Eunuch, a position acquired not without certain . . . sacrifices." Visually meagre, the film shows signs of post-production penny-pinching, including a cheap and unconvincing sea battle and indifferent process work. (Burton also complained that, as the costumes had been made for Stephen Boyd and never altered, his shoes pinched abominably.) Enormous amounts were spent on the triumphal entry of Cleopatra into Rome, semi-naked dancing girls (choreographed by Hermes Pan) expelling gold dust, birds and flowers before a huge black and gold sphinx on top of which Cleopatra and her son are enthroned; but veteran cinematographer Leon Shamroy has no opportunity to do more than record the spectacle. Only one scene, that of Caesar suffering an epileptic fit in his chambers while heavy bars of shadow lie across his body, shows genuine visual imagination.

It is said Miss Taylor did not want initially to make the film, and suggested her huge fee of $1 million plus percentages of gross—she eventually received between $2 and $3 million—to dissuade Wanger. The result of his acceptance was the immediate inflation of star salaries to risible proportions. Despite its four Academy Awards, all minor ones, *Cleopatra*'s $40 million cost made profit an impossibility, and it remains the gravestone of Hollywood's ambitions, as the empty slogan "Movies Are Better Than Ever" is its epitaph.

CHARADE. Universal-International. Produced and directed by Stanley Donen. Script by Peter Stone, from a story by Peter Stone and Marc Behm. Photographed by Charles Lang Jr. Art direction by Jean D'Eaubonne. Edited by James Clark. Music by Henry Mancini. Costumes by Givenchy. Players: Cary Grant (Peter Joshua), Audrey Hepburn (Regina "Reggie" Lambert), Walter Matthau (Hamilton Bartholomew), James Coburn (Tex Penthollow), George Kennedy (Herman Scobie), Ned Glass (Leopold Gideon), Jacques Marin (Inspector Grandpierre), Paul Bonifas (Felix), Dominique Minot (Sylvie Gaudet), Thomas Chelimsky (Jean-Louis Gaudet).

With Alfred Hitchcock largely inactive, the victim of short-sighted studios and tight money, producers hoping to achieve good suspense films without Hitchcock's investment of expertise and imagination imitated the school he had established. Among the best of the imitations, *Charade* set a durable fashion in *chic* thrillers and one-word titles. It was followed by *Mirage* (Edward Dmytryk, 1965), *Masquerade* (Basil Dearden, 1966, in UK), *Arabesque* (Stanley Donen, 1966, in UK), *Kaleidoscope* (Jack Smight, 1966, in UK), *Caprice* (Frank Tashlin, 1967) and *Blindfold* (Philip Dunne, 1966). Many shared the theme of Ernest Lehman's *North by Northwest* (see 1959), in which a rich, glamorous professional man—psychiatrist, academic, tycoon—is lured from his comfortable life, often by a woman, and finds himself the pawn in an elaborate plot. The villain was usually cultured and foreign, the setting Europe, the conclusion, after a bizarre chase, bloody. Peter Stone's *Charade* script—

Three *Cleopatras.* a) Theda Bara (1917); b) Claudette
Colbert (1934) with Cecil B. DeMille; c) Elizabeth
Taylor (1963).

a

b

Charade. **Cary Grant and Audrey Hepburn.**

he also wrote *Mirage*—played Hitchcockian possibilities from early on, with socialite Reggie Lambert sunning herself at an alpine resort, a gun emerging in a gloved hand and filling her ear with water. In succeeding scenes she finds her Paris flat stripped of its furniture, her husband, after his sudden death while fleeing the country, is revealed as an international criminal, and a grim group of Americans set out after her in their search for a fortune in gold they and her husband stole during the war. Calmly romancing the widow and representing himself variously as a thief, vengeful relative, FBI agent and tax investigator, Cary Grant manages well in a role essentially the reverse of that in *North by Northwest* where *he* was the innocent in love with somebody about whose motives and honesty he was in doubt. Except for an idyll on the Seine in a glass-roofed floating restaurant, Donen wisely avoids plush *salons* and tourist spots, setting the action in a convincingly ramshackle Latin Quarter hotel and the untidy clutter of the Tuileries. A black Hitchcockian humour marks the villains' characterisation: George Kennedy is a hook-

handed sadist, and James Coburn the folksily sinister Tex who jabs a corpse's hand with a pin to establish it is dead and terrorises Reggie in a phone booth by dropping lighted matches into her lap. The role is a signpost to Coburn's later eminence in a series of quirky roles culminating in *The President's Analyst* (see 1967).

HUD. Director: Martin Ritt. Patricia Neal received an Oscar for Best Supporting Actress in Ritt's downbeat drama of the archetypal cowboy slipping out of his relevance to society in the changing world of modern Texas. In a script that earned them unique standing as *auteur* scenarists, the husband-and-wife team of Irving Ravetch and Harriet Frank explored the dissolution of the old West into a scatter of self-contained communities uninterested in the old realities of personal power and possession, honour and mutual esteem. Both old man Bannon (Melvyn Douglas) and his son Hud, despite their personal frictions, embody the old West, one the cattle baron whose worth is measured in terms of land and cattle, the other the cowboy, relying on physical strength and honour to sustain him. The impressionable Brandon de Wilde becomes disenchanted with Hud's self-interest but it is really the West he has ceased to admire, and significantly his detachment from Hud is also a detachment from Hud's society. James Wong Howe's photography of empty skies oppressing a bare earth, the bravura handling of scenes like the destruction of Bannon cattle during an outbreak of foot-and-mouth disease and Paul Newman's animal relish in the part of Hud give the film impressive credentials among less energetic modern Westerns.

1964

20th. Century-Fox boomed briefly under the Zanuck administration, and announced an $11½ million profit, derived partially from successful TV series like *Peyton Place* and *Daniel Boone*. Sceptical about epics after the *débacle* of *Cleopatra* but finding the popularity of *West Side Story* (Robert Wise, 1961) a heartening symptom, most studios turned from historical block-busters to musical ones. Warner Brothers, having paid an unprecedented $5½ million for the film rights to "My Fair Lady," made a huge profit with George Cukor's stylish adaptation, and the Disney studios cleaned up with *Mary Poppins* (Robert Stevenson, 1964). Fox invested heavily in the film rights to "The Sound of Music," shortly to become the most financially successful film of all time.

As the Fifties slump in recruitment and a resultant lack of seasoned performers to sustain production made itself felt, studios promoted their TV newcomers and exploited actors who for twenty years had slaved in character and supporting roles. This was facilitated by a shift among minor studios from big-budget films to expanded B-pictures using Forties plots dressed up with wide-screen and colour. In the change to a B-film mentality, a whole generation of Hollywood actors and actresses disappeared. While stalwarts like Bette Davis and Joan Crawford exercised the shreds of their drawing power in chillers and horror films, personalities who would have replaced them—Anne Baxter, Dorothy Malone, Joanne Woodward—as well as the *jeunes premiers* with whom they should have been matched—Richard Egan, Cliff Robertson, Robert Stack—retreated, bereft of suitable roles, into TV or retirement. The Sixties stars, predictably, are B-movie talents who graduated, like the films in which they appeared, to disconcerting eminence. Often able, they nevertheless carry connotations earned in the programme picture, and *personae* that typecasting has made indelible: hard blondes

Kim Novak and Carroll Baker, heavies Lee Marvin and Anthony Quinn, teasers Ann-Margret and Lee Remick, scatter-brains Marilyn Monroe and Shirley MacLaine, and Rock Hudson, the Robert Cummings of the Atomic Age.

THE KILLERS. Universal. Produced and directed by Don Siegel. Script by Gene L. Coon from Ernest Hemingway's short story. Photographed by Richard L. Rawlings. Art direction by Frank Arrigo and George Chan. Edited by Richard Belding. Music by Johnny Williams. Players: Lee Marvin (Charlie), Angie Dickinson (Sheila Farr), Ronald Reagan (Browning), Clu Gulager (Lee), John Cassavetes (Johnny North), Claude Akins (Earl Sylvester), Norman Fell (Mickey), Virginia Christine (Miss Watson), Dan Haggerty (Mail Truck Driver), Robert Phillips (George), Kathleen O'Malley (Receptionist), Ted Jacques (Gym Assistant).

Don Siegel, with Joseph H. Lewis, Maury Dexter and Phil Karlson, was one of the many veteran Hollywood B-film directors who found themselves much in demand as TV drifted from its first dreams of live drama into a recreation of low-budget Hollywood production. Their work for television in the Fifties and early Sixties has none of the blandness characteristic of the lusher late Sixties product, being marked by a brutal vitality and often eccentric reappraisal of the myths with which they worked. Siegel's *The Killers* was originally commissioned as one of Universal's first exercises in feature production exclusively for TV, but when its network sponsors rejected the nihilistic and violent work Siegel had created, Universal issued the film for cinema release, and it was quickly recognised as a modern classic.

Hathaway in *Kiss of Death* (1947), where Richard Widmark played the sadistic killer Udo ("*Girls* are no good if you wanna have some fun"), and John

219

West Side Story. George Chakiris.

Mary Poppins. Dick Van Dyke, Julie Andrews.

Huston in *The Asphalt Jungle* (1950), in which the corrupt attorney, played by Louis Calhern, described crime as "merely a left-handed form of human endeavour," both articulated a new attitude to organised crime in which Hollywood abandoned the Forties' simplistic good/evil conflict to examine criminal morality and its rigorous ethics. It was Siegel, however, who took the development one step further to expose this morality of violence as a code often more strict, equitable and admirable than those of big business or city living which increasingly obsessed the outside world. "Ordinary people of your class," Eli Wallach's gunman Dancer says in *The Line-Up* (1958), "you don't understand the criminal's need for violence." *The Killers* is his most coherent statement of this belief, and a cornerstone of Sixties' cinema.

The Killers. Lee Marvin.

Little of Hemingway remains in the film, as was the case in Robert Siodmak's 1946 version in which Burt Lancaster made his film *début*. The author's fragment detailed only the arrival of two gunmen in a small town, their discovery of their quarry and astonishment on the part of townspeople that the man chose not to run away, but meekly accepted his death. Working from this premise—mechanic Johnny North meekly submits to his execution by cool hired killers Charlie and Lee—Siegel has the sardonic and unemotional assassin Charlie, played by Lee Marvin, become intrigued by this submission and trace the reason through a maze of commercial duplicity and cunning to its core, a crooked businessman (Ronald Reagan in his last role before beginning a political career) and the machinations of his mistress, played by the remarkable Angie Dickinson, with Marvin one of the Sixties' greatest rediscoveries. Dying of gunshot wounds but satisfied at last to find that North's

illogical death was owed to the joker of sex, a random element any professional despises, Charlie is almost amused when the girl offers herself to him as a bribe to save her life. At the point of death, he raises his pistol, with its bulbous silencer a bizarre phallic symbol, murmurs apologetically "Lady, I haven't got the time" and shoots her dead. Siegel went on with *Madigan* (1968) and *Coogan's Bluff* (1969) and Marvin in *Point Blank* (see 1967) to develop and expand this philosophy of violence, but *The Killers* remains their most assured work.

MY FAIR LADY. Director: George Cukor. Though the independent approach to stage musicals succumbed to a Hollywood fashion merely to expand the stiff tableaux of the original—a fault of *Funny Girl* (William Wyler, 1968) and *Hello Dolly* (Gene Kelly, 1970)—Cukor's *My Fair Lady* set the fashion and skilfully exploited the form's limited potential with a flair few later productions were to achieve. Although Audrey Hepburn (dubbed by Marni Nixon), Rex Harrison and Stanley Holloway give a good account of the superb Lerner and Loewe score, credit for the film's box-office success clearly goes to its designers: production designer Cecil Beaton (who, with Harrison and Cukor, also won an Academy Award), and set directors Gene Allen and George James Hopkins. The stately "Ascot Gavotte" sequence with dancers in elaborately recreated Edwardian costumes of black and white pacing in a stylised representation of polite society shows a respect for style to which audiences instinctively responded.

FATHER GOOSE. Director: Ralph Nelson. The script for this comedy, written by Frank Tarloff and the brilliant Peter Stone, arguably the Sixties' finest writing talent in film comedy-drama, deservedly won an Oscar. The promising situation, of Cary Grant's boozy drop-out coast-watcher stranded on a Japanese-occupied island during wartime with Leslie Caron and her class of fugitive schoolgirls, gives the stars liberal opportunity for comic technique, on which Grant capitalises with one of his finest performances, mocking the traditions of the romantic comedy as often as he falls in with them.

VIVA LAS VEGAS. Director: George Sidney. Elvis Presley and Ann-Margret are as much phenomena of the Sixties as Deanna Durbin and Mickey Rooney were of the Forties, grotesquely artificial performers who communicate by an indefinable *rapport* with their mainly adolescent audience. A *protégée* of director Sidney, Ann-Margret, whose early career he guided, was used in his films with an attention to her kittenish sexuality and "teaser" quality few others could equal. In *Viva Las Vegas* (*Love in Las Vegas* in some countries), a cheap plot of amateur racing driver romancing Las Vegas swimming instructor was enlivened by violent dance numbers showing off Ann-

Margret's calendar-girl figure, and a climactic car race guaranteed to bring teenage audiences to their feet. In 1966 Sidney produced and directed *The Swinger* as a vehicle for the star, but its failure damaged both their careers, although after several films in Italy Ann-Margret has recently returned, notably less carefree and teen-oriented, in Mike Nichols' *Carnal Knowledge* (see 1971)

Snake-bite cure via whisky in *Father Goose*. Cary Grant, Leslie Caron.

1965

All companies reported good gross incomes, though like many statistics issued by Hollywood since the Fifties slump, these were deceptive, most profits having been derived from TV, records or real estate sales rather than film production. Adolph Zukor resigned from the Paramount board after arguments concerning a take-over attempt, and control of the company passed to Gulf-Western Oil. With a feature bringing up to $400,000 on TV, and $1 million paid by ABC to Columbia for *The Bridge on the River Kwai* (which was watched by a record audience of six million) studios shortened to three years the period in the US in which a feature was embargoed for television, and rushed their recent productions on the TV market.

Universal and 20th. Century-Fox explored new sources of talent to replace those drained in the previous decade. Universal announced a "new talent" programme, gambling on the hope that young directors working in the idiom popularised by the French *nouvelle vague* might catch, as Truffaut and Chabrol had, the imagination of the elusive under-thirty audience. UCLA film school graduate Brian G. Hutton and Canadian TV director Harvey Hart were each offered a feature relatively free of studio control. Hutton's *Fargo* (also known as *Wild Seed*), with new stars Michael Parks and Celia Kaye as a wandering drop-out and the girl he befriends, used documentary style and rural locations with a flair that reminds one of the early Thirties. Hart's *Bus Riley's Back in Town* (1965), based on one of William Inge's less effective screenplays, again used Parks as a dissident hell-raiser who returns to his home town after Naval service and is absorbed, after a brief revolt, into suburban mediocrity. *Bus Riley* and the Universal project ended abruptly when box-office returns from *Fargo* manifested the film as a disaster, and the company hedged its bets on the Hart film by shooting additional scenes

for Ann-Margret and demanding cuts that caused Inge to take his name from the credits. Hutton went on to direct commercial but nondescript action films like *Where Eagles Dare* (1969), and Hart to a distinguished career in TV before again making features in his native Canada.

Zanuck, whose star-hunting activities in Europe and production of *The Longest Day* (Ken Annakin, Bernhard Wicki, 1962) earned notoriety and profits respectively—a board decision to mass-release this film rather than road-show it instigated his take-over from Skouras in 1962—embarked on a series of American features by European directors, beginning with Wicki's *Morituri* (1965), a war drama with Marlon Brando, the gloomy loquacity of which chilled its box-office hopes. He also imported Serge Bourguignon, whose *Les Dimanches de Ville d'Avray*, as *Sundays and Cybele*, had been a US art house success, to make a Western, *The Reward* (1965) and negotiated with Akira Kurosawa to direct *The Day Custer Fell* from a Wendell Mayes script. All these failed in the aftermath of *Cleopatra*, as publicity and merchandising costs multiplied the initial $40 million expense. *Morituri*, renamed *The Saboteur: Codename Morituri*, and *The Reward* had indifferent releases, and the suspended Kurosawa project went to Fred Zinnemann, only to be dropped when Robert Siodmak made *Custer of the West* in Spain with Robert Shaw in 1968.

THE CINCINNATI KID. Director: Norman Jewison. Jewison's film is as close to *The Hustler* in plot as it is in attitude, and except for changes in setting —New Orleans in the Thirties—and the game—poker, not pool—the stories are interchangeable, even to the implication that Steve McQueen's failure to overthrow Edward G. Robinson, "The Man," is due to a lack of "character." *The Cincinnati Kid* achieves a sur-

Vagrants, including Michael Parks, warned by a malicious sheriff in *Wild Seed*.

prisingly convincing evocation of the South's decaying gentility—the faded elegance of worn plush and smoky wood panelling, old furs, stained glass lampshades and dusty lace curtains. Real life intrudes often into the genteel conventions of the professional poker players, as when McQueen is cajoled into taking Ann-Margret, as fleshy and vulgar as a pin-up nude, to a rowdy sweat-soaked cockfight, or when Robinson finds himself severely tested, physically and mentally, by his younger opponent. Both, however, contrive to rise above it to a world of pure values and simple questions of power and weakness, where The Man eats oysters for breakfast off a silver tray and The Kid waits in the quiet darkness for his final test, studying mathematical tables with the absorption of a meditating priest.

THE SOUND OF MUSIC. Director: Robert Wise. William Wyler was to have directed a film of "Peter Pan" with Audrey Hepburn, but this was cancelled in the general slump of original musicals; the same team was mooted for *The Sound of Music,* with Romy Schneider a possible alternative star, but Julie Andrews, who had missed repeating her stage role of Eliza Dolittle in *My Fair Lady* when both Cukor and Jack Warner had decided a "name" was essential, had her revenge in Robert Wise's awesomely profitable adaptation of Rogers' and Hammerstein's Trapp Family Singers musical—now, with grosses nearing $100 million, the most financially successful film ever made. Its frank appeal to the family audience brought instant critical obloquy, and few writers bothered to find merit in this persuasive and restrained version of a syrupy romance. "We didn't have a tenth the *dirndls* we could have had," the director said defensively. Wise's exterior handling of the unremarkable but tuneful songs, and his atmospheric *mise-en-scène* of numbers like "My Favourite Things," sung to calm

225

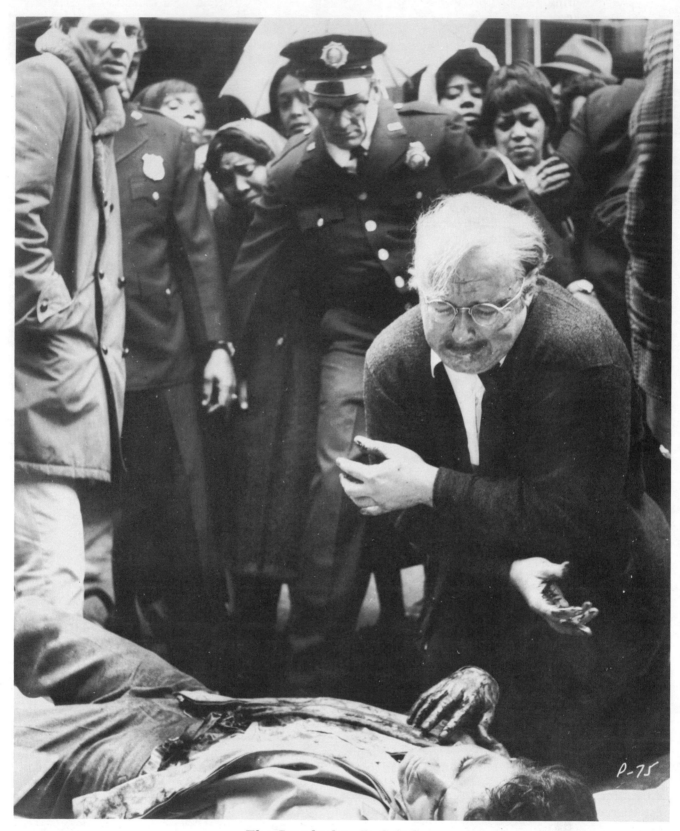

The Pawnbroker. Rod Steiger.

the children during a thunderstorm, show the imagination and taste of a man whose credentials include a spell as Orson Welles' editor (*Citizen Kane, The Magnificent Ambersons*) and some of Hollywood's finest realist dramas.

THE PAWNBROKER. Director: Sidney Lumet. Like Jewison a graduate of New York television, Lumet's career contrasts with that of the former, as it does with those of David Swift, Ralph Nelson, David Lowell Rich and the many slick craftsmen whose instant adaptation to Hollywood style shows that *in petto* they had always been studio men. In collaboration with cameraman Boris Kaufman, with whom he created a nervous, jumpy visual style appropriate to stories of mental distress and the tensions within small groups, he made a series of East Coast-oriented intellectual dramas, including adaptations of Eugene O'Neill's *Long Day's Journey into Night* (1962) and Mary McCarthy's *The Group* (1966). In the latter he overturned the myths of star-making by so effectively showcasing a number of young actresses, in a waspish examination of sexual and social frictions among girl college graduates, that the stars, notably Joanna Pettet, Elizabeth Hartman, Joan Hackett, Jessica Walter and Candice Bergen, all enjoyed highly successful film careers thereafter. Rod Steiger derived similar benefit from his performance in *The Pawnbroker* as a Jewish refugee in New York hiding the horror of his war experiences, in which he was forced to watch his wife sexually abused by Nazi officers and then killed in a prison camp, behind the indifference of a pawnbroker in the New York slums. Periodically, reminders of the past—a Negro prostitute's offer of her body in return for money, his assistant's involvement in the underworld—tear the frail fabric and he falls back into the horror, episodes in which Lumet uses fragmented intercut images to suggest mental disorientation. Lumet is occasionally guilty of excess in his evocation of Steiger's misery,

Major Dundee. Charlton Heston.

and in *Bye Bye Braverman* (1968) he gently parodied his own creation by casting Joseph Wiseman as a Jewish New Yorker who refuses to ride in Volkswagens and chills every conversation with reminders of "six million dead," to the good-natured despair of his other Jewish friends, but *The Pawnbroker* retains a unique standing in the Sixties from its harsh exploration of human misery existing behind the mask of the uncaring face.

MAJOR DUNDEE. Director: Sam Peckinpah. With *Ride the High Country* (also *Guns in the Afternoon*, 1962), Sam Peckinpah, like Budd Boetticher, Clair Huffaker, Gene Coon and Andrew V. McLaglen a graduate of series TV, established a reputation as one of the Western's new masters, and though his Sixties career suggested that, to him, Western myths were useful only as a vehicle for contemporary social comment, his frontier films are among the decade's finest. Of all his work, *Major Dundee* most impressively balances poetry and realism, unmarred even by producer Jerry Bresler, who altered Peckinpah's cutting, and refused, despite an offer by director and star Charlton Heston to work without salary, to shoot extra scenes when the film went over time and budget. Using a conventional plot—Dundee (Heston), a Northern officer, is forced to recruit Confederate prisoners, led by an old comrade (Richard Harris), to fight a renegade Indian band—Peckinpah discards heroics to dwell on the conflict between Heston's ruthless pragmatist and the visionary flair of his antagonist, an Irish mercenary whose pursuit of lost causes will, he knows, lead to violent death. "Damn you, Major Dundee," he rages. "I damn your name, I damn your flag." Ignoring the elements Ford took from this situation in *Fort Apache* and Robert Wise in *Two Flags West* (1950), Peckinpah concentrates on the men and their philosophical conflict. The battle is one of Titans, shown in almost Biblical splendour. Seen first in a barred pit, defiant in grey uniform and plumed hat even as chains weigh him down, Harris rises to be Heston's equal and confidant until a basic incompatibility leads them to the sacrifice of an assault against impossible odds. In a lakeside love scene between Heston and Senta Berger ending when an arrow pierces his leg, a fiesta in a square where executed leaders had hung, and in a scene of dissension between the two factions in an abandoned church, Peckinpah plays on the anomalies of collaboration to evoke a society where only fear, distrust and the will to death have any relevance.

1966

Seeing growth potential in failing film companies, corporations moved in to buy up even the giants. M-G-M fought to avoid takeover by real estate speculator Philip Levin, but Jack L. Warner, weary of the competition, sold his Warner Brothers holdings to Seven Arts, who in 1967 merged the two as Warner-Seven Arts, its output mainly for TV. With its Gulf-Western Oil money, Paramount, last major company to devote itself entirely to cinema, diversified into TV also. Feature-hungry world television radically changed the Hollywood pattern. "I don't know what's happened to motion pictures," comic Milton Berle quipped, "but I know what's happened to TV—it's become motion pictures." With feature prices rock-etting—ABC paid 20th Century-Fox $19½ million for seventeen films, and a further $5 million for two runs of *Cleopatra* at the close of its commercial release—networks found the purchase of Hollywood features an expensive practice, but since films consistently out-rated most series, an answer was found in the production of films primarily for TV. Universal, most TV-oriented studio, and independents like Commonwealth United took the trend to its logical conclusion and manufactured features specifically for TV, complete with commercial breaks, giving them brief theatrical release only after network telecasting. Fading stars and ambitious directors were hired to shoot thrillers in Yugoslavia, Spain, Australia and Hong Kong, an immediate network sale returning the small budgets overnight. Many series adopted the feature form, individual episodes running ninety minutes and employing "guest stars" to suggest the traditional "star billing." Occasionally, following a practice pioneered by Columbia, TV episodes were released in theatres as features. *Sergeant Ryker* (Buzz Kulik, 1968), starring Lee Marvin, was actually episodes of the "Arrest and Trial" series given theatrical release to cash in on Marvin's growing popularity,

and the practice had wide currency. The tail had indeed learned how to wag the dog.

GRAND PRIX. Joel/JFP/Cherokee-M-G-M. Produced by Edward Lewis. Directed by John Frankenheimer. Script by Robert Alan Aurthur. Photographed by Lionel Lindon. Second unit photography by Jean-Georges Fonteneille, Yann Le Masson, John M. Stephens. Visual consultant/Montages/Titles: Saul Bass. Supervising editor: Frederick Steinkamp. Edited by Henry Berman, Stewart Linder, Frank Santillo. Production designed by Richard Sylbert. Special effects by Milt Rice. Music by Maurice Jarre. Players: James Garner (Pete Aron), Yves Montand (Jean-Pierre Sarti), Brian Bedford (Scott Stoddard), Antonio Sabato (Nino Barlini), Toshiro Mifune (Yamura), Françoise Hardy (Lisa), Eva Marie Saint (Louise Frederickson), Jessica Walter (Pat Wilson), Geneviève Page (Monique Sarti), Phil Hill (Tim Randolph), Graham Hill (Billy Turner), Jack Watson (Jeff Jordan), Bruce McLaren (Douglas McLendon), Donald O'Brien (Wallace Bennett), Rachel Kempson (Mrs. Stoddard), Bernard Cahier (Victor), Adolfo Celi (Manetta), Enzo Fiermonte (Ferrari Crew Chief), Alan Fordney (Sportscaster), Brian Duffy (Photographer).

If John Frankenheimer can be said to have a single preoccupation it is the machine and its workings. A born tinkerer, his films invariably examine in detail the intricacies of some efficient and ingenious mechanism. *The Train*, with its hymn both to the steam locomotive and the subtle workings of the *maquis*, and *The Manchurian Candidate*'s depiction of a complex Communist plot, are the best examples of this, but one senses it also in the television-infested world of *Seven Days in May* and even periodically in the intramural *All Fall Down*, where the structure of a family is stripped down. It is because the theme has

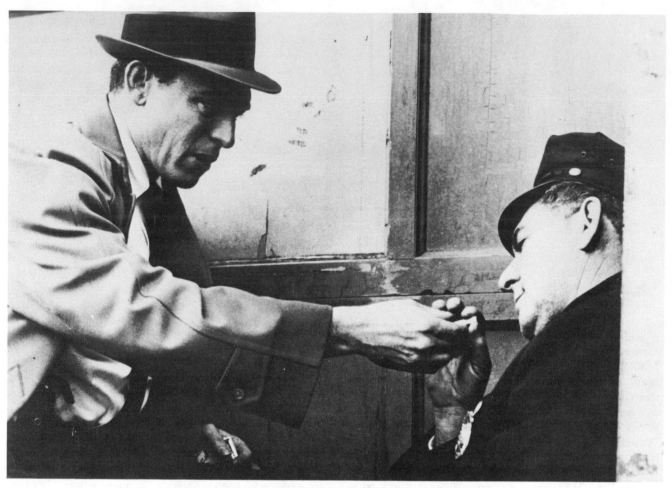

TV to cinema: Paul Burke in *A Death of Princes,* episode of the "Naked City" series, directed by John Brahm from a Stirling Silliphant script, released by Columbia as a cinema feature after telecasting.

its most ambitious exposition in *Grand Prix* (and because Frankenheimer is a racing driver *manqué*) that this is among his most interesting films.

Ostensibly *Grand Prix* concerns the fortunes of four drivers during a single Grand Prix season. Aron is an American, tough and careless, Stoddard an Englishman living in the shadow of a dead and famous racing brother, Sarti a Frenchman, ageing and tied to a loveless marriage, while newcomer Barlini is a dense but energetic Italian making the difficult transition from motor-cycles to cars. All have attendant women whose importance to the film is hard to underestimate. The phrase "film fugue" is a *cliché*. Nevertheless, Frankenheimer's development is fugal, offering not only the parallel recounting of four stories but also a simultaneous blending and counterpointing of them. There are *tutti* passages where a theme is stated by each of the drivers, a concept or belief reflected in the mind of one man at various times in his life. The fear of dying is stated

by all four, then worked-out in a split-screen composition where all appear to discuss their attitudes. Stoddard, driving at Monaco, is shown both racing in the afternoon and, by vertical split screen, walking the deserted course the morning before, while the soundtrack quotes his views on racing and superstition in an interview.

Motifs like the paintings of past victories, a car museum and the upkeep of traditions illustrate the ritualised lives of the drivers, and each race has its reflection in our attitude to the characters. Monaco is twisting and tricky, well-edited to give a sense of a maze in which all are caught. Monza, with its heavily-banked wall and long straightaways, is chosen appropriately as the location of Sarti's death; helicopter shots from above the hurtling cars and low-angled views of the banked wall combined with tense remarks by the drivers on the dangers build a fear and expectation adequately fulfilled when Sarti's car leaves the track, hangs briefly in the air and drops to explode

Producer Edward Lewis (left) and director John Frankenheimer during shooting of *Grand Prix*.

John Huston, who also played Noah, and friend on *The Bible . . . In the Beginning*.

on the ground below. On another circuit, subjective shots from road level stress immense speeds, the blurred detail of houses and onlookers preparing us for a car's sudden fatal skid into the crowd. Although spectacular, such sequences never sink to the level of mere spectacle, but contribute to the tone and point of the story.

Saul Bass adds an emotional dimension to an essentially documentary approach, his montages and split-screen sequences multiplying faces, hands and spanners a hundred times, filling the screen with postage-stamp facsimiles of a single motion or look. We sense a thousand hands working to keep the drivers going, a vast machine marshalled to their service. But Bass is capable too of designing a delightful interlude to illustrate the exhilaration of Sarti's love affair with Louise, ignoring a race's drama to show it as a lyrical game, cars waltzing, sliding and floating through shimmering air, a picnicking family looking on; girls, umbrellas, flowers. His ingenuity is all the more remarkable for the fact that he directed these sequences on a British circuit with two broken ankles, giving elaborate schematics to a horde of assistants and making only the occasional supervisory visit.

For an epic, the acting of *Grand Prix* is commendable, most performers responding to the literacy of Aurthur's script. Arguments between Stoddard and his mistress Pat achieve a razor-sharp viciousness, while her growing attraction to Aron is well organised. One senses no particular affinity and initially they are openly antagonistic. Then Aron apologises. "Why do we argue so much?" she asks, and he replies, "Probably because we hate one another." 'Speak for yourself," she says. Later, after dinner, they return to their hotel. Pat pauses by her door, the hint of sexual availability quite clear, but Aron ignores it, goes to his door—and pauses there until she joins him. Frankenheimer gives us insights into a life we know little about and teaches us something of how people respond to pressures we can only imagine. That it is done with impeccable style, restraint and imagination can be considered a bonus.

THE BIBLE . . . IN THE BEGINNING. Director: John Huston. An old-style epic the complications of which did much to sour Hollywood on co-productions with the mercurial Dino De Laurentiis. Advertised by De Laurentiis as a fifteen-hour feature to be directed by nine men, including Ingmar Bergman, Robert Bresson, Luchino Visconti, Federico Fellini and Orson Welles, each taking one book of the Bible, it was reduced to a feature of normal length by the ever-game John Huston—a visual scrapbook of Old Testament incidents from the Garden of Eden through Noah (played by Huston himself) and the Tower of Babel to Abraham and Isaac. Welles had visited the slopes of Vesuvius scouting locations for his episode, "Sodom and Gomorrah," suggesting that this section at least would have its problems, and Bresson, asked to find an Eve for his "Garden of Eden," brought back test footage of six potential stars, all of whom, to De Laurentiis's horror, were Negro or Indian. Appealing to the Vatican for a ruling, the producer was told, to no one's surprise, that Eve must be blonde, blue-eyed and white.

1967

Ignoring the fact that weekly admissions had sunk to fifteen million, a figure unthinkable even in the worst days of the late Forties, the IATSE & Basic Crafts reached agreement with the Association of Motion Picture and TV Producers for a 22% pay increase, absurd in an industry where unemployment was approaching 50%. Although cinema grosses climbed above $1 billion for the first time since 1957, this was attained mainly through the inflation of seat prices. The costs of gambling on big-budget production, the only type feasible in a cinema where "hard ticket" and "road show" systems had squeezed out most films of even moderate budget, were prohibitive for any studio not backed or owned by a major industrial concern. Publicity and distribution costs doubled the budget of any major feature, while the necessity to road show a film for an initial long run in selected cities before releasing it for saturation booking throughout the world delayed profits and accumulated huge interest charges on the money borrowed to finance the film.

Hollywood's establishment clung tenaciously to the shreds of its standing, cinematographer Harry Stradling resigning from *Who's Afraid of Virginia Woolf?* in protest over stage graduate Mike Nichols' insistence that Elizabeth Taylor shed her customary glamour image. He was replaced by Haskell Wexler, best of the new cinematographers and one familiar with the light camera technology pioneered by Éclair and Arriflex. Meanwhile, Leon Shamroy celebrated his thirtieth anniversary as a top cameraman with *Planet of the Apes* (Franklin J. Schaffner). In the hope of exploiting studio resistance to the union stranglehold on facilities, Mayor John Lindsay of New York appealed to film-makers to work in the East, a plan that collapsed when it was pointed out that labour in New York was more costly and restrictive than in Hollywood, with wages running

TV technique and light camera technology: Sidney Poitier in *In the Heat of the Night* (Norman Jewison, 1967); lighting by Haskell Wexler (at rear).

25% above California. As the unions bickered, an increasingly large number of producers by-passed the establishment to shoot features with non-union crews and distribute them through independent cinema chains.

THE GRADUATE. Embassy/United Artists. Produced by Lawrence Turman. Directed by Mike Nichols. Script by Calder Willingham and Buck Henry from the novel by Charles Webb. Photographed by Robert Surtees. Production designed by Richard Sylbert. Edited by Sam O'Steen. Music by David Grusin. Songs by Paul Simon, sung by Simon and Garfunkel. Players: Dustin Hoffman (Ben Braddock), Anne Bancroft (Mrs. Robinson), Katharine Ross (Elaine Robinson), William Daniels (Mr. Braddock), Murray Hamilton (Mr. Robinson), Elizabeth Wilson (Mrs. Braddock), Brian Avery (Carl Smith), Walter Brooke (Mr. Maguire), Norman Fell (Mr. McCleery), Alice Ghostly (Mrs. Singleman), Buck Henry (Desk Clerk), Marion Lorne (Miss De Witt).

Dustin Hoffman was a little-known twenty-nine-year-old with a few good reviews to his credit for Henry Livings's play "Eh?" and small roles in two films when Mike Nichols, ex-satirist and Broadway wonder-boy tested him for his adaptation of Charles Webb's slight novel about the hang-ups of a college graduate trying to square reality with his undirected sense of purpose. Trusting Nichols but feeling dubious about the story, Hoffman tested with little hope of success and promptly went back on relief. The film's popularity is as much a mystery to him as it was to the Hollywood studios, but in retrospect one can see why the film achieved its success. Like *Bonnie and Clyde* and the grotesque *Willard* (Daniel Mann, 1970), it catered to the dreams of the thirteen- to eighteen-year-old audience who found little in adult dramas that related to their problems. To them, Hoffman's shy but senstive hero fumbling through the subtleties of an affair with a married woman, unsure of how to attract a waiter's eye or book into a hotel without luggage, mirrored their own *gaucherie*. Hoffman mixes up his life by sleeping with the mother of the girl he loves, but finally his deep feeling, that which even the feeblest adolescent must possess, wins her from beyond marriage. His agonised cry as he sees her at the altar makes errors of taste, morality and etiquette unimportant.

The appeal to the lowest common denominator is sustained by Nichols's accurate rendering of the story in terms of physical feeling. Few modern films have had such a sense of the flesh, of neutral sensations

Adolescent dream of fulfillment: Katharine Ross and Dustin Hoffman in *The Graduate*.

like boredom, fatigue, depression, anxiety. In the first shot, Ben, blankly unaware of his surroundings, is borne along a moving footway as Simon and Garfunkel murmur "The Sounds of Silence," a hymn to detachment and non-thought. Enclosed in a full scuba suit, his parents' graduation gift, he potters about the swimming pool, immersed in his own breathing, and later drowses on the surface, stunned by the sun, dreaming of afternoon assignations with Mrs. Robinson which he keeps "because there's nothing else to do." The Robinsons—casually amoral wife, vicious cuckolded husband and elegant, distant daughter—are drawn from an adolescent's image of the archetypal family next door: the woman who sends him on errands, the man ill-tempered or beerily amiable by turns, the girl who becomes, through familiarity, an object of sexual fantasy. Nichols drew the world of American adolescence with an accurate and acid pen; it is the film's best joke that what they took as a dream he meant as a nightmare.

POINT BLANK. M-G-M. Produced by Judd Bernard and Robert Chartoff. Directed by John Boorman. Script by Alexander Jacobs, David and Rafe Newhouse from "The Hunter" by Richard Stark. Photographed by Philip H. Lathrop. Art direction by George W. Davis and Albert Brenner. Edited by Henry Berman. Music by Johnny Mandel. Players: Lee Marvin (Walker), Angie Dickinson (Chris), Keenan Wynn (Yost), Carroll O'Connor (Brewster), Lloyd Bochner (Carter), Michael Strong (Stegman), John Vernon (Mal Reese), Sharon Acker (Lynne), James Sikking (Gunman), Sandra Warner (Waitress), Roberta Haynes (Mrs. Carter), Lawrence Hauben (Used-Car Salesman), Ron Walters, George Strattan (Young Men in Apartment).

Canadian John Boorman, a director who has worked mainly in England, used Don Siegel's vision as a springboard for his ruthless thriller, a key Sixties film. A man's obsessional hunt for the wife and friend who betrayed him, leaving him for dead in the ruins of abandoned Alcatraz prison, becomes an exploration of the criminal power structure and an exposition of its brutal politics. Walker finds and kills Reese, tumbling him naked from a luxury penthouse, finds his wife and causes her death, eventually penetrates the centre of the crime industry from which he expects his rightful gains, but in each case the victory is hollow. Reese has used the money he stole to "buy into" the crime ring, his wife, abandoned by her lover and tormented by guilt, chooses to poison herself, and the top criminal, a nervous executive all of whose business happens on paper, proves to Walker that "real" money is an illusion in this new big-business underworld. Real money surfaces only once in the elaborate manipulations of the big time, during the midnight drop at Alcatraz in a robbery attempt on which Walker was originally double-crossed. He is promised a cut if he will collect it

in person, but naturally it is a trap. A helicopter lands in the dark, deserted compound; the money is waiting, but Walker does not appear. At last he has understood, and the shadows swallow him up.

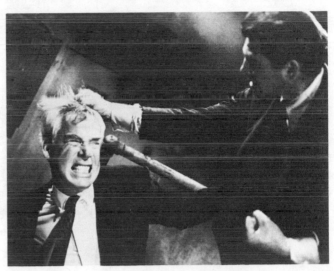

Point Blank. Lee Marvin.

Siegel must have approved. But *Point Blank* goes further than Siegel, showing that the new criminal morality must, if taken to its logical conclusion, supersede even basic human drives, offering a new sexuality of violence to replace them. Bursting into his wife's house, Walker empties his pistol into the bed, slow-motion emphasising the orgasmic shudder that runs through his body as the gun discharges. Tempting Reese from his penthouse, Walker sends his sister-in-law Chris to him, knowing that desire will make him careless, and although the girl is repelled by the man, her sexual choreography is precisely, cunningly judged, as is her estimate of her appeal. "How badly does he want you?" Walker asks, and Chris, on consideration, says, "Pretty bad." Love, shame, remorse have no place in a world built on force, as Chris realises when, despairing of ever attracting the attention of her phlegmatic protector, she attacks him as a mechanism, turning on all the electronic appliances in the gang-leader's villa (a *hommage* of Vidor's *Gilda*, where Rita Hayworth employs a similar device) and throwing herself at him with a fusillade of blows that leaves her exhausted and he, for the first time, both physically dazed and sexually excited. "This guy's beautiful," the professional gun says to his employer after Walker has killed one of their top men, "he's tearing you to pieces"—a phrase distilling the essence of this love affair with power.

THE PRESIDENT'S ANALYST. Director: Theodore J. Flicker. Leader of Chicago's "Second City" satire troupe and owner of the Premise Club in New

Two versions of Bonnie Parker: a) Dorothy Provine in *The Bonnie Parker Story;* b) Faye Dunaway with Warren Beatty in *Bonnie and Clyde.*

a

York—his first feature, *The Troublemaker,* 1964, is grotesquely funny about the problems of opening a night-club in the city—Flicker made an unclassifiable masterpiece in this comedy-thriller on the idiocy of cold war and the over-organised American environment. James Coburn plays a top New York psychologist whisked to Washington to be the President's private headshrinker, a spot that makes him America's most wanted man, pursued by spies friendly and unfriendly, the diminutive agents of the Federal Bureau of Regulation (a parody of Hoover's FBI) and the mechanical minions of the Telephone Company, incensed by complaints about wrong numbers into taking over the world. Flicker's own script and William Fraker's eccentric colour photography create a multi-coloured nightmare world too close on occasions to our own.

BONNIE AND CLYDE. Director: Arthur Penn. Not Penn's best film, this was probably his most popular. Precisely reflecting American myths, it elevated Thirties killers Bonnie Parker and Clyde Barrow to national heroes, focuses for the hopes of a generation to whom classic virtues were absurdly anachronistic. Unable to find anything worthy of emulation in a society devoid of social purpose, young audiences saw Penn's couple as saints for a disenchanted age: the bored but sensitive small-town girl who achieves national fame, and the minor thug, unimaginative and impotent, who conquers his inadequacies with a beautiful girl, then dies with her in a fabulous martyrdom. This is Bonnie and Clyde as the public

made them appear and they themselves would have liked to be; the reality, more accurately but less glamorously reflected in such films as *You Only Live Once* (Fritz Lang, 1937), *Gun Crazy* (Joseph H. Lewis, 1949) and *The Bonnie Parker Story* (William Witney, 1958), would hardly have had the same appeal.

THE DIRTY DOZEN. Director: Robert Aldrich. One of the year's most popular films was this brutal, amoral and unpretentious war film about the training of twelve convicted military criminals into a commando force for a suicide mission. Made in England mostly with a cast of minor personalities on which Hollywood was relying increasingly for anything below epic level, it tapped the same vein as *The Magnificent Seven,* glorifying the expert killer and his disdain for the moral rules of society. Audiences came to relish the brutal discipline to which the dozen were subjected by top-kick Lee Marvin, and to view without flinching the final onslaught on a Nazi base in which women were mown down with the same ruthlessness as men, and whole parties incinerated when the raid trapped them underground. Predictably, the film had a similar success to *The Magnificent Seven* in Europe, and imitations were a regular feature of the years that followed, with Brian Hutton's *Kelly's Heroes* (1971), featuring Clint Eastwood and Donald Sutherland (the latter from *The Dirty Dozen*), Hollywood's best variation on the theme.

b

1968

Jack Valenti, new chief of the MPAA, instituted a measure that its previous leader, the late Eric Johnston, had always opposed by replacing Hollywood self-censorship, now a dead letter, with a classification system that placed responsibility for censorship on theatre managers and audiences. Adapting the British system, MPAA ratings ranged from G for general exhibition through M and R to X, for adults only. Many independent exhibitors traded on the plethora of city, state and national hedges against obscenity by ignoring censorship altogether, showing a banned film just over a county border or, as in New York and San Francisco, defying the authorities to close them down at a time when the Supreme Court had made censorship on moral grounds near to a legal impossibility.

Though Cinerama had died off as a form, the Cinerama Corporation, now owned by Californian exhibitor William Forman, entered production and distribution, while Joseph E. Levine's Embassy Films, founded on the successful distribution of Italian epics like *Hercules* in the Fifties, accepted take-over by AVCO to become a powerful force in the evolving American film industry. 20th Century-Fox, on the other hand, slumped badly. *Star!*, Robert Wise's tasteful biography of Gertrude Lawrence with Julie Andrews, and *Doctor Dolittle,* an adaptation of Hugh Lofting's juvenile fantasies by Richard Fleischer, both lost large amounts, suggesting that the taste for Broadway musicals had become ingrained. Failure remained even when Fox re-edited *Star!* to a suitable length for saturation showing and changed the name to *Those Were the Happy Times* to exploit a minimal nostalgia value and cash in on the success of George Roy Hill's *Thoroughly Modern Millie* (1967), another Julie Andrews vehicle in which she had played a Twenties figure in a story trading on the conventional associations of "jazz babies," barnstorming pilots, Prohibition and the Charleston. Plans for a musical based on the "Tom Swift" stories with Gene Kelly directing were dropped, and Richard Zanuck, who had been made President of the company when his father ascended to the Chairmanship, instituted a ruthless austerity drive. Among the unpopular moves were the closing of the Paris office, his father's production headquarters during periods of voluntary exile, and the cancellation of a company contract with Geneviève Gilles, Darryl F. Zanuck's current *protégée,* an honour previously enjoyed by Juliette Greco, Bella Darvi, Irina Demick and other Zanuck discoveries. The cuts widened a rift between father and son without halting the slump in profits, and Richard Zanuck shortly afterwards moved to an executive position at Warners-Seven Arts (see 1970).

BULLITT. Warners-Seven Arts. Produced by Philip D'Antoni. Directed by Peter Yates. Script by Alan R. Trustman and Harry Kleiner from the novel "Mute Witness" by Robert L. Pike. Photographed by William Fraker. Art direction by Albert Brenner. Edited by Frank P. Keller. Music by Lalo Schifrin. Players: Steve McQueen (Frank Bullitt), Robert Vaughn (Walter Chalmers), Jacqueline Bisset (Cathy), Don Gordon (Delgetti), Robert Duvall (Weisberg), Simon Oakland (Captain Bennet), Norman Fell (Baker), George Stanford Brown (Doctor Willard), Justin Tarr (Eddy), Carl Reindel (Stanton), Felice Orlandi (Renick), Pat Renella (Johnny Ross).

To catalyse the new crime film's conflicting elements and make the most assured statement of its ethic was left to English director Peter Yates, who created a thriller precisely characteristic of the decade. Nothing in its plot, a straightforward but jumpily-told account of a gang skirmish, with San Francisco cop Bullitt unravelling the details of a dead grand jury witness' death and its significance before an ambitious young politician, silkily played by Robert Vaughn, has him demoted, suggests the film's excitement, which springs from a sophisticated manipulation of violence. Action erupts out of quiet, the click of a safety belt signalling the start of a vertiginous car chase around the city—stunt driver Bud Ekins doubled for McQueen, though the star is an expert driver—and later, in the final sequence, a wave of bystanders throwing themselves to the ground as the cop draws a bead on his quarry at the airport. Unlike Siegel's later films, *Bullitt* does not emphasise philosophy or motivation, except for a brief scene where Bullitt's girl rebels against the brutality of his life, and he, after killing his man, returns home to wash his hands in the film's last enigmatic shot. Siegel's postulation has become Yates's way of life. The suave politician runs with the aristocracy, unconcerned with the issues of social justice central to crime film of other decades, and the criticism of public indifference and political manipulation in Pike's original novel have been removed by the writers, along with Pike's unheroic and ageing detective. Yates's Bullitt lives comfortably, attended by a smart *équipe*, takes his pleasures as a right, and with little reference to those who provide them. At the hospital, when a nurse with a lunch tray, seeing Bullitt, asks "Are you the policeman who hasn't had anything to eat?", he gratefully grabs the tray and disappears munching, as the uniformed guard for whom the meal was intended stares stoically ahead, unable to complain. Even James Cagney could not have carried off such a scene in the dedicated days at Warners in the Thirties.

ROSEMARY'S BABY. Paramount. Produced by William Castle. Written for the screen and directed by Roman Polanski, from Ira Levin's novel. Photographed by William Fraker. Production designed by Richard Sylbert. Art direction by Joel Schiller. Edited by Sam O'Steen, Bob Wyman. Music by Krzysztof Komeda. Players: Mia Farrow (Rosemary Woodhouse), John Cassavetes (Guy Woodhouse), Ruth

Bullitt. Steve McQueen.

239

Rosemary's Baby. Mia Farrow.

Gordon (Minnie Castevet), Sidney Blackmer (Roman Castevet), Maurice Evans (Hutch), Ralph Bellamy (Dr. Sapirstein), Angela Dorian (Terry), Patsy Kelly (Laura-Louise), Elisha Cook (Mr. Nicklas), Emmaline Henry (Elise Dunstan), Marianne Gordon (Joan Jellico), Philip Leeds (Dr. Shand), Charles Grodin (Dr. Hill), Hope Summers (Mrs. Gilmore), Wende Wagner (Tiger).

Producer and director William Castle, who expended his talent during the Fifties on superficial experiments like "Emergo" and "Illusion-O" in which cardboard skeletons and trick glasses supplanted talent and imagination, at last returned to serious work with this adaptation of Ira Levin's compelling bestseller about the activities of diabolists in a rambling New York apartment house. (He even makes a brief Hitchcock-like guest appearance as the man who interrupts Rosemary during a frantic phone-call). Polish director Roman Polanski, exhibiting a characteristic Eastern European skill with fantasy, invests the story, of a young housewife impregnated by the devil and protected by devil-worshippers as she prepares to give birth to the anti-Christ, with an insistent horror that even Robert Wise's *The Haunting* (1963), one of the Sixties' finest horror films, could not quite attain. Shrewdly, Polanski gave the important subsidiary roles, and particularly those of the ageing ringleaders of the plot, to actors of substantial skill whose faces struck a chord of comfortable familiarity in audience's minds. Ruth Gordon and Sidney Blackmer as the Castevets have the avuncular amiability of an earlier decade, which makes even more terrifying their unmasking as instruments of the devil, malevolent and invincible. Fraker's colour photography and Polanski's direction create a rich sense of implicit evil contained in even the simplest surroundings, the central concept of Levin's novel. Even a love scene between Rosemary and her husband achieves a sinister air. The city looms coldly outside the window, while the bare boards of their as-yet undecorated rooms seem mocking and false, a stage set soon to be struck, revealing leering observers behind.

240

1969

Supported more by its hotel and television interests than by film production, M-G-M, having staved off take-over bids for the previous two years, came under the control of Las Vegas hotel tycoon and speculator Kirk Kerkorian, who installed James Aubrey, former CBS head known for his ruthless cost-cutting and managerial skill, as studio head. Warners-Seven Arts split, with ownership of the Warner Brothers half passing to the Kinney Group, a conglomerate of publishing and other interests. United Artists now being firmly in the hands of the Transamerica Corporation, only 20th Century-Fox remained as a studio owned by a primarily film-making group.

Despite a tax structure that made European tax havens less safe for runaway stars, frequent absence from America became a necessity for those anxious to avoid paying more than 90% of their earnings to the government. Since every known star and director had his own company, many problems were avoided, though roles were often chosen with an eye to the corporate income rather than for artistic criteria. Many stars frankly admitted accepting parts in poor films to pay taxes or alimony. For the films that made him famous (notably such successes as *Darling* (John Schlesinger, 1965) and *Death in Venice* (Luchino Visconti, 1971) English star Dirk Bogarde received no direct salary at all, since additional earnings would merely have increased his tax bill.

DOWNHILL RACER. Wildwood International/ Paramount. Produced by Richard Gregson. Directed by Michael Ritchie. Script by James Salter from "The Downhill Racers" by Oakley Hall. Photographed by Brian Probyn. Art direction by Ian Whittaker. Edited by Nick Archer. Music by Kenyon Hopkins. Players: Robert Redford (David Chappellet), Gene Hackman (Eugene Claire), Camilla Sparv (Carole Stahl), Joe Jay Jalbert (Tommy Erb), Timothy Kirk (D. K.

Bryan), Dabney Coleman (Mayo), Jim McMullan (Johnny Creech), Oren Stevens (Tony Kipsmith), Karl Michael Vogler (Machet), Rip McManus (Bruce Devore), Jerry Dexter (Ron Engel), Tom J. Kirk (Stiles), Robert Hutton-Potts, Heini Schuler, Peter Rohr, Arnold Alpiger, Eddie Waldburger, Marco Walli.

Paramount bought Oakley Hall's novel in 1966 as a possible project for Mark Robson and, when he dropped the idea, for Roman Polanski, himself a keen skier, but after the success of *Rosemary's Baby* Polanski could aim higher. It was then taken over by actor Robert Redford, a ski *afficionado* with strong views about US involvement in world ski competition. No American skier had ever won an Olympic gold medal, which Redford attributed to a lack of assertiveness in those chosen to participate. "Maybe one of our drawbacks," he said, "is that our athletes are usually college-trained kids. Maybe what we need is street-fighters. The character I play in *Downhill Racer* has a lot of street-fighter in him." Redford backed his belief by forming Wildwood International with his agent Richard Gregson to produce the film on location in Swiss and American alpine resorts with television director Michael Ritchie and a small crew, some of them professional skiers.

Hall's novel dealt with the dissensions and relationships in the American amateur skiing "circus" as it circulated from summer training camp to winter competition in Europe. Its central character, the most likeable of four friends, accepts second place to the team's best skier, even marrying his pregnant girl friend rather than have her impede the champion's chances, but at the conclusion it is the stooge who wins the big prize, sustained, like *The Hustler*'s "Fast Eddie," by the "character" his competitor lacked. In his script, James Salter, clearly at Redford's suggestion, argues the reverse: David Chappellet is the working-class outsider among the patrician career skiers, and although lacking character, a fact demonstrated by his boorish behaviour, his anxiety to excuse failures as due to chance or the malice of others, and his ungentlemanly response to a casual affair with a ski firm's pretty representative more anxious to gain advertising than to create an enduring relationship, he beats even the most polished college boy, and succeeds by the only standard that matters to him, the winning of races.

So substantially was the novel changed that Hall's name went unmentioned in the publicity, Paramount announcing that the film's script was a Salter original, but the novelist sued for his credit to be restored. *Downhill Racer* lacks the glamorous evocation of bigtime competition common to sports films. One sees the skiers mainly in moments of emotional nakedness, crouching frozen on the lip of the downhill run, aware only of the starter's chant and their own hyperventilated breathing, or in glum post-mortems when

recriminations or momentary triumphs are cushioned only slightly by the coach's reminders of team spirit. To Chappellet, team effort has little meaning, a fact that diminishes him as a person but makes him the perfect skiing machine. Team manager Eugene Claire, accurately played by Gene Hackman, isolates the reason when Chappellet tries to excuse an error that costs a race. "You never had any education, did you?" he says, ignoring the evasions. "All you ever had were your skis, and that's not enough." A glimpse of his home life bears out Claire's theory. Chappellet's father is a distant, disinterested rustic neither understanding nor wishing to understand his son's drive to succeed, and the aridity of his youth is suggested concisely in a brief coupling with an old girl friend in the back seat of a car, careless animal satisfaction that diverts neither of them from other preoccupations. Lacking objectivity, David enjoys but does not understand his affair with the European girl (well-played by Camilla Sparv, then the wife of Paramount's young

Director-star Dennis Hopper (left) and writer-star Peter Fonda in *Easy Rider*.

242

Bob Fosse works out routines for Shirley MacLaine on *Sweet Charity*.

studio boss Robert Evans), and is deeply offended by her casual termination of it, a scene set in the glittering world of *après-ski* and sleek sports cars to suggest the emptiness of championship and the goal to which he aspires. The rewards are hollow; but as one finally realises, when, in the last shot, he exults in the crowd's approval after a big win and sees the glint of resentment in the eyes of a beaten young competitor, for him they are enough.

EASY RIDER. Director: Dennis Hopper. No film more concisely sums up Hollywood's failure to gauge the needs of the emerging young audience than *Easy Rider,* Dennis Hopper's lyrical and exciting hymn to his own generation. Claiming to reject Hollywood traditions, *Easy Rider* is in fact the most professional of exercises in the commercial style, made by a director, producer, writer and star all trained in the studio system, and with a plot clear-headedly constructed to gain popular success. "It isn't hard to make a successful movie," Hopper says. "You just feed the elements into your computer and the answers come out." Even while making his appeal for a freer life, a less paranoid society and a return to the sensuous America of an earlier age, Hopper and writer Jack Nicholson, who also plays the drunken civil rights lawyer, evoke the fashionable music of the day, the glamour of the motor cycle, the trendy social phenomena—communes, pot, acid—whose virtues appear, superficially, to typify the best of the drop-out philosophy. The result is a film which, like *The Graduate,* offers escapism under the disguise of social comment, but this is not to invalidate the skill or seriousness of the film-makers. Fonda, Hopper and Nicholson realise that the traditions of Hollywood are not so easily discarded, that a language, however ill-formed or wanting, becomes with usage an instrument no artist can afford to ignore. Under the sweeping journey of Hopper's two outlaws across America—he specifically denies their status as heroes: "They're outlaws, as the men who kill them are outlaws"—there is both an evocation of the pure life that can exist in the United States and a condemnation of the elements, mainly heroin addiction, racial and social intolerance, and capitalism, which can destroy that purity. That a film of such force could have been made by the son of a major Hollywood star trained as a juvenile in 'teenage romances (Fonda), a character actor in Westerns with experience almost totally in that *genre* (Hopper), and a writer (Nicholson) whose cinema background consisted mainly of production credit on a rock musical (*Head,* Robert Rafelson, 1968) and second billing to Boris Karloff in a Roger Corman horror film (*The Terror,* 1963), merely confirms one's faith in the indestructability and merit of the professional film-making tradition which Hollywood exemplified.

SWEET CHARITY. Director: Bob Fosse. An agreeable exception to the vulgarity of Broadway show films, *Sweet Charity* boasted a script by the skilled Peter Stone from Fellini's *Nights of Cabiria (La Notte di Cabiria),* and Shirley MacLaine bringing humour and feeling to the role of a lonely prostitute (here a dime-a-dance girl) whose hope for a better life survives squalor, deprivation and unrequited love. Cy Coleman and Dorothy Fields provide an imaginative score, enlivened by the direction of Bob Fosse, agile second-lead dancer of Fifties film musicals and since then a talented Broadway choreographer/director. His imagination gives sparkle to the dullest numbers, and genuine depth to set pieces like "Hey, Big Spender," with dance-hall girls draped over a rail, languidly encouraging the attentions of patrons in a scene that has a stinging sense of the bought and their contempt for the buyer. "There's Gotta Be Something Better Than This," musically similar to *West Side Story's* "America" even to a rooftop setting, gets an even more frenzied treatment than Jerome Robbins gave, but "Rich Man's Frug," a clever parody of pop dancing in *élite* night clubs, is totally original in concept, Fosse's expressionless socialites jerking and gliding through a starkly modernistic set. Reviving a practice common in the Fifties, the studio offered exhibitors a choice of endings, one where Charity, abandoned by her lover, wanders off with some flowers hippies have offered to her, a symbol of continuing hope, and a second in which her reticent lover returns for a last-minute reunion. Neither ending, regrettably, offered a profit.

1970

Throughout Hollywood, only five features were scheduled to go into production after the Christmas break, the lowest figure of all time, though studio managers argued that rental to independent producers and the filming of TV series kept their facilities in constant use. Many companies recognised the new situation by forming smaller subsidiaries whose job was to manage studio rentals and supply film services. A changing pattern of distribution had turned the industry from big-budget films. Of 1969's top grossers, half had been made in Europe on limited funds, and many of the remainder by independents working with budgets and facilities the traditional Hollywood would have thought risible. The road-show system was crumbling, substantial losses by 20th. Century-Fox having shown that the trend had petered out. Only three features were scheduled for road-show release in 1970, compared with sixteen for the previous year. Exhibitors who, in the late Sixties, had talked hopefully of a technical innovation to revive mass audience interest in the cinema as sound, wide-screen and the drive-in had in their time, now resisted the most common suggestion for a Seventies exhibition industry, one relying on "intimate" theatres seating only a few hundred people and serviced by two or three staff members, including a single projectionist using automated equipment. Nevertheless, the trend had international popularity, with traditional "picture palaces" being rebuilt as two or sometimes three smaller cinemas. The logic of "small profits, quick returns" was shortly to force itself on the cinema.

Growing alarm among 20th. Century-Fox stockholders at the $47½ million loss incurred during Richard Zanuck's two years as President came to a head at the annual general meeting when only a $900,000 profit was announced. Richard Zanuck was deposed, and while Darryl Zanuck remained as Chairman his son moved to the new autonomous Warner Brothers as head of production. Resentment continued to simmer, with a committee of dissatisfied investors seeking a viable alternative to the Zanuck *régime*. Meanwhile, in May, M-G-M, in a move more valuable for publicity than profits, publicly auctioned the contents of its property departments. Tarzan's loincloth and Rhett Butler's top hat, weapons, furniture, boats, cars and planes from thousands of M-G-M productions were sold, and despite the poignant appeal of the Mayor of Culver City to keep them in the possession of Hollywood's children, even the Ruby Slippers from *The Wizard of Oz* went to a collector for $15,000. 20th Century-Fox quickly followed this lead, destroying the Hollywood mythology as earlier sales of features to TV had dissipated its artistic and financial heritage.

ALICE'S RESTAURANT. Florin/United Artists. Produced by Hillard Elkins, Joe Manduke. Directed by Arthur Penn. Script by Venable Herndon, Arthur Penn based on the song "The Alice's Restaurant Massacree" by Arlo Guthrie. Photographed by Michael Nebbia. Music and songs by Arlo Guthrie. Production designed by Warren Clymer. Players: Arlo Guthrie (Arlo), Pat Quinn (Alice), James Broderick (Ray), Michael McClanathan (Shelly), Geoff Outlaw (Roger), Tina Chen (Mari-Chan), Kathleen Dabney (Karin), William Obanhein (Officer Obie), Seth Allen (Evangelist), Monroe Arnold (Blueglass), Joseph Boley (Woody), Vinnette Carroll (Lady Clerk), Sylva Davis (Marjorie), Simm Landres (Jacob), Eulalie Noble (Ruth), Louis Beachner (Dean), Pete Seeger.

After the impact of *Bonnie and Clyde, Alice's Restaurant*, elegiac and calm, seemed an anti-climax, though its theme gave eloquent expression to the problems at which Penn's earlier films had merely hinted. Unlike *Mickey One, Alice's Restaurant* has a superficially amusing story whose humour partially disguises the lesson beneath. Arlo Guthrie's prosecution by the rural police for dumping rubbish on public land, and his subsequent rejection for military service because of this "police record" is described so as to blend a satire on American authority with a critical review of the myths *Bonnie and Clyde* so elegantly glamourised.

Independence, Penn suggests, has a darker side for the person without a sustaining belief and purpose. Following in the footsteps of his legendary father Woody—"Seems to me Woody might have taken this road once," he says, pausing by a tent revival meeting where the congregation sings the hymn "Amazing Grace"—Arlo makes his own way, rejecting, often harshly, those invitations to pleasure that his stoic morality cannot countenance—sex with an old comrade of Woody's, the wife of a drop-out friend, or with a brainless "collector" of pop stars ("I've made it with the drummer of the Democratic Convention. . . . You might be an album one day"). The unsuccessful search by the drop-out generation for a philosophy coalesces in the winter funeral of a young drug addict, a snow-shrouded rite where folk ballads—one of them significantly Joni Mitchell's "Songs for Ageing Children"—offer little comfort to the alienated, isolated mourners, and in the nervous tolerance of the small town where Ray and Alice hold open house in a deconsecrated church. (Although the story is true, one cannot help seeing Penn's choice as influenced by this useful symbol of new ideas coffined in the shell of the old.) At the centre of this confusion, through which Arlo moves with the moonstruck solemnity of a true ascetic, even those closest to the new ethic are ill at ease. Penn's final shot shows Alice silent among the trees, the camera zooming in and tracking back simultaneously to show subtle changes in perspective but none in actual proportions, a delicate device suggesting that the universal problems of man are not solved with mere variations in ritual. "No matter what the sense of motion might be," Penn has said of this image, "the final condition is one of paralysis."

BUTCH CASSIDY AND THE SUNDANCE KID. Director: George Roy Hill. Though a director of limited gifts, George Roy Hill's ability to catch the public imagination is unprecedented in Hollywood since the days of W. S. Van Dyke. Working from William Goldman's screenplay, for which the studio paid the highest figure ever recorded for an original script, he created a Western whose judgement of public taste seems in retrospect almost magical. His two stars, Paul Newman and Robert Redford, both figured in the "Hollywood Reporter" poll of the year's best stars, as the film ranked high in its financial table of top successes, spawning not only a number of imitations but a profitable TV series ("Alias Smith and Jones") as well. Despite its factual basis and the excursions into sepia for sequences suggestive of the 1890s, Hill's film belongs essentially to the Seventies, the wisecracking relationship of Cassidy and Sundance, their sharing of the schoolteacher (engagingly played by Katharine Ross) who is both lover and friend, and the friendship's conclusion in glamorous death providing a myth for a generation that has too few of its own.

1971

Though 20th Century-Fox edged its profits up to $41½ million, the dissatisfied action group approached a major stockholder, Broadway producer David Merrick, to accept the Presidency, while Fox countered by courting another large investor, Norman Alexander. When Merrick declined the nomination and put his power behind Zanuck, the company also withdrew its offer to Alexander, who then embarked on a campaign to obtain control with the help of several New York finance houses. At the Annual General Meeting in May, Darryl F. Zanuck stepped down from control of the company he had helped to create, the last original film tycoon to relinquish his place. M-G-M and 20th. Century-Fox now stood as Hollywood's two major film studios, and unsuccessful moves by the former to merge during the battles prior to Zanuck's resignation suggest that the tradition they represent will soon have only one representative, the last dinosaur in a changed world.

As exhibitors celebrated the astonishing success of Paramount's saccharine *Love Story* (Arthur Hiller) and pondered the new statistic that, though audiences were minuscule by pre-war standards—fifteen million weekly admissions remained a national average—more people were visiting the cinema than ever before, but less frequently, they grudgingly accepted that small suburban cinemas with frequent changes of programme would best exploit this new situation. Some linked it to an idea put forward by the Hughes Aircraft Co. for a satellite system beaming features to a chain of theatres across the country, replacing conventional projection with a new use of videotape and the "Electronovision" concept pioneered in the mid-Sixties, where films like *Hamlet* (John Gielgud, 1964) and *Harlow* (Alex Segal, 1965) were recorded first on videotape, then later transferred to film via an electronic process that erased the characteristic "lines" of TV. With a Supreme Court decision in 1970 clearing away legal objections to Pay-TV (though networks promised to fight the issue even into Congress) and a growing interest in cassette TV, replacing the telecast with privately purchased programmes or films played on a home video-recorder, there were signs that conventional cinema would soon be absorbed into a video industry which had expanded faster and more coherently than Hollywood ever had.

CARNAL KNOWLEDGE. AVCO Embassy/Icarus. Produced by Clive Reed. Directed by Mike Nichols. Script by Jules Feiffer. Photographed by Giuseppe Rotunno. Art direction by Robert Luthardt. Edited by Sam O'Steen. Players: Jack Nicholson (Jonathan), Candice Bergen (Susan), Arthur Garfunkel (Sandy), Ann-Margret (Bobbie), Rita Moreno (Louise), Cynthia O'Neal (Cindy), Carol Kane (Jennifer).

Audiences who expected, from the involvement of Mike Nichols, cartoonist Jules Feiffer and star Ann-Margret, to see a comedy, were jarred by *Carnal Knowledge*'s abrasive attack on male chauvinism, Nichols returning to the approach if not the style of *Who's Afraid of Virginia Woolf?* to expose and parody all the tricks men use to manipulate women. Feiffer, in a script closer to his play "Little Murders" than to his downbeat cartoon parodies of social relationships, employs the fragmented structure of the cartoons, but the observation is less flippant, more accurate and deeply humane. No man left the film with his self-esteem unshaken, so precisely has Feiffer rendered the inhumanity of man to woman. Following the sexual history of two college friends, Jonathan and Sandy, he shows them both falling for the cool Susan, instigating an elaborate deception for her sake —Susan sleeping with Jonathan but retaining a relatively chaste relationship with Sandy, whom she marries when Jonathan, preferring to hurt her rather than his friend, gives her up. After college, the mar-

Love Story. Ali McGraw, Ryan O'Neal.

Carnal Knowledge. Jack Nicholson, Ann-Margret.

riage of Susan and Sandy deteriorates, Sandy, now a successful doctor, taking a series of mistresses as Jonathan pursues a mindless playboy path, halted only when he meets Bobbie, whose lack of interest in housekeeping is more than balanced by her sexual ability and whom, under pressure, Jonathan finally marries. In the film's final section, now divorced, he gives a cynical slide show to Sandy and his latest (hippie) girl friend reeling off a list of his conquests, each dismissed with a caustic epitaph. Sandy offers his antidote for Jonathan's accidie—a pursuit of mental freedom and youth as empty as his friend's hedonism —and they part, Sandy with his disinterested girl, and Jonathan to a prostitute with whom, after an elaborate ritual, he is able to achieve sexual if not spiritual release.

Jack Nicholson's Jonathan perfectly embodies the "Playboy" illusion. Even as a student his "line" is fully developed, his brash charm and wheedling frankness toppling even Susan's *sang froid;* but by the time he meets Bobbie it has become reflex, a primer of seduction which, exercised in a plush nightclub (which Nichols shoots as if the room is centered around them, the golden couple on display like a prize pair of jewels), enchants with its utter obviousness.

Ann-Margret, a slightly over-ripe young matron, is perfectly cast as Bobbie, the sexual ideal, but one who, like all women, demands full payment of her small price, in this case a semblance of emotional security, preferably marriage. When Jonathan refuses, their life degenerates until only sex relieves the monotony. "Why do you put up with it?" Jonathan snarls, momentarily appalled at his grossness; and Bobbie replies, "You don't know what I've been used to." Her eventual suicide attempt is the last card with which she trumps Jonathan, forcing him to marry her but knowing it cannot last. Bobbie's bitterness and despair colours *Carnal Knowledge,* chilling one's amusement at Feiffer's lighter insights, as the joky obviousness of the lovers' relationship renders their sexual encounters lifeless, showing carnal knowledge but little feeling. Only the recurrent image of a girl skating on a frozen lake, glimpsed once by Sandy and Jonathan and thereafter evoked as the unattainable feminine ideal, the cold goddess in whose terms Sandy first conceived Susan, suggests a positive side to this pursuit of flesh and its momentary satisfactions, and her return as the film's last image offers all the hope Nichols and Feiffer are prepared to concede.

Summer of '42. Jennifer O'Neill, Jerry Houser, Gary Grimes.

SUMMER OF '42. Director: Robert Mulligan. Though never rising above amiable and good natured nostalgia (*To Kill a Mockingbird*, 1963) or downbeat realism (*Love with the Proper Stranger*, 1964), Mulligan's films are faultless in their popular appeal, and classic examples of the Hollywood film as generations have grown to enjoy it. Escapist, entertaining, employing a realistic insight only as seasoning to a palatable dish, they represent the deepest tradition of American cinema. Riding the waves both of nostalgia and unsentimental romance, *Summer of '42* softens the adolescent stirrings of sexuality with the untroubled mood of the mid-war vacuum. In love with a young wife on the island where he holidays with his parents, a boy is taken to bed by her on the night she receives news of her husband's death, an initiation delightful in its unexpectedness, its drama and its ease. Meticulous art direction and extracts from *Now Voyager* with Bette Davis and Paul Henried sustain the image of another, gentler age, an illusion which, though specious, cannot be resisted. If escape we must, such films offer incomparable vehicles.

Index

ILLUSTRATIONS OF DIRECTORS & PERSONALITIES